Disability and Psychology

Also by the editors

Goodley D. (2000) *Self-Advocacy in the Lives of People with Learning Difficulties*.

Goodley D., Lawthom R., Clough P. and Moore M. (2004) *Researching Life Stories*.

Goodley D. and Moore M. (2002) *Arts Against Exclusion*.

Disability and Psychology: Critical Introductions and Reflections

Edited by

Dan Goodley

and

Rebecca Lawthom

First published 2006 by
PALGRAVE MACMILLAN
Houndmills, Basingstoke, Hampshire RG21 6XS and
175 Fifth Avenue, New York, N.Y. 10010
Companies and representatives throughout the world

PALGRAVE MACMILLAN is the global academic imprint of the Palgrave
Macmillan division of St. Martin's Press, LLC and of Palgrave Macmillan Ltd.
Macmillan® is a registered trademark in the United States, United Kingdom
and other countries. Palgrave is a registered trademark in the European
Union and other countries.

ISBN-10: 1–4039–3601–3 paperback
ISBN-13: 978–1–4039–3601–1 paperback

This book is printed on paper suitable for recycling and made from fully
managed and sustained forest sources.

A catalogue record for this book is available from the British Library.

A catalog record for this book is available from the Library of Congress.

10   9   8   7   6   5   4   3   2   1
15   14   13   12   11   10   09   08   07   06

Printed in China

We dedicate this book to the memory of Mairian Scott-Hill (who also published as Mairian Corker) whose scholarship and true inter-disciplinary vision inspired us both to think about possibilities for the extension of disability studies. We deeply regret that she is not around to deconstruct this text.

– Dan Goodley and Rebecca Lawthom

Contents

List of Tables and Figures   ix

Acknowledgements   x

Notes on Editors and Contributors   xi

Preface   xv

1   Disability Studies and Psychology: New Allies?   1
    Dan Goodley and Rebecca Lawthom

Part I   The Psychology of Disability: From Infancy to   **17**
           Adulthood

2   Parents, Professionals and Disabled Babies: Personal   19
    Reflections on Disabled Lives
    Claire Tregaskis

3   Being in School? Exclusion and the Denial of   34
    Psychological Reality
    Pippa Murray

4   The Disability Discrimination Act and Lifelong Learning?   42
    Students with Disabilities and Higher Education
    Deb Viney

5   Disabled and Graduated: Barriers and Dilemmas for   71
    the Disabled Psychology Graduate
    Peter Stannett

6   Disability and Old Age: Or Why It Isn't All in the Mind   84
    Mark Priestley

7   Towards a Psychology of Disability: The Emotional   94
    Effects of Living in a Disabling Society
    Donna Reeve

**Part II   Disability, Psychology and Practice: From a   109
            Disabling to an Enabling Psychology**

  8   Against Stereotypes: Experiences of Disabled   111
      Psychologists
      Freda Levinson and Simon Parritt

  9   Understanding Intellectually Disabled Clients in   123
      Clinical Psychology
      Jennifer Clegg

 10   Enabling Practice for Professionals: The Need for   141
      Practical Post-Structuralist Theory
      Liz Todd

 11   Counselling with the Social Model: Challenging   155
      Therapy's Pathologies
      John Swain, Carol Griffiths and Sally French

 12   Doing Community Psychology with Disabled People   170
      *Carolyn Kagan, Rebecca Lawthom, Paul Duckett
      and Mark Burton*

 13   Conclusions: Making Enabling Alliances between   187
      Disability Studies and Psychology
      Rebecca Lawthom and Dan Goodley

References   205

Index   225

List of Tables and Figures

Tables

3.1	The words of exclusion and inclusion	40
4.1	Summary of the HESA statistics 1994–2002	44
4.2	Summary of the HESA statistics 1994–2002 – undergraduates	46
4.3	Summary of the HESA statistics 1994–2002 – post-graduates	48
4.4	The proportion of "working age" participants (16–60 years) who self-reported a disability in the Autumn 2001 Labour Force Survey	51
4.5	The type of impairment self-reported by participants in the Autumn 2001 Labour Force Survey	52
13.1	Two paradigms of disability thinking	201

Figures

12.1	Roles of community psychologists	184
12.2	Skills of community psychology	185

Acknowledgements

We would like to thank our commissioning editor Andrew McAleer for his consistent support from initial conception to completion of this text. We are also grateful to our anonymous reviewers for their constructive comments of the proposal, and to friends and colleagues who have offered critical insights, often unknowingly during fleeting conversations, into the troubled relationship between psychology and disability. These include Dr Rob Evans, Iain Carson, BA (Hons), Learning Disability Studies students at the University of Manchester, Ludo Schoeters and all at Onze Nieuwe Toekomst including coaches Griet Roets and Dries Cautrels, David Paré, Beth Omansky, Michele Moore, Ian Parker, Mark Rapley, Huddersfield People First. Finally, we would like to thank the contributors for their enthusiastic analyses now presented in this book.

Notes on Editors and Contributors

Editors

Dan Goodley is Reader in Disability Studies, University of Sheffield, with research interests in disability theory, activism and methodology. Recent publications include *Self-Advocacy in the Lives of People with Learning Difficulties* (2000), *Arts against Exclusion* (with Michele Moore, 2002) and *Another Disability Reader* (with Geert Van Hove, Garant, 2005).

Rebecca Lawthom is Principal Lecturer in Psychology, Manchester Metropolitan University and a member of the Research Institute for Health and Social Change. Her research interests are in disability, community and feminist psychology. Her publications include *Researching Life Stories* (with Goodley, Moore and Clough, 2004) and 'Epistemological Journeys in Participatory Action Research' (*Disability & Society*, 2005).

Contributors

Mark Burton is Head of the Manchester Learning Disability Partnership. Over the years he has worked as a clinical psychologist and head of quality and professional practice developments in the service. He pioneered the involvement of people with learning difficulties in National Development Team projects and has written widely about critical psychological thinking and practice.

Jennifer Clegg is Senior Lecturer, University of Nottingham, and Hon. Consultant Clinical Psychologist, Nottinghamshire Healthcare NHS Trust. She has reviewed intellectual disability research in 'Death, disability, and dogma' (with Lansdall-Welfare, 2003, *Philosophy, Psychiatry, Psychology*) and is currently researching transition to adult services.

Paul Duckett is a critical community psychologist and senior lecturer in psychology at Manchester Metropolitan University. His research interests on social issues include disability (including mental health), un/employment and education, and methodologies include qualitative, participatory action and emancipatory forms of work.

Sally French is an associate lecturer for the Open University and a freelance lecturer, writer and researcher. Her main interest is Disability Studies where she has (with others) authored and edited various texts including *Controversial Issues in a Disabling Society* (2003) and *Disabling Barriers – Enabling Environments* (2004).

Carol Griffiths (formerly Buswell) is a sociologist at Northumbria University. She has, over the years, researched and published across a wide range of social issues which include aspects of inequality, education, training and employment. She is currently working, with others in Northumbria University, on research into Sure Start programmes in the NE of England.

Carolyn Kagan is Professor of Community Social Psychology at Manchester Metropolitan University, where she is the Director of the Research Institute for Health and Social Change. Her work includes participatory evaluation research with those marginalised by the social system and she has worked for many years supporting service developments and citizen advocacy projects involving people with learning difficulties.

Freda Levinson is a consultant clinical psychologist with clinical and research interests in neuropsychology and learning difficulties, and wide therapeutic experience. She was the initiator and director, for twenty years, of the former North West Thames in-service training course in Clinical Psychology. She is a registered Disability/Action Trainer.

Pippa Murray is Director of ibk initiatives – a research, consultancy and training agency whose aims are to promote the inclusion of disabled children, young people and their families in their local communities and to challenge a disabling world that denies their right to an ordinary existence (http://www.**ibkinitiatives**.com).

Simon Parritt is a chartered counselling psychologist in private practice. He is Senior Lecturer at the Institute of Sexuality and Human Relations and was Director of the Association to Aid the Sexual and Personal Relationships of People with a Disability (SPOD). He has a particular interest in training and supervision of counsellors and health professionals working with disabled people and those living with long-term conditions.

Mark Priestley is Reader in Disability Studies at the Centre for Disability Studies, University of Leeds (UK) and Administrator of the international email discussion group disability-research@jiscmail.ac.uk. His research interests include generational and life-course analysis, and comparative policy analysis.

Donna Reeve is a PhD student in the Department of Applied Social Science at Lancaster University. Her research interests include disability, sociology of the body, post-structuralism and sociology of the emotions and has published papers in *Disability & Society*.

Peter Stannett currently works in psychopharmacology after having worked in diverse areas of employment such as mental health and mobile telecommunications engineering. He has published several articles on disability and employment.

John Swain is Professor of Disability and Inclusion at Northumbria University. He has published widely in the area of disability studies including Swain *et al. Disabling Barriers – Enabling Environments* (2nd edition, 2004).

Liz Todd is Director of Educational Psychology, Newcastle University. Her research interests are in the participation of young people in private/public decision-making and multi-agency working. She has published articles in a number of journals including *International Journal of Inclusive Education and Educational Psychology in Practice*.

Claire Tregaskis is a research fellow in the Faculty of Health and Social Work at the University of Plymouth. Publications arising from her research interests in applied disability studies include *Constructions of Disability* (2004) and 'Social Model Theories: The Story so Far' (*Disability & Society*, 2002).

Deb Viney has interests in neuropsychology (e.g. haemophilia and HIV research) and the teaching of psychology (all levels from GCSE to post-graduate). She has been a disability officer at the University of Southampton since 1997. Deb is also a member of the Executive Board of the National Association of Disability Officers.

Preface

This book is the first to bring together the disciplines of psychology and emancipatory disability studies. The latter discipline is a relatively new phenomenon, at least in Britain, in which disabled people and their allies have endeavoured to make sense of and challenge the exclusionary practices of disabling society. The former discipline has a longer history and a more dominant position in academia, research, policy making and practitioner worlds. Both boast a range of theorising and approaches to research that have influenced, often in very different ways, the lives of disabled and non-disabled people. Yet, while the disciplines of sociology, social policy, humanities, education, history and politics have critically engaged with disability studies, psychology has remained conspicuously absent from these debates. There are a number of reasons for this absence and the clear imperative to rectify it.

Firstly, psychology has commonly viewed disability in the domain of rehabilitation psychology (Olkin and Pledger, 2003). This approach places emphasis on individual factors related to a person's impairment, with the aim of improving a person's life through interventions associated with cure, rehabilitation and normalisation (e.g. Frank and Elliott, 2000), therapeutic adjustment (e.g. Waitman and Conboy-Hill, 1992) and pain relief (e.g. Gatchel and Weisberg, 2000). Psychology's preoccupation with such concerns has led to a disengagement with other more externalised and contextualised phenomena. In contrast, the disability community and the disabled people's movement have called for a concerted analysis of wider social, psychological, relational, cultural and political factors that must be tackled in order to change disabling society: constituting the inter-disciplinary focus of disability studies.

Secondly, there is an urgent need to reconsider psychological practices in the light of recent anti-discriminatory disability legislation. Whilst feminism, queer theory and critical race paradigms have had formal association with psychology, disability studies remains isolated. This may be due to ignorance of the view that disability is a socio-political category. The advent of anti-discriminatory disability legislation has forced disability into the foreground of some psychological arenas. For example, the *American Psychological Association's Committee on Disability Issues in Psychology* posits the following mission:

- promote the psychological welfare of people with disabilities;
- promote the development and implementation of psychological service delivery models responsive to the needs of people with disabilities;
- promote the awareness of disability issues in psychological research as well as specific research activity in disability areas;
- promote inclusion of knowledge about disabilities and disability issues in education, training programs, and professional development of psychologists. (http://www.apa.org/)

In Britain, at the time of writing, *The British Psychological Society* (BPS) has no similar committee with a specific interest around disability. While there have been recent discussions to consider a section of the society which will tackle discrimination and prejudice experienced by disabled people, there remains a clear need for psychologists to fully realise the seriousness of recent legislation in terms of their own practices. Just as there have been attempts to consider the impacts of disability legislation on the practices of psychology in a North American context (e.g. Bruyere and O'Keefe, 1994), this proposed book emerges at a time of major legislative changes: the *Disability Discrimination Act* (1995) and *Special Educational Needs and Disability Act* (2001). While there is a clear British focus here, much of what is discussed in this book will be of relevance and interest to audiences of other countries where reactions to disability legislation and policy are largely in their infancy.

Thirdly, psychology continues to ignore the contributions of disabled people and disabled psychologists to the development of inclusive psychological literature and practice. In Britain, and elsewhere, the psychological industry remains largely untroubled by the agitations of disabled people. Just as feminists have insisted on the need for psychology to attend to the perspectives of women and feminist researchers (promoting the formation of a separate section of the BPS, the *Psychology of Women Section*, and a distinct journal, *Feminism and Psychology*), so too this text pushes for acknowledgement of disabled people in psychology. Disability studies literature has long made the case for social science research to work *alongside* rather than *on* disabled people. Such approaches, characterised in community psychology as participatory action research, link into a key aim of disability studies: augment the participation of disabled people in knowledge production. Consequently, this proposed book includes contributions from disabled people – including disabled psychologists – which challenge the tendency to view disabled people as objects rather than arbiters of psychological intervention. Other contributions draw upon the experience and expertise of disabled people in their analyses. Hence, psychology is critically reviewed as a potential resource for developing disability studies – and vice versa – in ways that empower rather than pathologise disabled people. This text aims to add to this critical literature by challenging – via disability studies debates – taken-for-granted notions such as 'disability', 'impairment' and 'professional knowledge'.

The original proposal for this book was written at a telling time in disability politics. The strength of the International Disabled People's movement was recognised by the 2003 European Year *of* Disabled People. This book provides a timely opportunity to (re)consider the relationship between disability studies and psychology in ways that contribute to the emancipation – rather than the exclusion – of disabled people.

Chapter 1

Disability Studies and Psychology: New Allies?

Dan Goodley and Rebecca Lawthom

Introduction

This book aims to capture some connections between the inter-disciplinary nature of disability studies and the multi-variant theoretical/ practical discipline of psychology. In so doing, we bring together disability studies and psychology from a particular stance. For us, disability studies comes first and psychology second. Our overarching concern is to explore how disability studies can benefit from a critical and not unproblematic engagement with psychology, rather than how psychology can colonise disability studies. Our aim is to examine the ways in which psychology can work in ways that contribute to the individual and collective empowerment of disabled people. Our focus is not on the usual rehabilitative association of psychology and disability but on the ways in which psychology can contribute to those radical social changes demanded by disability studies. In this opening chapter, we provide an overview of disability studies, particularly as it is understood in our own British context. We outline some of its main tenets and key debates. We then begin to unravel some of the complexities of psychology that exist behind its public image. We suggest that there is much radicalism and diversity of theory to exploit. Such resources can be fruitfully used by disability studies; as demonstrated by the contributors of this book.

Disability studies: From disablement to emancipation

The disability studies we describe in this book is inherently a British disability studies. There are clear points of divergence between

1

different contextual (and conceptual) takes on disability studies, not least in the difference between North American (Linton, 1998; Albrecht *et al.*, 2001; Longman and Umansky, 2001), Nordic disability research (Traustadottir, 2004; *Scandinavian Journal of Disability Research*, 6(1), 2004) and British Disability Studies (e.g. Barton and Oliver, 1997; Oliver and Barnes, 1998; Shakespeare, 1998; Barnes *et al.*, 1999; Corker and French, 1999; Thomas, 1999; Barton, 2001; Barnes *et al.*, 2002; Barnes and Mercer, 2003; Swain *et al.*, 2003a). When we talk about disability we are discussing people who have the ascribed identities of being 'disabled people'. Such an identity term includes various people who have been historically situated in a whole myriad of impairment groupings including physical and sensory impairments, learning difficulties and people with mental health issues. As befits a British disability studies stance, however, we endeavour not to embrace impairment-specific considerations – as have many charities and organisations *for* disabled people – but instead consider disabled people as a heterogeneous group, with many impairment labels who face a number of overlapping experiences of exclusion or disablement. The disability studies that this book locates itself within is an *emancipatory disability studies*. It is tied to the development of the disabled people's movement – which we understand as a new social movement (Campbell and Oliver, 1996) – and many of the writers within the field are themselves disabled activists and 'organic intellectuals' in Gramsci's sense of this term (Oliver, 1990). Like other 'minority-group disciplines', including African/ critical race studies, feminist and queer studies, disability studies maintains close links with its own community and blurs the distinction between the researcher and researched (Olkin and Pledger, 2003, p. 296).

Crucial to the development of British disability studies has been the ubiquitous use and reuse of the term 'the social model of disability'. Many of the contributors to this book will make reference to this 'big idea' (Hasler, 1993).

> The significance of disability theory and practice lies in its radical challenge to the medical or individual model of disability. The latter is based on the assumption that the individual is 'disabled' by their impairment, whereas the social model of disability reverses the causal chain to explore how social constructed barriers have disabled people with a perceived impairment. (Barnes and Mercer, 1997, pp. 1–2)

The social model of disability has turned attention away from a preoccupation with people's impairments (and the associated 'consequences' on everyday activities) and instead focused on the ways in which disability is created – through the social, economic, political, cultural, relational – and psychological – exclusion of people with impairments (UPIAS, 1976; Oliver, 1990, 1996b; Barnes, 1991). Disability is therefore a socio-political category; a cultural artefact, a relational and psychological phenomenon. When we speak of disability in this book, the contributors are considering the ways in which people with impairments are constantly threatened with being excluded from mainstream life. Disablement – the exclusion of people with impairments – is a form of apartheid of the 21st century. From leisure settings to work, education and everyday social relationships, disabled people continue to struggle with and against the humiliation of marginalisation. In Britain, it took until 1995 for disabled people to receive some form of legislative protection on the form of the Disability Discrimination Act. In 2001, this act was eventually focused on educational institutions. Nevertheless, as we shall see, this legislation has failed to tackle the endemic discrimination faced by disabled people. Even in 2004, disabled people are threatened with a life on the margins of society. Disability is clearly a political phenomenon.

But, impairment itself is not unproblematic. For many writers in British disability studies, impairment is a biological given – a loss of a limb or mechanism of the body or mind (see UPIAS, 1976). For others, impairment of mind and body is itself a psycho-emotional, socio-cultural and/or political formation. Impairment is something discursively created (Hughes and Paterson, 1997), a remnant of modernist thought (Corker and Shakespeare, 2002), a phenomenon based on different epistemological stance (Goodley, 2001), an ontological position dependent on psychological and social processes (Reeve, 2002). When we speak of, label, react to, deal with, joke about, medicalise, professionalise, rehabilitate, drug, treat, think of or relate to 'impairment' then we reveal its fundamentally social nature. Therefore, the social model of disability brings with it a social model of impairment (Abberley, 1987). This is potentially paradigm busting. A critic of this text might well presume that just as organisations of disabled people and their allies reveal the political nature of disability then we unhelpfully refocus analysis on individual impairment – especially so because our text has the psychology word in the title. Such a focus is in danger of re-impairing disability politics. Our position is not this. Instead, this text positions impairment as a complex thing, fundamentally social in nature, and something which psychology must consider in the same socio-political formation as it considers disability. In bringing together psychology and disability studies, our aim is not to empower the former and colonise the latter. The aim of this book is to consider both as remnants of social thought and practice that require thinking through with the aim of challenging the disablement of disabled people. Our aim, then, is unapologetically political. So is our conception of the discipline and practices of psychology.

Psychology: Diversity and radicalism behind the pop-labels?

Psychologists are used to a response when disclosing their occupation: 'Are you analysing me?'. Psychology, in popular cultural terms, tends to imply the therapeutic counselling of another's problems. In our current climate of psychoanalytic culture (Parker, 1999), psychology appears to feed into a climate of Oprah-esque proportions; dulling the senses, uselessly reifying the trivial, promoting a naval-gazing and confessional culture. Simultaneously, while psychology-as-analysis is dismissed as trivialising nonsense, it is also treated with deep suspicion. Psychology appears to be obsessed with difference (usually referred to as deviance) and cattle-prodding back into submission that which stands out from the norm. Hence, displaying anger in the car is now a psychological label that requires the intervention of suitably qualified experts. Naughty kids are now kids caught up in a psychopathology of challenging behaviour, emotional behavioural difficulties, autism and attention deficit hyperactivity disorder (Billington, 2000). When disability is raised in the training of psychologists then it tends to be considered in terms of individual biological factors (Olkin and Pledger, 2003). Such a focus is allied to the advent of the psy-complex (Rose, 1989) – the institutionalisation of psychological interventions into people's lives. This clearly raises worrying concerns; particularly for people with impairments. Disabled people have extensive and intensive experience of the intrusions of professionals such as psychologists whose major aim of intruding appears to be one of enforcing normalcy (Oliver, 1996b). Psychology is to be distrusted because it is:

- Individualistic – the scientific study of mind and behaviour;
- Bourgeois – ideas of the majority (and ruling) are exercised over the minority (http://www.fireflysun.com/);

- Apolitical – changing individuals rather than society (Masson, 1988);
- Professional-led – experts over the lay;
- Pseudo-scientific – an emphasis on science and a poor version of it at that (Popper, 1997);
- Normalising – concerned with individuals adjusting to their impairment;
- Oppressive – disabled people are mere subjects of psychology's individualising practices.

However, a brief immersion in the discipline of psychology – the industry that exists behind the pop-labels – reveals a complex community. *Psychologies* may be a more apt disciplinary label. There are many psychological theories including: cognitive, behavioural, psychoanalytic, humanistic, existential, social, cultural, political, social constructionist, feminist, critical, critical race, postmodernist, discursive, forensic, spiritual, developmental, narrative and community psychologies, to name but a few. There are numerous practitioner roles, including educational, clinical, organisational, criminologist, child, counselling and therapist. Furthermore, like all viable social scientific disciplines, debates rage about epistemology, ontology, theory, methodology, method, analysis, ethics, application and political potency. To situate psychology as a bounded discipline engaged with enforcing normalcy does a disservice to the dynamic nature of knowledge disciplines. Psychology is but a collection of many different communities, each with their like-minded members, constituting a myriad of psychological paradigms (Kuhn, 1965); although many theories and practitioners are involved in the disability industry and implicated in the institutionalised oppression of disabled people, as with any loosely related collection of community members, discord and debate reign (Lawthom, 2004). The history of psychology is peppered with radical collectives and individuals challenging the (disabling) *status quo*. In terms of what may be of use to the development of an emancipatory disability studies, we can point to three key paradigmatic battles – if not exactly paradigm shifts – where the status and role of psychological knowledge and practice have been thrown open to debate and critique.

The crisis in social psychology
The 1970s saw a major shift in thinking about how psychology should go about its business. Parker (1989) suggests that a key crisis emerged in social psychology as ethnomethodologist and interpretivist

writers challenged the dominating forces of positivism. The text by Marsh *et al.* (1978) is a classic example of psychologists discarding psychology's mistaken model of science, instead turning to the hermeneutically rich world of ethnomethodological and qualitative studies of human behaviour as it naturally occurred in real-world settings. While there are traditions of qualitative research to be found in (social) psychology (e.g. Allport, 1947), the crisis refers to the increasing dissatisfaction with psychological functionalism: individualistic and consensus understandings of people that view them as atomistic beings in socio-political vacuums. Even now, psychological circles abound with debates about the psychology's relationship to science and positivism; the role of qualitative versus quantitative methodologies in accessing the social world; the place of subjectivity and objectivity in research and the place of partisanship in psychology. The crisis led to fragmentation and paradigm-shifts that have given rise to more meaning-oriented theoretical persuasions, often with political affiliations. It is no surprise that feminist psychologists were some of the most vociferous opponents of 'malestream' positivistic approaches to psychology (e.g. Ussher, 1991). Sadly, disability studies never really got represented in these crises, as the disability movement was still relatively in its infancy in the 1970s. However, as we look back now on the crisis in psychology and the challenges that were posed to override (ruling) dominating knowledge, it would seem that psychology has the potential for being opened up and radicalised.

The rise of critical theories

The theoretical and epistemological status of psychological knowledge and practice has faced some of its stiffest tests from critical theories such as social constructionism, discursive and critical psychologies and radical psychoanalysis. These four not necessarily inclusive nor bounded theoretical resources share the aim of contesting some of psychology's given truth claims. In essence, they provide not only alternative psychological theories but pose major challenges to the mainstream practices of the discipline of psychology.

First, *social constructionism* has challenged the concept of the self as an embodied and unitary human subject and opened it up as a distributed self, dependent on different contexts and the meanings in those contexts at given times (e.g. Nightingale and Cromby, 1999; Burr, 2003). The self and psychology become seen as constructed phenomena through meaning-making, language and human practice. The very concept of personality, for example, is ripped out of its usual embodied site and recast as a socio-cultural formation. Personalities are increasingly consumable entities of a society obsessed with identity. In contrast, the supposed undesirability of a disabled identity raises questions about what identities are deemed socially valued. Second, *discursive psychology* furthers an engagement with constructions by positing that there can be no truth without language and the ideologies and institutions implicated in the production of language. The various forms of discursive psychology are beyond the remit of this chapter, though two classic texts capture at least some of this diversity (for more details, see Nikander, 1995). Potter and Wetherell (1987) exemplify an approach to discursive psychology which is concerned with picking out the contradictions and variations of seemingly fixed entities such as attitudes. Their main thesis is that mainstream approaches to social psychology assume a stability of self that is actually far from the reality of everyday psychology. For Potter and Wetherell, self is always constituted by the language people use to account for self. Through the use of conversation analysis we can see how these very accounts reveal contradictions and complexities. The use of sophisticated conversational strategies and resources make a mockery of the fixed concept of the human psyche assumed by attitude tests and psychometric analyses. People make attitudes through their talk and attitudes shift and change according to context and the conversational strategies that are used. Rapley (2003) exemplifies a conversational analysis approach which takes a purportedly real, organic and individualised phenomena such as 'intellectual disability' and reveals how it is constituted by the talk about it. Parker's (2002) approach to discourse analysis is also concerned with providing a social account of subjectivity. His approach, though, leans more heavily on poststructuralist writers such as Michel Foucault and Jacques Derrida, whose aim is to deconstruct, subvert and account for societal discourses – what Lyotard (1979) terms 'grand narratives' (see also Burman and Parker, 1993). Hence, in an associated text, Parker *et al.* (1995) unpick the ways in which psychopathological conditions are the product of normalising institutions and professional practice. Mental illness is not a condition that exists prior to the psychologist intervening – mental illness is a social creation of institutions within society that psychology has helped to construct. Third, and obviously related, *critical psychology* challenges the tacit assumption that psychology is a progressive and enabling practice. Fox and Prilleltensky (1997) argue that psychology's traditional practices and norms hinder social justice, to the detriment of individuals and communities in general and of oppressed groups in particular. The task for critical psychologists is to confront the practices of psychology that sustain oppression, promote a politicised and aware psychology, work alongside users and survivors of psychology and link into wider social justice agendas as ethically responsible psychologists. Finally, *radical psychoanalysis*. The counselling room is perhaps one of the first places critics think of when thinking of the oppressive horrors of psychological practice. Pop-Freudian understandings, publicised incidents of therapeutic abuse and controversies such as false-memory syndrome have all contributed to a damning view of psychoanalysis. Yet, there is a long history of radical psychoanalytic thinkers, most notably evident in the pre-Second World War work of the Frankfurt school. Scholars associated with the Institute of Social Research, Frankfurt, Germany, include Theodor W. Adorno, Herbert Marcuse, Max Horkheimer and Jurgen Habermas (see Frosch, 1999). These writers shared the aim of bringing together the work of Marx and Freud, in order to promote radical social theory. Kovel's (1988) analysis is a more modern attempt to bring back the work of the Frankfurt school work alongside a celebration of spirituality and human worth.

The impact of community psychology

Following Goodley and Lawthom (2005), a community psychology (CP) perspective can be defined in a number of ways: a branch of psychology; a revolutionary paradigm of psychology; a counter-hegemony to mainstream psychology's individualism; an inter-disciplinary context that brings together politics, sociology, social policy, health and social welfare (adapted from Rappaport, 1977; Heller *et al.*, 1984; Orford, 1992; Duffy and Wong, 1997; Levine and Perkins, 1997; Kagan, 2002; Prilleltensky and Nelson, 2002). Crucial to most conceptions of CP is the idea of working alongside the primary source of knowing and instrument of research: 'the self-directing person within a community of inquiry' (Reason and Heron, 1995, p. 123). CP often embraces models of participatory action research. Here, CP researchers work alongside members of excluded communities to understand and challenge oppression and marginalisation. Such a model has many links with emancipatory disability research, which seeks to challenge the dominant modes of research production (research *on* disabled people; research *on* the pathologies of impairment) and, instead, foster a mode of research that works alongside disabled people in ways that understand and challenge disabling society (research *with* disabled people; research *with* disabled people on the pathologies of an exclusionary social world). The view of psychology promoted by CP is inherently political. It considers psychology as a liberatory space (Martin-Baró *et al.*, 1994; Kagan, 2002), in which researchers, who are armed with theoretical and practical knowledge of the social and interpersonal world, aim to work alongside communities towards positive social change. Psychology is up for grabs: particularly by those communities whose psychologies have been pathologised and alienated by labour markets, poor housing, welfare dependency and material poverty. Psychology is a social, cultural and political creation. CP is interested in communities, activism and political engagement. CP critically engages with qualitative research as a means to work alongside the agendas of community members. The psychology of CP is often of a social constructionist and structural bent: what Wetherell (1996) terms 'sociological social psychology'. CP emphasises the socially and culturally grounded psychologies of community members; recognises the distributed and multiple identities of community members and, of course, the significance of a healthy community to members' well-being.

Furthering emancipatory disability studies: Engaging with psychology's radicals

Our observation is that disability studies should critically engage with the resources outlined above and offered in this text. Psychology has a history of epistemological twists and turns, which in some places have left empowering and politicised visions of psychology. Psychology is not necessarily the disabling discipline that it might appear to be from first viewings. Indeed, a whole host of theoretical, methodological and analytical resources may be there for the taking by disability studies. However, before we continue, a word of caution: beware of psychology's seduction. We do not aim in this book to give over disability studies to the wants of psychology. Far from it. A recurring theme of this book is that psychology – its institutions, practitioners, theorists and researchers – have done some major damage. In contrast, what we aim to do is to examine some of the radical elements of psychology and carefully question what they might offer us in terms of promoting an emancipatory disability studies.

Psychology and disability: Critical introductions and reflections

Part I of the book explores disability – and impairment – as it is experienced and challenged throughout childhood and adulthood, in a variety of institutional contexts. The contributors examine the key psychosocial stages of infancy, childhood, adulthood and older age from a disability perspective. Rather than unpicking the tragedies and pathologies of impairment in these stages, the contributors explore various societal institutions of health and social care, schooling, higher education and psychological training in order to expose disabling practices which threaten to exclude disabled people. The task is to turn away from a dominant focus on the consequences of impairment to an examination of how disabled people's participation in stages of life are constantly shaped by disabling environments.

Chapter 2 by Claire Tregaskis draws upon the author's own early childhood experiences and her work as a researcher on a current research project entitled 'Parents, professionals and disabled babies: Identifying enabling care'. Tregaskis argues that little has changed down the years in the way that some professionals continue to objectify disabled people and render them as 'other' in ways that can have serious long-term negative effects on their subsequent life chances. Much of what might count as developmental psychology is infused with understandings of 'normal childhood and child development'. Deviation from the norm is often viewed as pathological and invites the intervention of a whole host of medical and psy-complex professionals (Rose, 1989; Burman, 1994). Tregaskis's chapter illustrates the ways in which the use of such pathological understandings can threaten to stifle the development of childhood as an artefact of the wider family. She notes the ways in which parents can be made passive by professional intervention but also that parents challenge and contest the professional knowledge that they are given. Significantly, she reminds us that the love and care of children – with or without impairments – remains the telling issue in the dynamic between child and family. Too often such basic emotional considerations are masked by a psychological preoccupation with specialised care for children with particular impairments. As families work together in formulating understandings of impairment and disability, we must remain mindful of the implications of psychological ideas that emphasise deficient understandings of impairment over more capacity-building understandings of children in which environments are made places in which to thrive.

Chapter 3 by Pippa Murray draws upon the author's extensive personal and research experience of disabled children and their experiences of social and educational exclusion/inclusion. Currently, in Britain and elsewhere, we live in a policy and legislative context of inclusion. Yet, much of what passes for inclusion may be seen to be merely rhetorical (Billig, 1996). The reality for parents, educational psychologists, teachers and school heads is one of an ideological battlefield (Apple, 1995). Significantly, disabled children are often the main casualties of these battles. For Murray, making visible the consequences of disablement, some of them less obvious than others, is the first necessary step in the process of healing and resolution. Here concepts of psychological reality are very useful for making sense of the processes of disablement. Murray argues that when we deny the psychological reality of others, our capacity for empathy is forfeit: they cease to be human in our innermost representations of them. The psychological reality described here is one infused with social and cultural meanings – (disabled) children can only be understood as the social beings that they are (Walkerdine, 2001). This may seem a rather obvious point but takes on more significance when we understand the ways in which children with impairments are denied basic human needs such as friendship as a consequence of them being viewed as solely those impairments. The task here is to bring together understandings from disability studies and psychology in order to challenge this denial of the psychological reality.

It is clear that the involvement of disabled people in psychology can and will only come about through the recruitment of students with disabilities to psychology training in Higher Education Institutions (HEIs). Just as, arguably, the increase of female and black psychologists has to certain extents demanded psychology to challenge its sexist and racist practices, then the input of disabled psychologists is crucial to the production of a non-disablist psychology. In Chapter 4, Deb Viney comprehensively reviews the position of students with disabilities in HEIs. Her analysis is thought-provoking. Clearly, disabled people continue to be excluded in many ways from educational institutions even in the current (British) climate of disability legislation. The number of students self-defining as disability is increasing. This calls for necessary support. In order to critique this support, Viney critically examines funding arrangements for students with disabilities: the Disabled Students' Allowance; gaps in funding for individual students and the provision of institutional funding. The latter element is crucial – supporting students with disabilities cannot be a reactive practice but a proactive element of HEIs anticipating the support that may well be needed by disabled and non-disabled students. Viney ends her analysis with a focus on a specific HEI. She concludes that the Higher Education sector has had to absorb many changes over the last few years. Against this background there have been significant changes in the ways in which funding for students with disabilities is channelled. These changes have the potential to make a substantial difference to students, but there remain issues to be addressed.

In Chapter 5, Peter Stannett reflects upon his experience as a qualified psychologist of disabling practices that have threatened to prevent him from studying and practising psychology. His analysis is a damning assessment of the institutionalised discrimination within the provision of psychological training and employment. From low expectations at school to an occupational therapist only viewing his ambitions to gain a degree in psychology as a means to itself, to difficulties at various stages of application and interviews for paid work in psychological services, we are reminded that there is much work to be done in challenging the discrimination faced by disabled psychologists. It is particularly important that psychology embraces diversity and difference within its professional population. After all, these very professionals often work with diverse people, some of whom have been pushed to the margins of society as a result of their difference. It is crucial then that psychology embraces disabled professionals in order to promote a truly accepting and participatory discipline. Yet, it is also not about impairment: as the social model of disability demonstrates, the exclusion of people with impairments from employment is indicative of disabling practices. Disabled psychologists should be employed as psychologists – with their impairment needs being respected and met. Stannett's chapter asks, as a stark reminder, of the barriers that exist and of the possibilities for change.

Chapter 6, by Mark Priestley, analyses an often overlooked aspect of disability – older age. Social theories of ageing have often over-looked the embodied connection between ageing and disability. The normalcy of impaired bodies in old age, and particularly in advanced old age, may help to explain why older people with impairments are rarely regarded as 'disabled' in quite the same way as younger adults or children. Furthermore, it could be argued that disability studies and activism have tended to emphasise the experiences of disabled adults of working age or disabled children and, primarily, their experi-ences of schooling. When they both come together, we are reminded that disability and old age challenge the individualistic project of modernity – competitiveness, autonomy and independence – and that such a project is often closely linked to the projected outcomes of psychological intervention. In contrast, this chapter reminds us of the cultural and political formations of human categories that psychology must be careful not to recreate in its theories and practices.

Donna Reeve, Chapter 7, opposes the psychopathology of psychology which generally views disability as being the domain of rehabilitation psychology rather than part of mainstream psychological training. Reeve argues for the specific inclusion of both structural and psycho-emotional dimensions of disability within an extended social relational definition of disability. This, she aims to demonstrate, contributes to the development of a psychology, rather than a psycho-pathology, of disability. She aims to examine the ways in which structural and cultural relations of disability impact on the psycho-emotional experiences of disabled people by drawing on the accounts of people with physical impairments. This chapter provides a useful link from disability as it is experienced and challenged to wider questions of how psychology can and should engage with disability and impairment.

Part II of the book examines some of the practices of psychology, in relation to well-travelled terrains of chartered, educational, teaching, counselling and community psychology. Rose (1989) under-stands these professional, disciplinary and institutional practices as contributed to the psy-complex. This tangled weave of knowledge production aims to govern the soul and psyche. This raises real concerns for disabled people. Historically, disabled people have constituted a specific grouping of the 'human subject' that these psy-complex practitioners aim to normalise, rehabilitate, cure and, in consequence, pathologise. The contributors to this book take a critical, perhaps distanced, position in relation to the practices of the psy-complex. Their remit is to think again about these practices from a disability studies stance and available social theories of disability.

Chapter 8 by Levinson and Parritt brings in the authors' own experiences as disabled psychologists. Their focus is on how they, as disabled professionals, have faced and challenged barriers within a whole host of professional contexts. Their chapter is a timely overview of the ways in which organisations such as the British Psychological Society (BPS) – the main professional organisation and affiliation of British psychology students, trainees, researchers and practitioners – should engage with the professional and human rights of students with disabilities and practitioners. Disabled psychologists may challenge the underlying perceptions of clinical and health psychologists and members of other health professions. Their professional roles clash with stereotypes of disability that are firmly linked to patients. The authors integrate their personal experience and observations with the prevailing approaches to disability. They also suggest how the BPS can foster more positive training, practice and research in the relevant applied disciplines of clinical, health and counselling psychology. These suggestions necessarily involve an engagement with models and understandings of disability. Significantly, their suggestions are timely in view of the pressing legislation confronting the BPS.

In Chapter 9, Jennifer Clegg critically reflects on her work as a clinical psychologist working with people with the label of learning difficulties or intellectual disability. Her analysis raises difficult questions about the potency of models and theories of disability in accounting for forms of professional practice which are subject to a whole host of institutional pressures, changing constructions of impairment and disability, legislative developments that promote inclusive rhetoric without associated funds and the relative powers of people with 'intellectual disabilities' and their carers/families. Set against this context, Clegg analyses some significant concerns faced by people with learning difficulties and clinical psychologists: responding to self-harm, tragedy, aggression and promoting empowerment. In contrast to psychological theories and professional interventions that individualise or pathologise such problems, Clegg traces a number of relational and systemic forms of clinical psychological practice which recognise and emphasise the psycho-social nature of distress. Her analysis answers Marks' (2002) demand to break the split between the psyche and the social – exploring differences while avoiding polarities in order to develop and keep an intervention in motion. Such a stance is at the heart of a social constructionist approach to psychology and disability studies, which engages with multiple realities, distributed selves and the mixing of associated discourses.

The process of deconstructing and unpicking disability and professional discourses is taken up by Liz Todd in Chapter 10. The arena of poststructuralist thought is drawn upon to unpick the meaning-making and creation of professional discourses in relation to disabled children, their parents and educational contexts. A particular concern of Todd is the way in which professionalised discourses of impairment and disability threaten to become totalising discourses, where individual nuances of children are blurred by impairment-centred professional practices of diagnosis, assessment and intervention. Todd argues that a process of deconstruction challenges professionalised tendencies to categorise and exclude children on the basis of perceived 'otherness' and instead puts forward ideas for the promotion of inclusive participative practice – which bridge critical psychological practice and disability studies.

Swain, Griffiths and French, Chapter 11, refer to a research project that explored the provision of counselling for disabled people in primary health care and a further education college, through open-ended interviews with both counsellors and disabled clients. They note that counselling and disability studies appear, at first sights, to be at opposite ends of the spectrum. The former seems to emphasise individual adjustment (perhaps to impairment), while the latter expects society to change (to include people with impairments). Their aim is to re-politicise the counselling room and to consider the ways in which practising counsellors can critically reflect on the dominant ideology of individualism and the pathologising of social problems. Instead, suggestions for externalising the aetiology of psychological difficulties are offered, in ways that are more in line with a disability studies perspective.

In Chapter 12, Kagan *et al.* introduce a particular form of psychology – community social psychology (CSP). Psychological practice associated with CSP differs from traditional professionalised approaches to psychology in that work is undertaken alongside people and their communities, psychological resources are shared and a range of stakeholders are involved (including community members and professional groups). Following this introduction, the authors present work undertaken with people with the label of learning difficulties. They describe a systemic and distributed approach to practice in which people with the label of learning difficulties, their families and professionals worked together to devise a meaningful programme of person-centred planning. An engagement with social systems challenges the dominance of expert knowledge and provides access to the huge intellectual and practical resources available from social groups. This chapter demands psychologists to broaden psychological theory and knowledge in ways conceptualised by co-researchers of under-represented and marginalised communities.

The concluding chapter, by the editors, identifies some key objectives that need to be addressed by a psychology that aims to promote the analytical qualities and emancipatory aims of disability studies. In the light of the theoretical and practical failings and potential islets of resistance and good practice, it is argued that psychology can contribute to the project of disability studies by adopting objectives including rethinking impairment, recognise the elusive psychological elements of disablement, assume an active/activist view of disabled people, promote a psychology of inclusion, seek radical psychological theories and develop emancipatory research practices.

Part I

The Psychology of Disability: From Infancy to Adulthood

Chapter 2

Parents, Professionals and Disabled Babies: Personal Reflections on Disabled Lives

Claire Tregaskis

Introduction

This chapter explores the experiences of families with babies and young children with impairments who have sometimes been disempowered by the experience of coming together with professionals who have not always been able to see the humanity that lies behind and within a diagnosis of impairment. Drawing both on my personal life experience as a disabled person and data from a current Economic and Social Research Council (ESRC) project, *Parents, Professionals and Disabled Babies* (http://www.shef.ac.uk/inclusive-education/disabledbabies/), it shows what effects a wholly medicalised and depersonalised approach to diagnosis and treatment may have both on the disabled person themselves, and on family dynamics as a whole, and how in turn this may lead to the creation of what we might term 'disabled families'. Such considerations are crucial to the development of psychological theory and practice that provides enabling concepts of disability, impairment, childhood and family.

In drawing comparisons between the experiences of families in the current research sample and those of my own family from 40 years ago, it is suggested that little has changed down the years in the way that some professionals continue to objectify disabled people and render them as 'other' in ways that can have serious long-term negative effects on their subsequent life chances. More positively, however, data from the current study also suggests that families today are clearer about wanting ordinary lives that enable their disabled children to have equal opportunities alongside their non-disabled siblings and peers. In terms of delivering high-quality services to families in the future, the data suggests that professionals – including those who are practising from a (particular) psychological perspective – will need to take more account of this desire for ordinary lives in shaping and delivering the services they offer.

Birth, infancy and childhood: The beginnings of a disability career

Mine was a blue-light birth – a loud, confused environment characterised, so my mother tells me, by ambulance men telling her repeatedly to 'hang on, missus' as they struggled to complete her emergency transfer from the cottage hospital she had been booked into for my birth to the bigger maternity unit seven miles away. It emerged later that the cottage hospital had suspected a breech birth from the outset, but had decided they could cope anyway...until towards the end of the labour, when they suddenly realised that they couldn't. Cue the blue lights and the last-minute transfer, and my traumatic introduction to a world where I was to discover that over time my life course would continue to be affected by medical snap judgements like this one that characterised my birth. So bruised and battered was I by the delivery that for some time I was not expected to survive. My dad was in an understandably panicked state, and kept ringing the special care baby unit to ask how I was, until the staff had to gently explain to him that having to answer the phone all the time was taking them away from the job in hand of keeping us babies alive. So he had to rein in his fear and keep it hidden. That was the way of things then.

A hurried baptism followed, with only two other family members present due to bad weather conditions that prevented the rest from making the trip. And then gradually as the bruising on my body subsided I was able to abandon my original frog-like pose, and instead lie on my back like other babies. I think that was when they started to realise that I would survive. From what I can gather, though, at this stage nobody mentioned the possibility that the trauma of my birth might have resulted in any sort of long-term impairment. For my parents, the memory of numerous previous miscarriages meant that their over-riding feeling now was one of relief, at having a live child to take home with them. Yet it was still a bitter-sweet moment, made even more poignant by the fact that on the same day I was born another baby had been found abandoned on the hospital doorstep. My mum said she couldn't help but compare their own struggle to keep me – a desperately wanted but seriously ill baby – alive, at the very same time that this other poor baby had been left by its own parents. From what she's said, I think this contrast made her and my dad even stronger in their resolve that, if they had anything to do with it, I was going to survive.

I had cause to reflect on this experience some years ago, when I was struggling to make sense of what had happened when I was born. I was talking to my then GP about it, and he explained that given my mother's pre-existing gynaecological problems I would never know if my impairment was caused *in utero* or by the emergency circumstances surrounding the time of birth itself. He then continued by reading me an extract from my early medical notes. These confirmed that early on in babyhood I had been 'very poorly'. However, the doctor had also written that I was 'clearly a much loved and well cared for baby'. When he read this out it made me want to cry, because it cut through all the subsequent muddle and confusion of my life and highlighted the fundamental truth, which was that my parents had always loved me. At that point I realised that actually it didn't matter exactly what had happened to cause my impairment. The thing that counted most was that they had loved me enough to support me through all the traumas that were to come as a result of my being labelled as a disabled person.

In fact, though, from what I can gather it was not until I was 18-months old that the diagnosis of 'cerebral palsy' began to be talked about. Before then, my grandmother had apparently kept on at my mum, telling her 'there's something wrong with that child' because I was slower to reach developmental milestones than was usual in her experience. But my mum didn't really listen at the time, dismissing it as an example of an interfering mother-in-law (though she took it all back eight years later when my non-disabled sister was born, and she realised how much more quickly she developed than I had done). It must also have been really hard for her to hear anyone cast doubt on the apparent perfection of her longed-for baby, so it's not surprising that she chose to ignore the hint that was being made.

Even when the diagnosis was formally made by the medical profession, it appears that little further information about the condition was forthcoming, leaving my mum to conclude that it just meant I would be a bit slower to reach my developmental milestones than other children. It seems that nobody explained to her that there might be some things I would never be able to do, or suggested adaptive strategies to get around any such restrictions. I suspect that this lack of information was compounded both by the doctors' relative lack of knowledge about cerebral palsy at that time, making them unwilling to commit themselves to saying something they might later have to retract, and by geographical barriers, in that by this time we had moved down to Cornwall with my dad's job. However, 40 plus years ago, Cornwall had no resident paediatrician. Hence each time we had an appointment we had to make a 200-mile round trip back to where I was born, in order to be seen by the specialist there. The stress imposed on my parents by having to undertake this journey on a regular basis, and its knock-on effect on the possibility of enjoying an ordinary family life, may easily be imagined. Further, I suspect that having made the sacrifices needed to undertake this trip, they would have been looking for a positive outcome from each consultation, to in a sense justify the effort they'd made in getting there. In such circumstances, I can imagine that it must have been difficult for them to challenge the information (or lack of it) they were being given, especially as new parents who, like others, will have doubted their own ability and understanding at times, preferring to defer to expert knowledge instead.

Yet from my mother's reactions after subsequent consultations that I can actively remember, I know that they didn't always believe what they were being told. As soon as we were outside the consulting room she would belittle the doctor's negative comments about me, and so I would learn to bury the hurt in what they had said about me, and about the negative prognosis that was being offered. She would never have dreamt of missing an appointment – that would have been too openly subversive a strategy. Instead we would meekly go along, and not challenge anything that was said, only to burst out laughing afterwards as we reviewed the latest outlandish statement about my lack of ability and poor future prospects. Sometimes indeed these diagnoses seemed so wide of the mark that it felt as though they were being made of somebody else, and it was often hard to take seriously a judgement that was being made on the basis of a five-minute consultation from someone whom we had never met before, and would be unlikely to see again. Because that was another thing – throughout my childhood we never saw the same paediatrician twice, not even once Cornwall had developed its own paediatric service. This organisational barrier meant that each time we went along it was to meet someone new, and to whom I was just a set of symptoms rather than a whole person. Hence it is perhaps unsurprising that the experience was routinely one of being made to feel coldly judged by a stranger who had no need or desire to get to know who I was beyond the boundaries of that one consultation. Each time I was made to feel like a sub-standard object – making the opportunity to subvert the experience through laughter afterwards an essential survival strategy.

In retrospect I sometimes wish we had been brave enough to actively challenge such oppressive behaviour at the time. However, in truth we are talking about a different era here, one in which all doctors were treated as gods, and where it was unthinkable that anyone, especially not an ordinary working-class family, might challenge what they said. Also, my mum had herself had her fair share of serious illness in her life, involving several long stays in hospital. Such experiences must have coloured her approach to the doctors in my own case, even though as I was a small child she would hardly have shared any private misgivings with me at the time. They may also have been at least partly responsible for the fact that we didn't really openly discuss my impairment or its effects when I was growing up, an approach which had the unfortunate effect of making me think that probably one day I would wake up and be 'better'. This misconception persisted until I was 14, when a neurologist put me straight by explaining that I would always have 'CP', a revelation that although crushing at one level, at the same time came, as a massive relief, because now I knew the true extent of what I was dealing with, and so could get on with the reality of my life as it was. It was still a day of huge grief for my dad, though, as he felt that what the neurologist had told me represented the denial of the possibility of all hope for the future. Perhaps it would be more accurate to say it marked the end of his own hopes that life would get easier for me in the future, a loss which I suspect took him some time to come to terms with.

For myself, on the other hand, I learned to utilise this irrefutable factual knowledge alongside my mother's strategy of not believing most of what we were told by other transitory consultants down the years, an approach which had bred in me a strong resistance to unproven negative medical judgements. This proved an important survival mechanism for me down the years. Thus over time I learnt to extract the most important (by which I mean the most value-free) bits of information from each consultation, whilst defending against the doctors' negative responses to my impairment. In at least three memorable cases, such a defence was necessary to the preservation of my very self-hood.

In the first instance, when I was three, we were still having to make our 200-mile round trip to see the consultant. On one particular occasion the consultant we saw was black. Growing up in Cornwall in the early 1960s meant that I had never seen a black person before. As a result, according to my mum, I was spellbound by his appearance, and remained speechless throughout the consultation as I gazed at him in wonder. And apparently once we got outside again I repeated to her word-for-word the answers for all the questions he had asked me, and for which I had failed to answer at the time. Unfortunately, however, my silence during the consultation had serious diagnostic repercussions, as the doctor took this to mean that I had learning difficulties, thus creating another label to be added to my ever-growing file of medical notes. What was most disturbing about this incident was the extent to which it demonstrates the individualisation of disability and impairment issues. Here this doctor did not consider any environmental factors that might be contributing to my silence, or do anything to put me at ease during the consultation that might have helped me open up to him. Instead, he straightforwardly assumed that my silence represented an individual learning difficulty on my part, and so that's what went on my notes. And of course, once something is written up in your medical notes, it can be very difficult to have that opinion revised. Furthermore, his snap judgement will have been used for guidance by many of the subsequent transitory paediatricians whom I saw, and so may well in turn have affected how they viewed and treated me.

Being attributed this learning difficulty diagnosis represented a particular barrier given the potential power it had to affect my future, coming as it did before the 1970 Education Act, which guaranteed access to education for all children, including those with learning difficulties. Certainly it may well have influenced the later actions of the school doctor at primary school who, when I was five, tried to insist that I should go away and board at a special school, because I wouldn't speak to him when he tried to examine me. Again this was really down to my inherent shyness with strangers, but like the previous consultant he could only see it as a sign of learning difficulty. I was only saved on that occasion by my headmistress, who knew me far better than he did. She apparently had a fierce three-hour row with him over the issue, and insisted that I stay in her mainstream primary school. Luckily she won the day, and my educational future was assured. However, it was a terrifying reminder of how shyness and difficulty in verbal communication could be turned by professionals into something far more sinister. They seem like poor reasons to condemn a child to a life of social exclusion.

A further example of overt discrimination that sticks in my mind happened much later again, when I was 14, thus demonstrating a disturbing continuity of negative behaviour by the paediatricians I met throughout my childhood. At 14, I still had difficulty talking to strangers, so during medical consultations my mum would normally speak on my behalf. This time the consultant asked me what I wanted to do when I left school, so mum replied that the family hoped I would go to university. His response to this aspiring statement was wholly negative and dismissive, as he told us that his own daughters were far more intelligent than me, and they weren't clever enough to go to university. He suggested that my hopes were unrealistic, and that it would be far better for me to do something less stressful instead, like working in the outdoors planting potatoes. Needless to say, this was one of those occasions when mum and I came out of the consultation room and doubled up with laughter, because we both knew I would go on to university. Yet at another level his comments continued to rankle with me, and looking back I know they had an effect in increasing my competitiveness in ways that weren't always constructive, to try and prove him wrong. Indeed, that particular monkey stayed on my back for many years, until the day when circumstances conspired to bring us together again as trustees of the same charity. Perhaps strangely, when it came down to it I felt no need to challenge him about his past behaviour – indeed, he didn't even realise that he'd met me before. Instead I realised what was most important was that he could see me as a competent disabled person and a professional in my own right, doing a valuable job in the here and now. It was only at that point that I was able to let go of his negative value judgement on me from all those years ago. Such is the long-term power of medical professionals to affect the self-image of the clients they work with.

Given the persistence of attitude and labelling barriers like those detailed in here, I was actually extremely fortunate that my impairment needs meant that, in addition to the intermittent inspections by paediatricians, I was also seen routinely throughout my childhood by an orthopaedic surgeon. Even more fortunately, unlike with the paediatricians, I saw the same man regularly every three to six months from the age of three onwards. Several factors contributed to this being a more positive experience than those previously described. First, his surgeries often took place in a town near to where we lived, so mum and I only had to miss half a day of normal activity to see him, as opposed to the all-day excursions needed to see the paediatrician at a city 30 miles away. So it was easier to see these local visits as a temporary nuisance, rather than something that affected the whole way we lived. Second, being an orthopaedic surgeon meant that this consultant saw a wide range of patients – both children and adults, and both disabled and non-disabled people. In my view, this predisposed him to be more able to see his patients as ordinary people who happened to have a skeletal problem that he could deal with, rather than objectifying us purely in terms of our diagnosis. Certainly when I was growing up I always felt that he could see the whole of who I was, not just the part of me that was CP-related. This made it easier to trust him, because I was reassured that he had my best interests at heart, and wasn't going to start experimenting on me in the way that happened to some of my friends who lived in other parts of the country. Third, he was enormously well respected and admired, both by his patients and within the medical profession as a whole. Thus over time I noticed that if he said something, or challenged someone else's decision, his view tended to prevail.

In very practical ways, these factors positively affected my ability to grow up and develop in a mainstream environment, in ways that the negative statements of other medical professionals had seemed to preclude. Throughout my childhood there were occasions when I had reason to be grateful for his intervention in challenging their negative value judgements, and thereby ensuring that my ordinary life course remained on track. It was he who openly questioned the diagnosis of learning difficulty, and also a subsequent IQ test which gave me a very low rating. Thirty plus years on I can still recall him dictating my case notes to his secretary on that occasion, and saying bluntly that 'this result is unfair'. I remember, too, the raised eyebrows of his secretary as she noted it all down, and anticipated the fireworks that would follow this statement. But it had the desired effect of challenging perceptions of me as being 'different', 'special' and 'sub-normal', and of thus keeping me in the mainstream. Additionally, he was the one consultant whose views my mum and I didn't have to constantly filter through to expose negativity. He was trustworthy simply because he did not need to objectify me in the way that the paediatricians did, but could instead see me as an ordinary person with normal aspirations, who happened to have additional physical support needs. This suggests the value of a multi-disciplinary approach to dealing with children with impairment, so that nobody's future prospects have to rely on the opinions and actions of any one set of medical professionals.

Forty years on: What happens now?

At the time of writing this chapter, I was nine months into my involvement with the ESRC-funded research project *Parents, Professionals and Disabled Babies: Identifying Enabling Care* (http://www.shef.ac.uk/inclusive-education/disabledbabies/). This research is being carried out jointly by two universities, and is exploring families' experiences of health and social care when they have a baby or young child who needs ongoing specialist support. A key aim of the research is to identify enabling care practices that support the families in maintaining ordinary family lives. Though much fieldwork remains to be completed, the pilot phase of the research has already suggested a number of areas in which, although in many ways services have undeniably improved in the past 40 years, a range of structural barriers persist. The data discussed in here is drawn from the 'Southtown' part of the research sample, which I was working on until August 2004. Some of these improvements and ongoing barriers are discussed in here, as a way of exploring both how far we have come in 40 years, and what barriers to effective care giving and support remain.

In terms of drawing comparisons between then and now, a key difference is that the current research project draws primarily on an urban-based sample of research participants. Thus for these families nearly all the services they need are based in the town where they live, and so travelling long distances for appointments is not the norm in the way it used to be for disabled families in Cornwall. Also, because the Southtown consultants are all locally based, the families appear to receive continuity of care from the same team – although not always from the same person in that team – over time. In addition, the development of a multi-disciplinary assessment process, whereby a child is seen over an intensive two-day period by all those health care professionals required to manage the effects of their impairment, is said by the professionals to be having positive benefits in terms of establishing a unified treatment regime. These locally based services are an important way in which the inevitable disruption to ordinary family life caused by the need to keep health-related appointments appears less severe nowadays. That said, analysis of the preliminary research data suggests that those mothers in the sample who work outside the home experience difficulties in managing the multiple appointments necessitated by a diagnosis of impairment alongside

their work commitments. One mother, herself an NHS professional, expressed particular concern at what she saw as the inflexi-
bility of the appointment system:

> It's just the age old problem with the NHS – they cater for people
> on the basis that they go in work time, and I was working full time,
> and the group sessions were at 2pm in the afternoon so that you
> couldn't even go to work and then come back, go and come back.
> Also 2pm is not practical, as many children have their nap time
> then. Maybe if we'd known it was as serious as autism we might
> have made more effort at that stage. In a way we were penalized
> for the fact that we were working. (Rebecca Portman)

At least two of the mothers in the sample have had to cut down
their work commitments as a result of the need to attend multiple
appointments and treatment sessions with their child. This in turn
has naturally had a negative impact on their family income levels,
which the award of Disability Living Allowance to meet some of
their children's mobility and care needs has done little to alleviate.
This finding corresponds with that of Kagan *et al.*'s (1998) study
into the experiences of working parents of disabled children, who
also uncovered economic disadvantage amongst (usually) mothers
of disabled children. Naturally, neither woman in the current
study begrudges the input of time when they can see that it is
helping their child. However, even when attending appointments,
there was a feeling that sometimes the time could be used more
effectively:

> The only thing I have felt at the Children's Centre is that every time
> we go we end up . . . sort of going back to the birth, telling the story
> and then writing it all down, which I don't really understand
> because I don't know why they have to write it down every time we
> go . . . because obviously we've been going since her birth. Y'know
> you're there a long time for all the paperwork . . . rather than
> thinking 'oh yeah, well we know Izzy, let's move on to what she
> needs now'. . . (Josie O'Hanlon)

Thus the data suggests that at present Southtown's multi-disciplinary
approach does not appear to continue beyond the assessment process.
Partly as a result of this, it also appears (from the families' accounts
of service provision) that not all families automatically get access to

all the services their children are entitled to. Some are clearly aware of this:

> I read the magazine, the Down's magazine and some areas seem to give a lot more of one thing than another . . . like . . . things like speech therapy, some people seem to be getting it every fortnight . . . and, y'know, we don't . . . get it every fortnight, so I don't know how they get it. I don't know if the resources are more in some areas . . . (Josie O'Hanlon)

Others are either not aware of this disparity or feel themselves to be isolated and engaged in a constant battle to get the services their child needs, as illustrated by my fieldnotes from a meeting with one group of parents:

> The parents again brought up the lack of integration of services and the frustration of trying to get in contact with the correct person for their needs. They felt that the bottom line was that service providers aimed to frustrate, and to try to put parents off until they were too tired to ask any more. Again there was a call for one person (at the top of the tree) to whom you could apply for multi-disciplinary services. All agreed that they cannot get a straight yes or no answer.

In terms of learning more about their child's impairments, and the benefits and services available to them, even those parents who did express general satisfaction with the services they received stated that they had obtained most information about what was on offer from other parents of disabled children, impairment-specific support groups or voluntary sector children's information services. Only one parent, herself an NHS worker, named NHS staff as key informants. Thus it appears that there is an ongoing barrier in information delivery to families by health and social care staff. This lack of information was also prevalent around the time of diagnosis of the child's impairment, despite previous research findings on the desirability of telling parents about the diagnosis more than once, to give them time to take in the information, and of reinforcing the message through the provision of appropriate written material (Sloper, 1999; Smith and Daughtrey, 2000). Again, most of the parents interviewed to date have reported that they were given relatively little information by medical staff, and that most of them had instead resorted to searching books and the Internet for the knowledge they needed to be able to understand the diagnosis and its implications. Post-diagnosis, some parents acknowledged that they knew how to 'play the system' in order to get quick access to the services they needed. One father was even forced into threatening to abandon his child with social services unless an urgently needed medical appointment was forthcoming. The tactic worked on that occasion, but it should not have needed to come to that.

More positively, there has in this study been a real sense of families being prepared to fight for their children's rights, because they see no reason why disabled children should be seen as second-class citizens. This is a real step forward from 40 years ago, when disabled people were often objectified, viewed purely in terms of their impairments, and seen as departing from expected norms of appearance, behaviour and performance (Finkelstein, 1980; Oliver, 1990, 1996b; Goodley, 2000; Tregaskis, 2004). Some of the parents I have spoken to openly acknowledged that things are easier for them nowadays, in that although society is more competitive nowadays, there is also more scope for individual self-expression. Thus, as one mum put it:

> In the early days, when I took him out I used to really worry in case he made too much noise and drew attention to himself. But over the years I've begun to relax, and to think instead 'Yeah, bring it on, make as much noise as you like'. I know now that he has a right to be himself.

Despite this increased acceptance of difference within families, too often there appears to be an ongoing gap between their aspirations and the treatment they receive from professionals. Specifically, most parents in the current sample have compared the services on offer to their disabled and non-disabled children, and feel their disabled child is missing out. In terms of equipment, for example, one group reported their unhappiness about an apparent double standard around both cost and availability, as this meeting report suggests. Here the families complained that:

> Non impaired children did not require special aids; and standard equipment was freely and instantly available in large stores at reasonable prices. Their parents had more time as the children quickly became independent, and this was an area of discrimination for parents of disabled children. Equipment for disabled children was

not freely available in the same way, and even if the parents of disabled children offered to pay for equipment themselves – an expensive alternative – they were advised by professionals against this course of action as safety standards (whose standards referred to here were not specified) may not be met. (Fieldnotes)

Another parent, whilst generally happy with the treatment her child was receiving, noted a certain impersonality in the approach of some consultants:

sometimes I felt that . . . they referred to her as 'the child with Down's Syndrome', rather than 'Izzy, with Down's Syndrome'. (Josie O'Hanlon)

This type of data suggests that at least some parents are becoming increasingly aware of, and resistant to, the depersonalised and objectified approach to working with disabled people that was fairly common in my experience from 40 years ago (see also Murray and Penman, 1996, 2000). Others have also had to resist an apparent inability amongst some medical staff to see their parental desire to bond with their disabled child as being natural:

I got nagged by the social worker that I should be taking some fresh air and going for a walk, and I thought 'I don't need you to tell me to get out and have some fresh air, there's time for that, I'm not suffering, I'm fine but I don't have time'. What was important to me at that time was caring for my son, and they were a bit trying to force it down your throat that you have got to look after yourself. And I am thinking 'I am grown up, thank you'. . . . They were thinking that I was going to go mad in the hospital because I was just confined to the ward and not getting out . . . What they were getting at . . . they thought I had got this bond problem where I couldn't leave him and it wasn't that I couldn't leave him or that I didn't want to leave him it was just practical, you know. It was just I'd rather sleep, thanks, than go for a walk. (Mags Hardcastle)

Luckily Mags was strong enough to be able to resist the apparent negative projections of the staff on the ward, and continued to happily bond with her son. Taken together, these data suggest that the parents are able to see impairment as part of the mainstream continuum of human experience, and that as a result they expect their family experience to be recognised as ordinary rather than as 'special' and 'different'. Today's parents are also more aware of their own rights and those of their children, and seem more prepared to complain rather than go along with second-class treatment of their child. In seeking to respond to these attitudes within families, it is suggested that more staff in health care related professions will need to move from an individual pathological treatment approach to one based on an understanding that, in working with disabled children, they are also going to be working with that child's family, who love that child and expect them to be accorded the same level of service and respect as is offered to non-disabled people.

Within psychology, Developmental Systems Theory (DST) (Ford and Lerner, 1992) would seem to offer staff a conceptual framework that could support them to work more holistically with disabled families, by stressing the importance of understanding the needs of individuals within a social context (ibid., p. 46). Although the DST model does assume that illness and impairment represent 'decremental change' to the individual (ibid., p. 52), when talking in more general terms about the power of human potential, Ford and Lerner make clear that 'the initial conditions of life do not determine one's life course' (ibid., p. 205), 'there is no "one right way" for human development to proceed' and that 'there is great adaptive and social value in the human diversity that exists' (ibid., p. 230). If these general principles were applied rigorously in analysing disabled as well as non-disabled people's life experiences, I suspect that more psychologists would be able to view impairment, and disabled families' achievements in overcoming disabling environmental barriers, more positively. They might then also be able to recognise that impairment factors are just one aspect of people's lives, and not all-encompassing negative determinants that prevent all possibility of personal incremental change and wider social inclusion.

In turn, where psychologists are able to view impairment in these more positive ways, there appears to be great scope for them to develop more effective working partnerships with disabled families that can in turn support disabled children to develop to reach their full potential. Professionals can also provide essential out-of-family support direct to children, not least by recognising the 'pressures and stressors that children can be under which they might elect to conceal from the adults around them' (Moore *et al.*, 1996). I suspect that some disabled children may feel under particular pressure to act as if all is well, because they do not want their families to feel that they have let them down by not conforming to normative standards of appearance, behaviour or performance. In such circumstances, having an external party to turn to, and in whom to confide and explore these fears, would be invaluable.

Conclusions

In this chapter, I began by describing aspects of my own life experience as a disabled person, and explaining how the presence of both structural and attitude barriers routinely acted to disable my family as a whole. I then moved on to discuss what the emerging data from the current research project, *Parents, Professionals and Disabled Babies*, may be able to tell us about how the families of disabled babies today experience the health and social care system. Some of the data presented here suggest that fundamental inequalities in accessing health and social care remain, and that some health and social care staff remain unduly wedded to an individual pathologising treatment approach that can disable the whole family in both economic and social terms. More encouragingly, other data suggest both a degree of service improvement over time, and a greater sense of families being able to see impairment experience as part of the ordinary continuum of mainstream life, in a way that wasn't really possible 40 years ago. I hope and believe that this more inclusive approach, when supported by wider social initiatives such as the further development of inclusive education, will give their children a greater sense of inherent self-confidence and self-worth that will in turn help them to make their way in the world as they grow up.

Chapter 3

Being in School? Exclusion and the Denial of Psychological Reality

Pippa Murray

Introduction

The current policy climate is one of social inclusion, in which the entitlement of disabled children and young people to mainstream education has never had better legislative support (SENDA, 2001). Unfortunately, for those children and young people, policy and practice are two very different things. Just how wide the gap really is depends to a considerable degree on how we define our terms. It is one thing to see inclusion in mainstream schools as a matter of 'allowing disabled children to attend', and quite another to see that as a necessary but far from sufficient condition of inclusion. When we take the latter view, and insist that inclusion also requires the humanising qualities of care and respect, then, as this chapter shows, all is far from well.

Educational stories of disablement

Craig, fifteen-years old, has attended his local secondary school (with support worker) on a full-time basis for the past three years. In spite of the fact both he and staff are happy with his placement there, Craig has no real friends at the school. Nor does he receive a meaningful education as his impairments prevent him from learning in a conventional fashion, and his teachers have failed to make the curricular adaptations necessary for his learning. Consequently Craig, though an accepted presence, is visibly set apart from the majority.

Similarly, seven-year-old Tanya's experience within her mainstream primary school is one of differential treatment because she cannot conform to 'normal' developmental or social expectations. She loves to paint alongside her classmates, and is proud of her work. But one morning her mother, looking at the artwork on the walls of the classroom, noticed that none of her paintings were on display. On questioning this she was told, 'it is impossible to know what Tanya's scribbles are – a tree doesn't look like a tree, a house doesn't look like a house'. On this basis the class teacher had decided her paintings did not merit being shown alongside those of the rest of the class. Sadly, such experiences are not unusual . . .

- Jonny is asked to go home for dinner as there is no one to support him during the lunch hour . . .
- Jasmine comes home from school with her body arched in a fixed position because she has not been taken out of her chair all day. Although her mother asked that Jasmine be allowed to lie on the floor from time to time, the school responded by saying that to do so would be against their lifting and handling policy . . .
- Katie is made to sit apart from the rest of her class during school assembly so that she is beside her classroom assistant . . .
- Since Abdul's system of communication is unrecognised, there is no one at school who can interpret his gestures . . .
- Calum is asked to repeat a year (for the third time) in order to 'catch up with his peers'. At the same time Calum's parents are told he is socially immature and finds it very hard to maintain friendships!
- Before she can read her English texts, Isabella has to wait until she receives them in large print – by which time her peers have usually moved on to the next book . . .
- Dominic sits beside the class teacher while all his classmates perform a play to the rest of the school . . .
- Having succeeded in getting to university – a rare thing for any disabled young person – Tina has to miss a series of lectures as she is physically unable to get into the classroom . . .
- Jamie is given only half an hour extra to complete his GCSE English exam – in spite of the fact it takes him more than twice as long as his non-disabled peers to express his thoughts on paper . . .
- Rosa is asked to stay at home when her support worker is sick . . .

. . . and so on. These stories are not limited to any particular school, region or grouping of disabled young people. Sadly, they are common experiences for children and young people of all ages and with all types of impairment. Being seen as different at school has a knock-on effect on relationships elsewhere, since it usually means having no one to go out with afterwards. Such collective activities as swimming, going to town, park, bowling alley or football match all form a vital part of socialisation (Corker *et al.*, 2001; Murray, 2002). This being the case, differential treatment in the classroom cannot but have far-reaching consequences.

It is not my intention in this chapter to go into these stories or to comment on their frequently dubious legality. Rather, my aim is to focus on the emotional and psychological consequences for disabled young people and to note the effects on their non-disabled counterparts who, through such examples, learn the core messages of a disabling world: that it is OK for Jonny to be sent home for dinner, for Calum to repeat Year One three times and for Tina to miss her lectures. In sum, that it is normal and natural for disabled young people to be *absent*. Making visible the consequences of disablement – some obvious, others less so – is the first necessary step in the process of healing and resolution.

A personal account

I was first introduced to the subtleties of being in but not belonging to the mainstream some fifteen years ago. I learned about them by observing the experiences of my own son, perceived by many as too difficult to include in the mainstream. Having begged, pleaded and fought for a place in the school his non-disabled sister attended, I naively thought his presence there would be all that was required. I knew that staff would be on a steep learning curve, and that it might take some time for things to work out, but I could not have anticipated the reality he encountered: of exclusion wearing the face of inclusion; of his being there without in any real sense belonging.

The past five years as a researcher have allowed me to explore further this tension between appearance and reality. In talking to young disabled people with a wide range of impairment and experience of mainstream education, a universal theme to emerge has been that of being present but not belonging. As one young man told me, 'mainstream schools treat you differently from other students'.

The consequences of my son's impairments made it necessary to spend time with him, observing his responses carefully in order to gauge his opinions and pick out his preferences. Like many children with complex impairments, his sensitivity to others was such that he would detect their attitudes towards him from the sound of a voice or the touch of a hand. By watching and listening, within the context of enjoying his presence and valuing his being, I realised that the 'bottom line' for his inclusion in any setting lay in his being accepted exactly as he was by whoever was supporting him. If his support worker was open to his ways of being, and enjoyed his company, my son seemed instinctively to know he was safe, and could allow himself to relax. If, on the other hand, his support worker had fixed ideas that denied those ways of being, he would become tense, withdrawn and at times openly distressed.

The quality of support my son received had marked consequences for his experience. Though his impairment was a given, the sense he himself made of it was not, and it was of the utmost importance to me that he was supported in developing a positive self-image. He lived in a disabling world, and there were serious limits to my powers to protect him from its harsh realities. What I could do, however, was strive to counteract any tendency on his part to internalise the core message from that world, relayed in ways gross and subtle, that he was of less value than others. I therefore took any sign of withdrawal or tension very seriously. In doing so, I began to see how the nature of his support affected the degree to which his right to be there was acknowledged, his presence accepted.

At first both my son and I were excluded from the process of selecting his support worker: only after a considerable struggle did we win this 'concession'. Where support workers themselves doubted my son's right to be there, his peers took little interest in him. Conversely, when support workers enjoyed his company and were able to develop positive relationships with him, classmates accepted his presence with greater equanimity. It will come as no surprise to parents of disabled children that my attempts to argue the need to pay close attention to my son's emotional well-being went largely unheeded. The collective mindset of a disabling world was too strong, and I rarely, if ever, succeeded in convincing those charged with his education of the importance of his internal experience. The undisguised disregard for *his* emotional well-being stood in stark contrast to the value nominally placed on that of his non-disabled sister. On more than one occasion I was told that her well-being would be threatened by his presence in the same school. As a matter of fact, this disparity of concern was not only unjust, but inaccurate: my daughter was forever sad that her brother could not be there with her. Contrary to the perceptions of a disabling world, she suffered from his absence.

The denial of psychological reality

This deep-seated failure to acknowledge their internal experiences typifies societal attitudes to virtually all disabled young people, who are simply not seen as psychologically 'real' by the majority. When we deny the psychological reality of others, our capacity for empathy is forfeited: *they* cease to be human in *our* innermost representations of *them*. And when that happens there is every cause for alarm. Not a single one of the countless atrocities committed by human beings down the ages could have taken place without being preceded by this same denial. Of course, the practices described here do not justify the label *atrocity*, but they do amount to a form of *abuse*. The denial of psychological reality gives licence to the assumption that relationships are not central to the well-being of disabled young people, as they are to everyone else. And the more complex the impairment, the greater that licence. Owen's is a case in point:

> That his psychological health depended on him having opportunities for interaction with a range of people became clear when, after leaving school, he was without any provision at all for nine months due to the refusal of our local authority to pay any attention to his clearly stated choice ... Owen was deteriorating daily as a result of his isolation. (Murray, 2004)

By contrast, Alison tells how her sister Leanne is happiest when she is in valued, respectful relationship:

> She just likes the company of other people, people talking to her, not about her but talking to her. I don't know if Mum told you, but we had some of Chloe's friends down and she loved it. One of them came up to her and held her hand when he was talking to her and she loved that. She likes Chloe's boyfriend Joe as well, she's got a big soft spot for him ... she just likes people to have a conversation with her, likes to be around people. (Murray, 2004)

As I listen to other young disabled people I hear the same story – of how the deep pain of exclusion lies in the denial of access to 'ordinary' relationship. Although we have journeyed a long way in the last thirty years, it seems that the emotional and psychological structures shoring up a disabling world stem from the idea that impairment indicates some kind of 'sub-human' state. That idea can itself be traced back to a failure of imagination whereby disabled young people are seen as cardboard cut-outs, lacking psychological depth.

The anxieties of one young man, prior to meeting someone new, demonstrate how the constant experience of being rebuffed has taught him not to take acceptance of his humanity for granted:

> I was a bit worried that she would find me awful and very gratified to find that she was not put off by my impairments. I think it will be easier to go there next time, now that I know that she is OK with me. I wish everyone was the same, and then my life would be much happier. (William, personal correspondence, 2002)

William, like so many before him, pays a heavy price for being perceived as different. In the damage done to self-esteem, and in his dangerously low level of self-confidence, he is not alone:

> As far as relationships go many disabled people have nothing to offer a normal peer.... I am a rather awkward person... I just lack a presence that fits in. (Tyler, personal correspondence, 2004)

Are Owen, William and Tyler so very different from us? Don't we all know what it feels like to be excluded from relationships? Over the past few years, in workshops with both disabled and non-disabled people, I have explored the experiences of inclusion and exclusion (Table 3.1), and their effects on emotional well-being. There is a striking similarity in the words used by participants to describe their experience.

These universal responses speak volumes. In all the complexity – some of it unavoidable at this point in time – that surrounds the issue of inclusion, it is good to remind ourselves that at root we are speaking of something very simple, very ordinary and very much within the experience of every one of us. From this perspective the failures of empathy that necessarily accompany exclusion amount to a denial not only of the other, but of our own humanity. As we have already noted, the adverse consequences of a disabling world touch all of us.

Table 3.1   The words of exclusion and inclusion

Exclusion	Inclusion
Useless, unwanted, depressed, lonely, isolated	Warm, secure, anything is possible
Sad, angry, frustrated	Important, self-worth, loved, respected
Isolated, unhappy, unconfident, unfair	Happy, fulfilled
Hurt, dismayed, confused, betrayed	Valued, needed, loved, safe
Unsure of myself, lacking confidence, dependent	Able, creative, healthy, alive
Frightened, can't take anything in	Relaxed, involved, warm, comfortable
Different, stressed, afraid, unloved, ridiculed	Safe, calm, hopeful, light hearted
Insecure, low self-esteem, inadequate, not good enough	Involved, wanted, able to contribute
Embarrassed, anxious, depressed	Valued, strong, confident, human

Conclusion

We began this chapter from the premise that inclusion requires more than allowing the other in; that also required all the care and respect always due from one human being to another. Care and respect depend on *empathy* – on our recognising, deep down and not just as a 'head thing', that *this is a real person I'm dealing with*. Seeing the other as having a psychological reality equal to our own is the start *and* end point of the empathy I am speaking of.

Empathy has the mysterious quality of being self-enriching. How? Because not only it is a necessary *condition* of the care and respect which, when added to 'allowing the other to be here', create an inclusive environment, it is also a *product* of that care and respect. We only begin to attend, in any meaningful sense of the word, to another's well-being when we acknowledge the reality of their internal experience. Such attention in turn elicits richer and more complete pictures of that internal reality. Just as absence of empathy and absence of respect operate as cause and effect of one another in a vicious circle of exclusion; so do their presence, working in mirror image of the same dynamic, create the virtuous circle of inclusion.

To understand the problem, then, is to understand the solution. The stories told here, of exclusion dressed up as its opposite, reflect a near total lack of empathy. That lack of empathy stems, as lack of empathy always does, from fear: in this case the fear of impairment engendered by a disabling world. By understanding the dynamic by which exclusion is not only caused by, but causes, the failure to see disabled children as real people, a way out is revealed.

Chapter 4

The Disability Discrimination Act and Lifelong Learning? Students with Disabilities and Higher Education

Deb Viney

Introducing the position of students with disabilities in Higher Education

Students with disabilities have been attending Higher Education Institutions (HEIs) for decades, although their numbers appear to have been small until recently. A few HEIs developed specialist residential accommodation and facilities (e.g. Clarkson House at the University of Southampton; Kulukundis House at the University of Sussex) from the 1970s onwards to support the residential and personal care needs of students with severe physical impairments. No national statistics are available prior to 1994; however, anecdotal evidence from Disability Officers suggests that, at least until the 1990s, the HEIs were usually aware only of those students with relatively severe physical and sensory impairments. The needs of those with "hidden impairments" (e.g. dyslexia, mental health issues) were seldom considered, except perhaps where their individual health issues directly affected their grades (when, e.g., "special consideration" might be permitted at an examination board). Typically, particularly prior to implementation of the Disability Discrimination Act (DDA) IV in 2002, where HEIs made adjustments to the needs of students, they were individualised and reactive changes, rather than the result of proactive services supported by institution-wide strategic planning.

The official statistics for Higher Education

Higher Education Institutions report an increasing number and proportion of students with disabilities. In the academic year 1994–95 the institutional returns to the Higher Education Statistics Agency (HESA) indicated that 2.65 per cent of students had disclosed a disability. However, readers should note that in the early years of the HESA returns the reported non-response rates (including where information was reported as "not sought") were very high: in 1994–95 non-response was reported for 29.03 per cent of the sample. By 2001–02 the total had increased to 4.65 per cent of students reporting a disability, despite a substantial increase in the total number of students in Higher Education (HE). The non-response rate had dropped to only 3.16 per cent, this improvement probably reflected institutions' increased attention to the collection of these figures; since 2000 the HESA return figures have been used to calculate the "disability mainstream funding" amounts. Tables 4.1–4.3 provide summaries of the national HESA returns from 1994–2002. No data are available for the preceding years. The HESA "disability categories", which are largely impairment-defined, reflect those used in the undergraduate admissions process, that is, those adopted by the Universities and Colleges Admissions Service (UCAS) which are typically also "borrowed" for post-graduate admissions processes. Table 4.1 has the overall figures for all levels of study. Table 4.2 provides the undergraduate-only figures. Table 4.3 covers the post-graduate cohort. The final row of each table indicates the total increase in the number of disclosures for that category and what factor (multiple) of increase this represents over the eight-year period. These HESA data indicate that for both undergraduate and post-graduate populations there has been an increase in the number of people disclosing in each of the identified categories. For some categories this increase has been particularly marked:

Overall disclosures of "dyslexia" were $n=2359$ in 1994–95 and increased by more than fivefold ($\times 5.8$) to $n=13,800$ in 2001–2002.

Overall disclosures of "mental health difficulties" were $n=303$ in 1994 and have increased by a factor of more than five ($\times 5.3$) to $n=1302$ in 2001–2002.

It seems likely that at least some of this large increase is the result of an increase in *disclosure* of these largely "unseen" conditions.

Table 4.1 Summary of the HESA statistics 1994–2002

All levels of study	Total no. of HE students	Total known to have a disability	Dyslexia	Blind/partially sighted	Deaf/hearing impairment	Wheelchair user/mobility impairment	Personal care support
1994–1995	592,839	15,699	2,359	677	1,144	1,080	32
1995–1996	574,973	17,885	3,170	687	1,322	920	44
1996–1997	624,665	22,091	4,364	860	1,453	1,545	39
1997–1998	622,634	23,940	5,381	858	1,518	1,057	60
1998–1999	677,329	26,432	6,575	912	1,605	1,292	61
1999–2000	677,100	26,720	8,370	930	1,630	1,260	70
2000–2001	755,095	30,970	10,430	1,020	2,060	1,550	100
2001–2002	818,445	38,020	13,800	1,255	2,450	1,955	110
Increase between 1994 and 2002	225,606 [× 1.4]	22,321 [× 2.4]	11,441 [× 5.8]	578 [× 1.9]	1,306 [× 2.1]	875 [× 1.8]	78 [× 3.4]

Table 4.1 (Continued)

All levels of study	Mental health difficulties	An unseen disability, e.g. diabetes, epilepsy or asthma	Multiple disabilities	Other	No known disability	Not known/not sought
1994–1995	303	7,617	750	1,737	405,063	172,077
1995–1996	319	8,596	629	2,198	477,299	79,789
1996–1997	546	9,461	1,039	2,784	558,439	44,135
1997–1998	512	10,695	1,195	2,664	568,324	30,370
1998–1999	724	10,335	1,721	3,207	624,705	26,192
1999–2000	860	8,140	1,870	3,590	608,610	41,770
2000–2001	1,290	8,430	2,015	4,080	694,370	29,750
2001–2002	1,605	9,400	2,690	4,750	754,550	25,875
Increase between 1994 and 2002	1,302 [× 5.3]	1,783 [× 1.2]	1,940 [× 3.6]	3,013 [× 2.7]	349,487 [× 1.9]	Reduced by 146,202 [× 0.2]

In this table from 1999 onwards 0, 1, 2 are rounded to 0. All other numbers are rounded up or down to the nearest 5 (by HESA).

Source: Copyright © Higher Education Statistics Agency Limited 2001.

These data are available on the HESA website (www.hesa.ac.uk) and are reproduced here with permission.
Readers should please note that HESA cannot accept responsibility for any inferences or conclusions derived from the data by third parties.

Table 4.2 Summary of the HESA statistics 1994–2002 – undergraduates

Undergraduates	Total no. of HE students	Total known to have a disability	Dyslexia	Blind/partially sighted	Deaf/hearing impairment	Wheelchair user/mobility impairment	Personal care support
1994–1995	451,840	14,034	2,112	597	985	925	30
1995–1996	448,199	15,754	2,822	617	1,118	769	37
1996–1997	491,474	19,337	3,854	743	1,233	1,367	35
1997–1998	479,329	20,486	4,737	705	1,204	849	53
1998–1999	522,887	22,469	5,731	743	1,298	1,047	52
1999–2000	525,140	22,290	7,280	780	1,300	980	60
2000–2001	595,155	25,955	9,025	840	1,700	1,270	80
2001–2002	649,680	32,165	11,965	1,085	2,055	1,600	100
Increase between 1994 and 2002	197,840 [× 1.4]	18,131 [× 2.3]	9,853 [× 5.7]	488 [× 1.8]	1,070 [× 2.1]	675 [× 1.7]	70 [× 3.3]

Table 4.2 (Continued)

Undergraduates	Mental health difficulties	An unseen disability, e.g. diabetes, asthma, epilepsy	Multiple disabilities	Other	No known disability	Not known/not sought
1994–1995	267	6,960	675	1,483	317,760	120,046
1995–1996	287	7,651	575	1,878	375,928	56,517
1996–1997	487	8,270	943	2,405	442,391	29,746
1997–1998	452	9,241	1,048	2,197	437,873	20,970
1998–1999	630	8,756	1,495	2,717	482,589	17,829
1999–2000	740	6,630	1,630	2,900	471,000	31,860
2000–2001	1,115	6,690	1,755	3,480	545,455	23,745
2001–2002	1,440	7,490	2,405	4,030	596,715	20,800
Increase between 1994 and 2002	1,173 [× 5.4]	530 [× 1.1]	1,730 [× 3.6]	2,547 [× 2.7]	278,955 [× 1.9]	Reduced by 99,246 [× 0.2]

In this table from 1999 onwards 0, 1, 2 are rounded to 0. All other numbers are rounded up or down to the nearest 5 (by HESA).

Source: Copyright © Higher Education Statistics Agency Limited 2001.

Table 4.3 Summary of the HESA statistics 1994–2002 – post-graduates

Post-graduates	Total no. of HE students	Total known to have a disability	Dyslexia	Blind/partially sighted	Deaf/hearing impairment	Wheelchair user/mobility impairment	Personal care support
1994–1995	140,999	1,665	247	80	159	155	2
1995–1996	126,774	2,131	348	70	204	151	7
1996–1997	133,191	2,754	510	117	220	178	4
1997–1998	143,305	3,454	644	153	314	208	7
1998–1999	154,442	3,963	844	169	307	245	9
1999–2000	151,960	4,430	1,090	150	330	280	20
2000–2001	159,935	5,015	1,400	175	360	280	20
2001–2002	168,760	5,855	1,835	170	395	355	15
Increase between 1994 and 2002	27,761 [× 1.2]	4,190 [× 3.5]	1,588 [× 7.4]	90 [× 2.1]	236 [× 2.5]	200 [× 2.3]	13 [× 7.5]

Table 4.3 (Continued)

Post-graduates	Mental health difficulties	An unseen disability, e.g. diabetes, asthma, epilepsy	Multiple disabilities	Other	No known disability	Not known/ not sought
1994–1995	36	657	75	254	87,303	52,031
1995–1996	32	945	54	320	101,371	23,272
1996–1997	59	1,191	96	379	116,048	14,389
1997–1998	60	1,454	147	467	130,451	9,400
1998–1999	94	1,579	226	490	142,116	8,363
1999–2000	120	1,510	250	690	137,620	9,910
2000–2001	175	1,740	260	600	148,920	6,005
2001–2002	170	1,910	285	725	157,830	5,075
Increase between 1994 and 2002	134 [× 4.7]	1,253 [× 2.9]	210 [× 3.8]	471 [× 2.9]	70,527 [× 1.8]	Reduced by 46,956 [× 0.1]

In this table from 1999 onwards 0, 1, 2 are rounded to 0. All other numbers are rounded up or down to the nearest 5 (by HESA).
Source: Copyright © Higher Education Statistics Agency Limited 2001.

The changes in the number of disclosures of the more visible mobility/sensory impairments are more modest, but are likely to reflect an actual increase in the number of people with these impairments:

> In the "wheelchair user/mobility impairment" category, overall disclosures were $n = 1080$ in 1994–95 and increased to $n = 1955$ in 2001–2002 ($\times 1.8$).
>
> In the "visual impairment" category, overall disclosures were $n = 677$ in 1994–95, and almost doubled ($\times 1.9$) to $n = 1255$ in 2001–2002.
>
> For the "hearing impairment" category the original overall disclosures in 1994–95 were $n = 1144$ and increased by a factor of 2.1 to $n = 2450$ in 2001–2002.

Students will usually have self-identified by entering the appropriate numerical code on their application or enrolment form and this information is then included in the HESA return. This self-disclosure results in some cases where the student selects a category such as "other", rather than, say, "mental health issues". In a few cases this categorisation is deliberate and results from concerns about possible discrimination if they disclose such "conditions". Despite the increased proportion of students with a disability, disabled people are under-represented in HE compared to the general population. A recent Labour Force Survey (LFS) (Smith and Twomey, 2002) indicated that the overall proportion of people with long-term disability in the general UK "working age" population is 19.3 per cent. The proportion increases with age.

Table 4.4 shows the proportion of people self-reporting a disability in the "working age" population, stratified by age group and gender. Overall the male and female groups have similar proportions of people with disabilities: 19.3 per cent of each gender group. The overall figures mask some small differences between the genders within each age group, though neither gender has a consistently higher proportion. There is a broad variation between the age groups since the proportion of people self-reporting a disability proportion increased with age (from 8.8% of 16–19-year olds to 33.75% of 50–59-year olds). The 16–19-year group had the lowest proportion of people with disabilities, 8.8 per cent of all (males 9.2% and females 8.4%). The 20–24-year group had 10.45 per cent of all (10.3% males and 10.6% females) and the 25–34-year group had 12.85 per cent of

Table 4.4 The proportion of "working age" participants (16–60 years) who self-reported a disability in the Autumn 2001 Labour Force Survey

Age group (years)	Percentage of people with a disability		
	All	Males	Females
16–19	8.80	9.2	8.4
20–24	10.45	10.3	10.6
25–34	12.85	12.1	13.6
35–49	18.50	17.5	19.5
50–59	33.75	33.9	33.6
Overall	16.87	19.3	19.3

Source: Adapted from Smith and Twomey, 2002.

all (12.1% males and 13.6% females). The rise is sharper for the over-35s: of all those aged 35–49 years, 18.5 per cent reported a disability (17.5% males and 19.5% females). Among all those 50–59 years of age, 33.75 per cent reported a disability (33.9% males and 33.6% females). The type of disability reported to the LFS (2002) was also of interest (see Table 4.4). The categories used for the LFS do not match those used for the HESA statistics collected for HE. Even where the categories do coincide, it is difficult to compare with the HESA figures in Table 4.1 because the LFS statistics are expressed as the proportion of those with a disability.

Table 4.5 shows that for the LFS 2002 the largest single category (34.8% of those with a disability) was "musculo-skeletal disorders"; followed by "chest/breathing difficulties" (13.0%); "heart/blood pressure/circulatory disorders" (11.2%); "mental illness" (9.0%); "other" (8.2%); "stomach/liver/kidney/digestion difficulties" (4.8%); "diabetes" (4.7%); "progressive illness not elsewhere specified" (4.4%); "epilepsy" (2.2%); "learning difficulties" (2.1%); "visual impairment" (1.9%); "skin conditions and allergies" (1.9%); "hearing impairment" (1.7%); the smallest category was "speech impairment", where the sample size was too small for a reliable estimate. We should note, however, that it is unclear whether the LFS category "learning difficulties" includes both those with learning disabilities and those with specific learning difficulties.

Table 4.5 The type of impairment self-reported by participants in the Autumn 2001 Labour Force Survey

Type of impairment	All (%)	Males (%)	Females (%)
Musculo-skeletal	34.8	34.7	35.0
Back/neck	18.0	17.2	18.9
Legs/feet	11.2	12.2	10.0
Arms/hands	5.7	5.3	6.2
Visual impairment	1.9	2.3	1.6
Hearing impairment	1.7	1.7	1.6
Speech impairment	*	*	*
Skin conditions and allergies	1.9	2.0	1.7
Chest/breathing problems	13.0	12.3	13.8
Heart/blood pressure/circulatory problems	11.2	14.1	8.1
Stomach/liver/kidney/digestion	4.8	4.4	5.2
Diabetes	4.7	5.5	3.8
Epilepsy	2.2	2.1	2.4
Mental illness	9.0	8.1	9.9
Depression, "bad nerves"	6.1	5.2	7.1
Mental illness, phobia, panics	2.9	2.9	2.8
Learning difficulties**	2.1	2.7	1.4
Progressive illness not elsewhere classified	4.4	3.8	5.0
Other problems, disabilities	8.2	6.0	10.6

Source: Adapted from Smith and Twomey, 2002.
The percentages refer to the proportion of respondents with disabilities.
* Sample size too small for reliable estimate.
** The report did not define "learning difficulties" and therefore it is unclear whether this includes both people with general intellectual disabilities and those with specific learning difficulties or just one of these groups.

Setting targets?

The 19.3 per cent overall proportion of disabled people in the working age population reported in the LFS provides a possible target for HEI populations. However, it cannot be applied simplistically, as one must also take into account disabled people's lower educational attainment, which would tend to limit entry to HE. For example, 19 per cent of disabled people aged 16–24 years have no educational qualifications, in comparison to 9 per cent of non-disabled people of the same age (Smith and Twomey, 2002).

Does Higher Education make a difference to employability?

The LFS 2002 also reported 52.1 per cent unemployment of disabled people compared to 18.8 per cent for non-disabled people. Furthermore 35 per cent of people with disabilities had been unemployed for more than one year, compared to 21 per cent of those without disabilities. A recent survey indicates that HE can be effective in improving the employment prospects of disabled people. In 2002, for the first time, the Association of Graduate Careers Advisory Services First Destination Survey of recent graduates (AGCAS FDS, 2004) allowed reporting and analysis of specific data about respondents' self-reports of disability. This data is a snapshot of a single year, and further research is needed, but the report showed that 48.4 per cent of disabled graduates were in full-time employment, compared with 53.4 per cent of non-disabled graduates. Hence, given the necessary support, graduates with disabilities are roughly as likely to be employed as graduates without disabilities.

Increasing numbers in Higher Education: Just more disclosure or a "real" increase?

A review of the HESA data (Table 4.1) indicates that the frequencies of all of the categories show some increase, with the greatest increases among students with dyslexia and those with mental health issues. Two informal student feedback surveys conducted at the University of Southampton showed that some students, particularly those with "hidden conditions", were concerned about whether to disclose their disability on application (summaries of these small-scale surveys are available from the author on request). The students, or their parents or teachers, were concerned about the possibility of negative discrimination in the admissions process. Some of the increase in disclosure probably results from applicants being more willing to declare a disability. The reasons for this may include:

- greater awareness of the institutional support services available and consequent disclosure in order to access those services;
- increased access to additional funding for disabled individuals who disclose, for example the Disabled Students' Allowances (DSAs) are available via Local Education Authorities (LEAs) and other funding bodies for UK students;

- many institutions have a long history of accepting people with disabilities, yet among the public there persists a belief that institutions will discriminate; the increased disclosure may reflect a lessening of those expectations of prejudice; possibly this increased disclosure is related to greater visibility of support services.

It seems likely that, aside from increased disclosure, there is also an increase in the actual number of disabled people applying for courses. Changes in government policies may have contributed to increased numbers of students with disabilities reaching HE. For example the Warnock Report (1978) and the subsequent Education Act (1981) should have resulted in increased numbers of pupils with disabilities receiving mainstream schooling and further education (FE). Moreover, those changes in policy should in turn have led to increased numbers of pupils with disabilities achieving exam grades at a level commensurate with application for HE. Readers may wish to note that it was not possible for the author to readily identify published government statistics which would allow these anticipated increases to be verified.

Anecdotal evidence from HE Disability Officers suggests that increasing numbers of students are being identified for the first time *during* their University career. This "new diagnosis" cohort ranges from relatively small numbers of people who acquire a mobility/dexterity/sensory/other impairment through injury or illness, to the relatively large number of people for whom a specific learning difficulty (SpLD) is "diagnosed", for the first time, during their studies in HE. This latter group, of those newly diagnosed with SpLDs, could be loosely grouped as follows:

- *Strugglers*: Those who have always barely coped with academic activities and yet have achieved sufficient academic grades to enter HE. They have not accessed an assessment previously, though some difficulty may have been suspected. Students who struggle in this way sometimes do not come forward for assessment until they have failed one or more assignments/examinations/course modules.

The strugglers' experience of HE may well be that their practical or oral work (e.g. in seminars) is comparable with other students. However, their research and written work may often take as long as, or longer than, their peers, and then they still do not achieve marks at a similar level to their peers. Strugglers may have a particularly strong initial reaction of relief when the SpLD is identified.

- *Returners*: Left their original education relatively early, possibly in part due to their [then] unidentified learning difficulties, and have returned via one of the "non-traditional" routes such as "access" or "vocational" courses.

It is likely that returners will not come forward for assessment early in their course. They may lack awareness of the support services available and their difficulties may be "masked" by a relative lack of experience of "traditional" study skills (i.e. both the student and staff may initially attribute their difficulties to "not having studied recently" or "not having taken A levels").

- *Copers*: Students whose learning strategies were sufficient to allow them to cope well, up to HE level. For these students the additional demands of higher levels provide a challenge which exceeds the capacity of their usual strategies.

It seems likely that these students may be surprised and/or confused by their difficulties at HE Level and they may be particularly vulnerable to their self-confidence being undermined; however, they may also show particular benefit from being taught explicit new coping strategies.

An increasing range of impairment labels?

In addition to the increasing numbers of students reporting a disability, there appears to have been an increase in the range of conditions and impairments experienced. This increased range may result from a number of factors. First, the increased number of students in HE (increased by 225,606 since 1994) raises the probability that the cohort will include some students who have exceedingly rare conditions, simply due to chance. Second, the prognosis for people with certain medical conditions (e.g. cystic fibrosis, muscular dystrophy) has improved over the last half-century to the point where a person may now reasonably expect to reach their twenties or thirties, hence completing a degree becomes a more viable aspiration. Third, improvements in the institutional facilities and services (e.g. the development of in-house specialist Disability/Dyslexia Services) make it more likely that the institutions will be able to support the needs of those with complex or extensive requirements (e.g. 24-hour personal care and academic support workers plus specialist IT equipment). Fourth, certain forms of impairment are now being diagnosed more frequently than in the past. An example here is Asperger's Syndrome.

The increased proportion/range of people with disabilities now apparent in the HE population is likely to have implications for pedagogy. For example best practice suggests that teaching activities should be planned with a range of needs in mind, using a range of teaching, learning and assessment styles or formats, so that no one is persistently disadvantaged because they have difficulty with one style or format. The Learning and Teaching Subject Network, Subject Centres and other sources (e.g. Skill – the National Bureau for Students with Disabilities) have begun to produce advice and information aimed at academics from the various disciplines (see reference list for more detail on these resources).

The current national and international legislation

The Human Rights Act provided a legal context in which disabled people may choose to pursue their rights, since it included reference to a right to an education. The original DDA was implemented in December 1996: however, education was explicitly excluded from the remit of the original DDA. It is important to note that this is civil rights legislation, which is similar in intent to sex/gender and "race" legislation. The Special Educational Needs and Disability Act (SENDA, 2001) amended the original DDA and became Part IV of the DDA, implemented in stages from September 2002. This legislation affects virtually all aspects of education, including HE. It applied the same broad definition of disability and duties concerning less favourable treatment and reasonable adjustments as the original act. In addition to the duties in relation to specific individuals, the DDA IV also imposed a general duty on education providers to:

* anticipate and plan for the needs of disabled people "at large";
* provide "auxiliary aids and services" from September 2003;
* make physical adjustments from September 2005. As is usual in such legislation, the requirement to make physical changes applies mainly to new buildings and occasions when a major refurbishment of an existing building occurs, otherwise there is *no* requirement to "retro-fit" adaptations, unless a specific request for access is received and is deemed to be reasonable.

Any adjustments must then take account of any request for confidentiality or for limited disclosure. If the institution fails to meet these obligations, any affected person may either request conciliation by the

Disability Rights Commission (DRC) or they may take a case to the County Court. Claims may address actual damages (e.g. tuition fees and living costs), psychological harm and lost potential earnings. The amount which may be claimed is not subject to any formal limits.

Certain justifications are permitted for not making "reasonable adjustments" and for "less favourable treatment". For example, health and safety legislation overrides DDA, though it cannot be used as a "blanket" justification – the individual circumstances are considered. In extending the DDA to education, the government found it necessary to add to the list of justifications, in particular the "maintenance of academic standards" and "maintenance of other standards" (e.g. professional body requirements – professional bodies themselves are not yet covered by the DDA, but there are planned developments in this area). There is also some protection of the educational experiences of other students, since institutions can argue that a particular adjustment would have a "significantly detrimental effect" on those other students. Other justifications allow institutions to argue that an adjustment is "not practicable" or "too expensive" – though the latter may prove difficult to argue, as it is expected that the entire institution's income would be taken into account in considering any specific adjustment.

Criticisms of the DDA by organisations representing groups of disabled people have included concerns about inadequacies in the definition of disability and the Act's (perceived) "lack of teeth" – for example the staggered implementation of the various aspects of the Act and the decision not to require retro-fitting of physical access changes to existing buildings (unless there is a specific request or during a major refurbishment). These criticisms have contributed to the decision to introduce the 2003 Amendments and the forthcoming Disability Bill (2005).

The DRC provides a conciliation service for students and institutions. The DRC website (http://www.drc-gb.org.uk) also provides a summary of recent court cases. The DRC worked with Skill (the National Bureau for students with disabilities) and other organisations to produce a Code of Practice (CoP – see References for detailed source information) for providers of post-16 education and related services. This CoP includes many useful examples of good and bad practice. However, as seems inevitable until some case law can be established, most of the examples deal with situations which are relatively straightforward and clearcut. The "real life" situations which institutions and students face are often more complex and hence some matters will require conciliation and possibly a court case to obtain resolution. Further changes to the DDA are under discussion and are likely to be implemented within the next two to three years. These include the 2003 Amendments to the DDA and the Disability Bill (2004/2005). These changes will include:

- an extension of the DDA, imposing a duty on "public authorities" to eliminate unlawful discrimination and promote equality of opportunity;
- an extension of the definition of disability;
- the introduction of the concept of *direct* discrimination on grounds of disability (which cannot be justified under any circumstances) as distinct from disability-related (indirect) discrimination.

The Higher Education Funding Council for England (HEFCE) Equality Challenge Unit will be producing a document summarising the implications of the 2003 Amendments to DDA for HEIs. The National Disability Team will also publish a document concerning the implications of the changes to DDA for HEIs. The "public authorities" would include at least some "professional bodies" which either certify professionals to practise or set the standards which apply to professional qualifications. This would include the British Psychological Society in its roles in the various criteria for achieving Chartered Status.

These legislative changes are likely to raise discussion about the criteria used for "fitness to practice" in some professions and also to trigger close scrutiny of the academic standards, personal skills and "competencies", which form parts of professional qualification criteria. The DRC is to be absorbed into the new *Commission for Equality & Human Rights*. This body will have the authority to issue "compliance notices" to Institutions where it believes there is a disability-related issue, *without* a specific individual having made a complaint.

Institutional responses to Disability Discrimination Act IV

Institutions have had guidance from several sources which should help them to determine what is good practice and what responses they need to make both to individual students' needs and also to the new legislation. These documents include: the HEFCE "Baseline provision" document (January 1999); the Quality Assurance Agency's Code of Practice for Students with disabilities; and the Disability Rights Commission's Code of practice for post-16 education and various DRC guides aimed at education providers (see References for full titles and sources).

It is difficult to establish an overview of HEIs' actual responses to DDA IV, since there is no obvious source for such information. For example it is required that institutions' Annual Operating Statements to HEFCE comment on the use of funding provided for students with disabilities, but these comments are typically only a few sentences per institution. Anecdotal comments from Disability Officers suggest that institutional responses have been variable. A few institutions have used the legislation as a spur for major reviews of policy and practice; a few institutions are making only minimal changes, perhaps choosing to await developments in case law, which will hopefully give a clearer indication of how the Act will be interpreted. Most institutional responses are somewhere between: they have made improvements on some aspects of policy and practice, yet are awaiting developments in case law to determine the responsibilities of each institution.

The various funding arrangements for students with disabilities

Funding arrangements: The Disabled Students' Allowances
The DSAs are available for UK students who are undertaking a certain amount of study: equivalent to 50 per cent of a full-time (FT) course (50% FT).

The allowances are not means-tested (the original DSA was means-tested, but the test was dropped in the late 1990s) and are available to any student who is prepared to both:

* provide suitable "evidence of disability" (e.g. a doctor's letter or a Chartered Educational Psychologist's report identifying specific learning difficulties)

and

* establish their study needs relating to the disability (e.g. by attending an Assessment Centre for an assessment of need).

The DSAs funding comes from either central government, administered through the LEAs or the student's course funding body (e.g. NHS Student Grants Unit, Research Councils for post-graduates).

The allowances relate only to the academic aspects of a course: for example where students require personal care, which would be necessary regardless of whether the person was studying or not, that responsibility remains with their home area Social Services Department. The DSAs consist of four elements:

1. An "equipment" allowance, typically used to purchase computer equipment and/or a minidisk recorder to help with note-taking.
2. Another element covers "non-medical helpers" such as academic support workers (e.g. dyslexia tutor, note-taker, sign language interpreter, visual orientation trainer, mentor).
3. The "general" allowance covers the formal assessment of need and other items (e.g. additional books, photocopying and computer consumables).
4. A "transport" allowance may be available in some circumstances.

An FT undergraduate could claim up to £38,000 (approx.) over the duration of a three-year course, part-time (PT) students may claim the DSAs *pro rata* to the "weight" of their course, that is, a PT award which will earn 60 credit points = 50 per cent of a FT course and therefore 50 per cent of the FT DSAs amounts are available to the student. Since 2001, post-graduates have also been eligible to claim DSAs, but they are allocated a total of £5000 (approx.) per annum, rather than the larger amounts permitted to undergraduates.

From a theoretical viewpoint the DSAs system may be criticised because it is essentially based on an individually focussed, medicalised model of disability, rather than a social model which addresses the wider context. Yet, the DSAs system is generally very popular with students, who like the fact that they have direct access to personalised equipment and human support, especially if they have struggled to obtain such support in school (where the funding is allocated to the institution, not to the individual person).

There are dilemmas. The following remarks are based upon various comments made by Southampton students about the possibility of making a DSAs application. Some students have initial concerns about whether they "should" make a claim – especially those with less visible conditions who feel that they are "not disabled enough" to "deserve" this support, believing that it is intended only for wheelchair users. Students also sometimes express (unjustified) concerns about whether claiming the DSAs will affect other benefits (e.g. Disability Living Allowance [DLA]); or whether it may have long-term consequences for the students' employment prospects; or whether it will make the person "registered disabled". Unfortunately the DSAs system does not cover the needs of every student. Even setting aside for a moment European Union (EU) and International students, who are not eligible for the DSAs under any circumstances, the financial limits on the allowances sometimes mean that those with the most severe impairments find that their needs exceed the funding available.

An example: a student who is profoundly deaf and a user of British Sign Language (BSL) could need both a BSL interpreter and a notetaker for each taught session, possibly 15+ hours per week. The cost of this combination of support workers would almost certainly exceed the £11,000 (approx.) available per annum through the DSAs. If the student happens to be a post-graduate, then DSAs funding is only £5000 per annum, hence cases where the student's needs exceed the DSAs funding are more common among post-graduates. Some Institutions are able to identify add-itional funding for such cases, but many struggle to do so, and hence the student may be either unable to access the full package of support they need or may be refused a place because those needs cannot be met. In addition there are serious problems in many areas of the country in recruiting sufficient BSL interpreters with adequate BSL qualifications, especially for subjects where there is also a need for understanding of specialist or technical jargon.

A further example of the limits of the DSAs system could be a student who, for any number of reasons, is not able to undertake 50 per cent FT and who chooses to study PT, completing perhaps two modules per annum (equivalent to 25% of an FT course). Such students are ineligible for the DSAs, even if their reason for not undertaking a greater amount of study is directly related to their disability; or where their PT course is organised in such a way that it is not equivalent to 50 per cent FT.

Funding arrangements: Gaps in funding for individual students with disabilities

European Union and International students are ineligible for the DSAs, yet the DDA IV provides them with the same rights to support as "home" students, regardless of the (lack of) available funding for that support. Institutions have no obvious source of funding from which to provide support for these students, especially as HEFCE funding cannot be used for non-UK students (there are similar bodies for Scotland and Wales). Many International students come from countries where there is no government assistance available to meet disability-related needs. It is well-recognised that most FT and PT students undertake paid employment, in addition to their studies, because of the increased financial pressures on them. A further source of financial hardship for many students with disabilities results from their limited access to paid employment and the financial benefits thereof. This appears to result from a number of interacting factors:

- Some students with disabilities experience fatigue as an aspect of their impairments and therefore have limited energy available for studying, and no extra energy available for additional work.
- Some students can manage their studies without excessive fatigue becoming an issue, but would simply find it impossible to undertake paid work in addition to studying because of fatigue issues.
- Many academic tasks simply take longer for many students with disabilities than for their non-disabled peers; therefore they have a much more limited amount of time available for external employment.
- Even where a student is willing and able to work in addition to their studies, they then enter a highly competitive PT employment market where they may well face all of the barriers faced by disabled people at large in employment.

The recent decision (Autumn 2004) to extend means-tested Housing Benefit to some students with disabilities who live in institutional Halls of Residence may help in some cases. However, the decision to apply this to only some students with disabilities, but not other students with disabilities, seems likely to result in inequalities. Those deemed eligible for Housing Benefit are:

1. those claiming DSA because they are deaf, but not for others those with impairments who are claiming DSAs; and
2. those who are in receipt of DLA.

Funding arrangements: The provision of institutional funding specifically for meeting the needs of students with disabilities
The provision of funding to FE and HE institutions for disability issues comes closer to an application of the social model of disability than the DSAs system. FE Institutions have worked with an institutional funding model for some years, whereas institutional funding

has only been introduced in HE relatively recently. During the 1990s the HEFCE provided a number of opportunities for institutions to bid for "special initiative" project funding. These projects allowed the development of good services in some institutions, but there was criticism in the sector that resources were not made available to every HEI and that such project activity was sometimes not "embedded" and was therefore lost after the end of the project funding. HEFCE indicates that there are unlikely to be more "special initiatives" and that in future the Widening Participation funding should contribute to disability-related activities. From academic year 2000–2001 HEFCE introduced "mainstream funding" based on a formula applied to the number of students with disabilities and the number in receipt of the DSAs, as reported in the Institutional HESA return from the preceding year. This mainstream funding is welcome. But HEFCE has been criticised because this funding is not "ring-fenced" for disability issues.

The HEFCE have also acknowledged the extent of institutions' tasks, required under DDA IV, in improving access to their physical estates and have so far made available two rounds of "Disability Capital Allocation Funding" (DCAF), which is designated for improvements to physical access and IT facilities. The bids for such funding had to be supported by formal access audits and there has been criticism because, to date, the DCAF available will address only a fraction of the work identified in those audits.

Evaluating the varying funding mechanisms
Comparing a solely institutional funding model (in FE) with a solely individual funding model (pre-2000 in HE), and the current "mixed" model in HE (individual DSAs plus institutional mainstream funding post-2000), it appears that the mixed funding model offers the most flexible mechanism. The "mixed" model allows for both changes to institutional infrastructure and provision for the individual student's needs in terms of tailored equipment and human support. The annual variation in the institutional mainstream funding makes it difficult to plan ahead in detail, but the knowledge that there will be some regular funding has allowed institutions to begin to take a more proactive approach – including the beginnings of strategic planning for the needs of students with disabilities. Similarly, the introduction of two rounds of "Disability Capital Allocation Funding" has enabled institutions to begin programmes of improvements to existing premises, though there are inevitably difficulties in deciding which works have greatest priority.

A case study of one institution: How things have changed at the University of Southampton

The University of Southampton has a long history of supporting students with disabilities, though actual numbers of people who disclosed a disability were small until relatively recently. The University co-operated with the British Council for the Rehabilitation of the Disabled and the Clarkson Foundation to open Clarkson House in the 1970s. This small residential hall (25 beds) was close to the centre of the campus and was purposely built for students with severe physical impairments and featured a fully accessible kitchen, bathrooms and so on, as well as a "24 hour care team" arrangement available throughout the academic year. The residents were a mixture of undergraduate and post-graduate students without any impairments, some students with physical impairments and a small number of people with variable "hidden" conditions which could result in an unpredictable need for large amounts of personal care.

By the late 1990s the University typically recorded approximately 300 students per annum (approx. 2%) with disabilities, mostly students with "hidden conditions". In 2003–2004 it is expected the University HESA return will report approximately 2000 students with disabilities (approx. 9%). Up until 1997, when Southampton became a member of the Southern Higher Education Consortium (SHEC, the regional group which undertook one of the HEFCE "special initiative" projects), the elements of the institution's support were:

- an academic allocated a few hours per year for the role "Adviser to Disabled Students";
- five spaces for students with relatively severe physical disabilities in the Clarkson House specialist accommodation which also provided 24-hour personal care provision in one "mixed" Hall with non-disabled students;
- two "specialist workstations" – one for students with visual impairments, provided through the Royal National Institute for the Blind (RNIB), and one for students with dyslexia.

The SHEC project established 1.0 full time equivalent (FTE) disability specialists in each of the participating institutions. At Southampton this provision was initially created as an 0.8FTE Disability Co-ordinator and an 0.2FTE "software specialist". The provision has increased gradually, particularly following the introduction of mainstream funding.

From September 2004 the University of Southampton's provision will include the following.

- *Four parallel professional services for intra-institutional students with disabilities*
  - The *Disability Service* which provides support for prospective and current students with all forms of disability and chronic medical conditions
  - *Dyslexia Services* (Learning Differences Centre) providing assessment and specialist tutorial support for students with specific learning difficulties
  - The *Mentor Service* for students who are especially "vulnerable to the effects of stress", for example due to a mental health issue or the effects of a physiological condition
  - The *Assistive Technology Service* which provides specialist IT suites on several of the University's campuses and advice and information to all students with disabilities on IT issues.
- *An Assessment Centre* – the *Centre for Enabling and Learning Technologies* (CELT) which provides assessments of need for the DSAs process to students with disabilities from across the region (including, but not limited to, the SHEC institutions).
- *Academic support workers* (e.g. notetakers, library assistants) provided in several ways, usually funded by the DSAs.
- *A range of residential accommodation choices* for students with disabilities. Personal care provision is negotiated with the student, usually funded by Social Services and provided by an external professional care agency.
- Regular staff training activities.
- Representation of the various services and students with disabilities on University committees.
- Inclusion of the needs of students with disabilities in strategic planning.

The impact of the legislation and funding changes on students with disabilities: Some examples and dilemmas

The following cases have been anonymised as far as possible. Where details could identify individuals, those former and current students have given informed consent to the inclusion of this material in the chapter, and they are aware that this may allow some readers to identify them as individuals. Note that some case histories mention mentoring, this is one-to-one specialist study skills support which is provided by professional mentor staff who typically have some formal counselling skills training and experience of teaching in HE.

In 1997, just before the "means test" was removed from the DSAs process, one Southampton student who had a visual impairment was refused DSAs funding because his parents' income was a few hundred pounds above the financial limit. He needed equipment to facilitate his studies which was costed at several thousand pounds, some of which was eventually provided by his family and the RNIB. He struggled, but did eventually complete his degree course.

In 1997 a young woman ("A") with cerebral palsy began studying at Southampton. She met the Disability Co-ordinator in Year 1, but she initially decided that the DSAs process was not for her. Later she developed a brain tumour and needed both treatment and additional assistance with studying; at this point she went through the DSAs process, and became one of the strongest advocates of this funding mechanism. With a Mentor and other support, she worked incredibly hard, despite continuing health complications and graduated First Class. Student A stayed on as a post-graduate, with continuing support, and completed her Masters, with Distinction. Her thesis was of such interest that the external examiner asked to read an additional chapter, which had been cut from the final draft.

In 1999 a young woman ("B") came for a prospective visit. The previous year at another university she had developed serious mental health issues. She re-commenced her studies at Southampton with a Mentoring arrangement in place and other support, all funded by the DSAs. This support was continued throughout three years, during which her mental health varied quite considerably. She graduated with a First Class degree in the sciences and has published at least one article in a national newspaper about the excellent support she received.

Also in the late 1990s a young woman ("C") applied for a paramedical course: at the time she had no known health issues. This student has told her story publicly (including to the House of Commons) on a number of occasions. During the first year examinations she had her first epileptic seizure and was required by her academic department to suspend her studies, because of both "fitness to practice" issues and concerns about patient safety, until she had been "seizure free" for a set period of time. The student was very unhappy about this decision and eventually chose to re-commence her studies as a Law student. She graduated with a strong 2.1 and went straight into the Law doctoral programme.

In 1999 a young woman ("D") with quite severe cerebral palsy came for a prospective visit, she had a mobility and speech impairment and needed some personal care plus academic support. In her first year, D lived in the Clarkson House specialist facility with 24-hour care. She also had specialist IT equipment and two Community Service Volunteers for academic and other activities throughout her studies, funded partially by the DSAs. Following some health complications she deferred for one year. Following her return she re-located with other students from Clarkson House to a self-catered Hall of Residence and her personal care needs were met with an individual package. In 2004, D graduated in the sciences.

Between 2000 and 2003 a young man ("E") who had been treated for a brain tumour attended a paramedical course. Among the multiple consequences of his treatment were acquired SpLD and a moderate-to-severe visual impairment. E repeatedly found that his supervisors on clinical placements (who are not employees of the University) were unduly concerned about the effects of his visual impairment, despite reassurances and risk assessments having been conducted by course staff. E was eventually failed on a clinical placement by one supervisor and decided to exit at the end of Year 2 with a Diploma in Higher Education instead of completing his degree. He went on to a more practical and less academic training course in a related profession.

Implications of the new legislation for academics

The current and forthcoming legislation will mean that in future academics will need to consider more carefully the learning outcomes and assessment strategies which they utilise in their courses. For example (these are based on possibilities, not real examples):

- If it is not possible for a person with a current serious mental health issue to take part in a counselling course, then the course selection criteria and course publicity literature need to make this clear.
- If the reason that students are subjected to four × three hour examinations in one week is because it is necessary to test their ability to cope with stress in preparation for working in a highly stressful work environment, then that requirement for examination

scheduling should be identified among the learning outcomes and in course materials.

- If it is essential that all earth sciences students undertake some fieldwork, is it absolutely essential for that to be undertaken up a mountain somewhere in the tropics? Or could the student obtain suitable field experience in more accessible terrain?

Clearly there are still many issues to be resolved. One major issue, for institutions and students alike, is what to do in the small number of cases where the person's needs exceed the available external (DSAs) funding and all of the institutional funding has already been used (e.g. to provide specialist services for other students with disabilities). There follow two recent examples:

In 2003 a student ("F") with a total visual impairment applied for a mathematics course. He is a braillist and can also use electronic materials. There remains a difficulty with access to mathematical materials, such as formulae, for people with visual impairments, since the technology is not fully able to support translation of materials into alternative formats. F's academic support requirements (for readers and notetakers with maths knowledge and specialist tuition on specific mathematical IT software) have exceeded the available DSAs funding in Year 1 by a substantial margin.

Also in 2003 a post-graduate student ("G") with a profound hearing impairment applied for an MA course. G needed specialist notetakers for all taught sessions. The cost of this support will almost certainly exceed the available Post-graduate DSAs funding for the year, since that funding is limited to £5000 per student for all needs including helpers (in contrast to £11,000 per annum available just for non-medical helpers for under-graduates). G was aware of the financial strain involved in providing her support and this may have contributed to her decision to suspend her studies at the end of Semester 1 and resume next academic year.

Institutions are struggling to determine how the funding available to individual students through the DSAs and the strands of institutional funding should interact. In particular the institutions would appreciate guidance on which services and facilities will be required in each institution, which might be "bought in" from external agencies and so on. Other funding issues for some individual students are likely to remain outside the DSAs remit.

Where a student needs personal care or domestic support, the expectation is that their home area Social Services will provide the funding. Unfortunately the national situation concerning personal care is under considerable strain and some Social Services Departments are either reluctant to fund students at University or completely unable or unwilling to do so. This leaves students and institutions in difficulties as, until there is case law, it is unclear whether the educational institution has to provide this funding if other agencies cannot or will not. The issue of funding for general maintenance where the student cannot work to supplement their income (discussed in page 59 onwards) remains to be addressed. One possible solution would be for the government to add a small personal maintenance allowance to either the DSAs or other funding, such as the Student Bursaries and Loans, for students with disabilities who are unable to work in addition to studying. For all institutions there remain a number of difficult issues including:

- the development and maintenance of robust bi-directional systems for communicating students' needs between their academic staff and specialist services;
- addressing the Occupational Health or "fitness to practice" issues (where applicable) so that all parties can be clear about what criteria will be applicable;
- achieving any remaining necessary attitudinal changes among teaching staff and senior management, particularly in a sector where there are so many competing demands on staff time and institutional resources;
- obtaining student feedback and ensuring the quality of services provided for students with disabilities.

Conclusions

There is little doubt that social and physical barriers continue to impede the progress of people with disabilities in HE to some degree; however, national legislative and policy changes are contributing to a positive change in attitudes. The HE sector has had to absorb many changes over the last few years and there are more to come with the implementation of further legislation concerned with various forms of discrimination. Against this background there have been significant changes in the ways in which funding for students with disabilities is channelled. These changes have the potential to make a substantial difference to students, but there remain issues to be addressed, some of which have been identified in this chapter. It is too soon to evaluate fully the effects of the new "mixed" funding model. A period of relative stability is needed for the new legislative changes and funding resources to work their way through into institutional services and future planning.

Chapter 5

Disabled and Graduated: Barriers and Dilemmas for the Disabled Psychology Graduate

Peter Stannett

Introduction

I am a person who studied psychology and who happens to have athetoid Cerebral Palsy. After graduation, I decided to embark upon a career in psychology because I wanted to pursue a challenging and rewarding career in a field that I found both interesting and intellectually stimulating. I also wanted to reconcile these scientific interests and abilities with the apparently conflicting deficits in motor control resulting from Cerebral Palsy. One of my initial and perhaps naïve assumptions was that psychology would be a relatively caring occupation that valued individual differences. However, the advice I received, the applications process itself and the 'can't do' attitude that I encountered were the perfect mirror image of the struggles I first faced at school. The fact that these struggles occurred at school level and then continued seamlessly into my working life is a sad reflection of the deeply entrenched negative attitudes towards the capabilities of disabled people. This leads to a tendency towards convenience, expedience and NIMBYism, a lack of good quality information, advice and support plus a half-hearted implementation of the Disability Discrimination Act (1995) (DDA) that extends from the initial application and selection process through to the day-to-day working life of a disabled person. There is no evidence to suggest that these attitudes are changing, but without centres of excellence for disabled people that provide sound advice, employers adopting transparent application and selection processes plus a more comprehensive and enforced DDA, there is little hope for an improvement for other talented disabled people.

The early years

Poor advice and lack of encouragement started at school. I fought to sit 'O' levels, but my school prevented me from following and sitting exams except in four subjects – I still have the letter from my head-master to my parents stating that undertaking 'O' levels would be virtually impossible due to the extent of my disabilities. I disagreed strongly with this assertion, so that when I left that school, and that headmaster, I gained another 6 'O' levels, 3 'A' levels, a BSc, an MSc and a Certificate in Professional Management. I think it is safe to say that my headmaster's beliefs were unfounded! My academic record speaks for itself, but it also reflects my determination to overcome the obstacles that have been strewn in my path. For example, I funded these courses myself and chose correspondence courses so that I was always available for work. I also needed a typewriter to produce all written work and I sought out an examination centre that would provide a room where I could use a typewriter without disturbing other students.

The weight of expectation

It was an Occupational Psychologist who first suggested I went to university. He also then suggested that gaining a degree could be viewed as an end in itself, that is, rather than it representing the beginning of a challenging and fruitful career. This may have been a well-intentioned advice designed to bolster my self-esteem in the event of my degree not leading to employment. However, it betrayed a lack of positive expectation for the future and my view is that this advice is patronising. Most non-disabled people would view a first degree as a means to employment or a foundation for higher degrees – not as an end in itself. Egan (1985) states that:

> It takes little experience in life to realise that people who are called experts are not always competent – you can draw this inference without being cynical.

My experience is that professionals tend to underestimate disabled people's ability and potential ability, and this in turn leads to poor advice being given. Furthermore, when a disabled person makes a career choice and is met with a professional's belief that the aspirations are unrealistic, this can undermine a disabled person's self-esteem and confidence. I believe that good advice is that which establishes a reasonable level of probability that a disabled person is likely to be able to achieve his/her aim or not. There may be no certainties, but there are probabilities. Most of those non-disabled graduates I know also had careers plans and detailed advice backed up with tangible support. I and other disabled people I am aware of were given advice such as 'suck it and see', and the majority of interviews I had included the opening 'There are no guarantees'.

Whilst this may be true, there are, once again, probabilities. The impression, which comes across to me, is that the statement is used as a disclaimer of responsibility rather than an attempt to manage expectations. I would have thought that any reasonably educated person, disabled or not, who be aware that there are no certainties therefore, the disclaimer, if that is what it is, seems to be patronising to me. I also think my judgements of what I am able to do have proved to be reasonably accurate and those of professionals reasonably inaccurate.

Worksearch

After graduating I began to look for posts such as a research associate or psychology assistant. I had no success. I did, however, find work in a disability organisation run by disabled people. Although this provided some much needed experience and income, it was not what I wanted to do. I thought that if I had a professional qualification, such as an MSc, then that should be ample evidence for employers that I could work as a psychology assistant/psychologist. Because I was now at the end of my twenties and still with only a few years work experience, I opted for a day-release course. Although this meant study on top of a full-time post, I considered it would have been a retrograde step to go back to being a full-time student because, after all, the reason for studying in my case was to secure employment.

I began my MSc in counselling psychology because I wanted vocational training rather than simply further academic qualifications, as I believed that this would increase the likelihood of obtaining employment. I discussed some of my difficulties with the university before beginning the course. For example, I requested the use of a tape recorder in lectures. The university's approach was very flexible.

I started the academic component of the course well; however, problems came when seeking clinical experience. I spent two and a half years approaching numerous clinics, disability organisations and counselling centres asking for the opportunity to gain counselling experience. Most cited dysarthric speech as a reason for not allowing me to gain experience at their establishment. Dysarthric speech refers to speech which is poorly articulated due to interference in the control of muscles, usually caused by damage to a central or peripheral motor nerve. Frequently, it was argued that the patient/client would find me difficult to understand. This is perhaps an example of projected anxiety? Nonetheless, when employed in advocacy organisations and interviewing a wide range of people, it presented few problems. Eventually, I had to change to the MSc Health Psychology programme where there was no clinical component but a more detailed research component.

After I was awarded the MSc, I arranged by letter to see one Occupational Psychologist asking about work in psychology. I outlined my academic qualifications and some of the work I have undertaken with disabled people. The psychologist was very enthusiastic and seemed to be sure that it would be relatively easy to secure employment as an assistant psychologist. So I arranged to visit the professional to discuss options. That Occupational Psychologist appeared to be shocked when she saw I had Cerebral Palsy and, in my opinion, took some time to compose herself.

The British Psychological Society's Code of conduct, ethical principles and Guidelines (1998) states that psychologists shall 'not allow their professional responsibilities or standards of practice to be diminished by considerations of religion, sex, nationality, party politics, social standing, class, self interest or other extraneous factors'. In my view, this psychologist failed this standard. During the hour-long consultation, she offered no useful information or support whatsoever (but still received a fee). I was able to inform her far more readily about disabled people's search for appropriate employment. She argued that I should have informed her initially that I had a disability. I disagree. If a psychologist cannot inform a disabled job seeker with the same degree of competence as they inform a non-disabled person with comparable qualifications, then by any definition I understand they are discriminating. One solution or partial solution might be Disability Equality Training. Oermann and Lindgren (1995) found that student nurses developed and maintained positive attitudes towards people with disabilities as a result of attending an educational programme on caring for disabled people. However, Pinfold *et al.* (2003), for example, found that 'educational workshops can have a small but positive impact on students' views of people with mental health problems'. They discovered that the change was very small, the criteria superficial and was poorly maintained. It appears that Disability Equality Training probably does little to change attitudes of adults. If attendance is voluntary then it suggests that those with well-established negative attitudes will not attend and it is these attitudes which are in most need of changing. Conversely, if an employer compels staff to attend, reluctant compliance may result without real benefits. If short courses prove ineffective, it would be useful to assess the influence of longer courses for those professionals working with disabled people.

One aspect, which initially surprised me, was the attitude of other disabled people towards my wish to enter the psychology profession. I spoke to one ex-clinical psychologist, who happens to have a disability, about my attempts to enter the profession and he stated that he was not surprised at the difficulty I was having. He described that the only way he entered the profession was to take a post in a department where no one else would work due to its reputation. Meeting other Disabled Psychologists at the British Psychological Society Conference at the Bournemouth Conference Centre in 2003 also endorsed the view that there are discriminatory views and practices within the profession. Other disabled people questioned why I wanted to enter what most perceived as a highly discriminatory and unhelpful profession. Many professionals have the position of greatly influencing the lives of disabled people based on their judgement. Most disabled people I know would question the accuracy of professional assessments concerning disability because they are aware of the inaccuracies and yet these assessments can influence the direction of a disabled person's life. Poor advice and negative attitudes of professionals who work with disabled people, over time, have a cumulative effect. Not only are disabled people ill-advised, but also they are continually ill-advised. This limits opportunity but also has an effect on self-esteem, and this can reduce an individual's expectation which, in turn, can fulfil the prophecies of the advisors; so they do more harm than good. This situation needs to be turned around. This can be done by recruiting advisors who are of the highest calibre and are monitored on the quality of service given, in addition to their attitudes towards disabled people being audited by those who will not collude with those under scrutiny.

Convenience and expedience

In general, one of most discriminating dispositions is that of expediency. By this I mean, in my experience, career advisors tend to give information and guidance, which would lead to easier routes to employment instead of the preferred career path. There seems to be an established history of 'bright' disabled people working in Information Technology since it is relatively easy to assist someone into that field. Choose a field where there is no history of people working in a field and it is much more difficult to enter, and therefore apparently support a disabled person. In my case, I have been discouraged from careers in the areas of science and health.

Much of the advice I have received has been poor in my view. There is a keenness to suggest that a person with Cerebral Palsy is able to work in a number of fields such as social or clinical psychology. Nonetheless, there is a tendency, even among those who worked with disabled clients, to find reasons why it would be 'extremely difficult' to work in their own particular department or field. An admissions tutor for a clinical course outlined a number of reasons why he thought the practical difficulties would be 'insurmountable'. There are solutions to every objection he offered. A common strategy, which has been used by psychologists in the past, is to substitute good-quality advice with praise, which presumably is to encourage me to feel better despite their inability to give good advice.

A further example of expediency is that employers can interpret anti-discrimination law as it suits them. An example might be putting a ramp in where there are a few steps. This may be viewed as reasonable by some but not to others. If the employer does not build a ramp, perhaps because it would change the appearance of an entrance, the employer could argue that image is an important part of their business at a tribunal. It is possible that the tribunal will find in favour of the employer, particularly if those on the panel have similar views. A number of psychologists I have met have judged it 'inappropriate' to share research information about disability, including attitudes towards disabled people, because they believe it may do damage to a person with low self-esteem. It is also possible, I think, that they will discover research on negative attitudes of professionals towards disabled people as I have done. My view is that it is far better to understand where one stands no matter how unflattering than 'protect' someone because it is judged that they are emotionally fragile. The less information the disabled person is given, the less able they

are to question procedures, practices and attitudes. Withholding information would make me question the competence of psychologists. The
fact that I have the skills to find relevant literature seems to make
decisions to withhold information to be of dubious merit. I was
taught that the important thing is the way information is given rather
than to deny it. The question which needs to be asked is how effective
are psychologists at assessing or judging the abilities of disabled
people. For example, Gillingham (1999) writes in an information
letter to the psychologist that as a clinical psychologist working with
people with neurological disabilities, his professional understanding
of disability only became more insightful as a consequence of experiencing a heart attack and a stroke.

Application process

The application process is littered with obstacles. I have applied for
numerous posts in psychology over the last 12 years. I have applied
for many other posts in small and large organisations. A constant
dilemma for me with regard to responding to advertisements for posts
both in and outside psychology is a stated requirement for excellent
communication skills. If I have published several articles, produced
dissertations, essays, advocated for people with disabilities, worked in
cross-functional teams and given presentations to those outside my
company, do I have well-developed communication skills?

However, I have dysarthric speech and all my writing needs to be
done using a keyboard. I suspect a prospective employer is likely to
emphasise the latter. A study by Stevens (2002) found that limited
writing/keyboard was the most 'important' obstacle to employment
and the next most important obstacle was impairments of speech and
vision. Therefore, the barrier is the interpretation of 'good communication' skills. Some advertisements only give a telephone number as a
contact for application forms or an informal discussion about the
post. This presents difficulties since not all people can or want to
understand dysarthric speech. I have had the experience of the receiver
being replaced numerous times. Another difficult area concerns the
attributions presumed about a person with a speech impairment and
the difficulty the speaker has in modifying the listeners' attributions.
I much prefer to make my initial contact in writing although this is
not always possible when only a contact telephone number is given.

The initial stages of applying for posts can be a major hurdle. For
instance, I have applied to numerous employers, all of whom claim to

have an equal opportunities policy. When asked for the application form in a different format, such as a soft copy, the reply is usually 'Sorry, not possible.' I have spent many hours aligning an application form in a printer so that I can use a computer to fill the form in. It is not an efficient process. Using a typewriter involves the removal of staples and folding the form back and forth to type on the appropriate page. This tends to strain the fold which needs the pages to be re-stapled. A further difficulty can be an application form printed on paper or card which is too thick for the typewriter or printer to cope with and these difficulties will automatically exclude many.

Section 5.9 of Code of Practice for the elimination of discrimination in the field of employment against disabled persons or persons who have had a disability (2003) states that producing application forms in alternative formats 'may be a reasonable adjustment'. So there is no compulsion and a degree of ambiguity, hence producing application forms in alternative formats is something that an employer can avoid with impunity. Nonetheless, there are some employers who are extremely good. It is often more convenient for me (or anyone) to submit a CV if writing is difficult. However, many employers disregard them. Various employers have been asked why they do not employ disabled people and the response is that disabled people do not apply. With so many barriers, it seems unsurprising that some disabled people do not apply. When I apply for a post, my qualifications often are above the minimum required. On a number of occasions, I have been interviewed and I have been successful in completing the assessment centre. Then there is a period between 6 and 12 months when one waits to be called for an interview at local level. Four times this period has elapsed and I am informed that no 'suitable' vacancy has been found. It is not possible for me to find the information concerning non-disabled applicants so that a comparison can be made about relative success rates. I am also informed that the conclusion that no suitable vacancy has been found is not open for discussion, so I do not know what assumptions have been made. It might be that no vacancies appeared at all, or it may be that in their judgement my disability made me an unsuitable candidate for any post, which did arise.

One large national employer sought a medical opinion as to my suitability for a post. I asked whether all applicants or just disabled people have medical examinations. The employer did not address the question. Section 5.23 of the Code of Practice for the elimination of discrimination in the field of employment against disabled persons or persons who have had a disability (2003) states: 'However, if an employer insists on a medical check for a disabled person and not others, without justification, he will probably be discriminating unlawfully.' How does one ascertain whether other candidates are given a medical examination and hence how can one check whether they are discriminating or not? Who assesses what constitutes justification? This process also assumes that the medical practitioner is able to make an accurate judgement of the disabled person's ability. My experience is that they do not and allow little discussion so that the judgement remains largely unquestioned. By contrast, one of the key messages in the paper by Rothwell *et al.* (1997) is that patients can accurately assess their own physical disability. Doyle (2003) states that 'An applicant with a disability might be prematurely excluded from further consideration and may lose the opportunity to demonstrate ability and merit' as a result of a medical examination. If I refuse a medical examination, it terminates the application process. Although medical examinations can be used to inform reasonable adjustments, to date I have never received an accurate medical assessment of my abilities.

Also, when attending a medical examination for employment I am anxious due to previous experiences of inaccurate judgements of my physical ability. This means that athetoid movement increases and my speech deteriorates. It is then that a judgement is made that can affect my future life. I can explain this to the examiner but I do not know if they take my view into account or not. One aspect I find extremely curious is that with a couple of degrees and a professional qualification, medical practitioners still seem to find it necessary to comment on my cognitive abilities in pre-employment medical assessments. Why? Further, Marks (1999, p. 51) points out:

> Medicine's drive to make normal that which it considers to be pathological and dysfunctional claims to be value neutral. Yet in practice, medicine contains a series of normative assumptions about value, beauty and function which influences its practices.

Is this a fair recruitment process? It is unlikely and unfortunate that any Disability Equality Training would reverse such long-held and deep-seated beliefs.

In the Code of Practice for the elimination of discrimination in the field of employment against disabled persons or persons who have had a disability (2003), in Section 18 of annex 3, it is stated that

'Applications to an industrial tribunal must be made within three months of the time when the incident being complained of occurred.' The company who undertook the medical examination for my prospective employers choose, despite my repeated requests by letter for a copy of the medical report, to delay sending it to me until the appeal period had almost expired. It would not have been reasonable to initiate proceedings within the terms of the Disability Discrimination Act (1995) without the report. The Access to Health Records Act (1990) provides individuals with a right, subject to certain conditions to apply for access to records relating to the health professional who holds the records. However, there is no compulsion for the company who undertook the examination on behalf of the prospective employer to give a copy by a specific date. On this occasion, the medical practitioner was able to tell me that I was fit for work when I was in full-time employment and had been working for 12 consecutive years.

Before attending one assessment centre, which was for a post as a psychologist assisting disabled people into work, I was asked what provisions I needed to allow me to undertake the exercises. I stated that I would need a computer for all written work. During one exercise, which involved applicants assuming roles and discussing a scenario of a person looking for work, the instructions at the beginning of the exercise included recommendations to take notes. However, because this was not a written exercise, the computer was removed. I asked for it to be returned which disrupted the exercise. This indicates that when I state that I need a computer for all written work it is not taken at face value. This experience occurred in the process of securing employment in a government department that among other remits helps disabled people into work! Such ironies are common.

However, even with the shortcomings of current assessment centres, they are far more disability friendly than those I attended over 10 years ago. In those days, there was no opportunity to use a computer. Instead an amanuensis sat with me and I was to dictate my answers and they wrote my response on the form. This was a system I was unused to, a system which did not allow me to do calculations or try things out on paper and a system which often involved long explanations to the person assisting me to produce the answer I wanted. There was little extra time and in my view this was a profoundly unfair process. There was computer technology available then, although the attitude to allowing disabled people access to employment was less developed than it is currently and yet they claimed equality of opportunity.

A frequent dilemma is, despite assurances of equality of opportunity, whether I declare my disability on the application form. Not to might be viewed as withholding important information and, anyway, if I am invited for interview, I could be rejected at that point because I have a disability or because hitherto I have not disclosed it. If I do declare a disability, I may be rejected because I have a disability, and perhaps the perception is that too many alterations will have to be made or resulting from prejudice. Most employers claim they welcome applications from disabled people. The emphasis is on the disabled person applying, not on the employer employing disabled them. Therefore, does such a claim mean anything? The second dilemma is that if I apply for a post, should I, before or during the application process, contest the employers' claims of equality of opportunity in application process? To do so may put one at a disadvantage, but not to may mean that one continues to be discriminated against on the grounds of disability.

For equality of opportunities in the application process to occur, employers should offer a variety of formats, as a few employers already do. In my case, this is either a 'soft' copy, which can be emailed to me, or an application form, which can be downloaded from the Internet. If successive British governments are serious about helping disabled people into work, perhaps they should provide funds to allow employers to provide accessible application forms.

One positive experience occurred when I wrote to a London-based clinical psychologist explaining the difficulty I had in trying to find work in psychology, largely as a result of disability. He offers short-term work for graduates who want to enter psychology. I undertook several pieces of work for him and gained some experience. Unfortunately, it does not seem to be sufficient to assist in getting more permanent work in the profession. I have often considered self-employment as a possible solution to the barriers psychologists among others have erected. However, I suspect that it would be difficult to launch a career without first gaining experience with an established employer. Of those I am aware of who have successfully become self-employed, most gained experience and established a reputation whilst working for an existing organisation. Many also developed a network via which work and support would flow when working for oneself. In a sense, becoming self-employed for this reason does not solve the problem but merely circumvents it in my view.

Some have suggested when I have complained of the difficulties that I have not tried hard enough. Occasionally, I have reduced my effort in seeking employment because of the lack of quality advice.

One Occupational Psychologist suggested that if I was serious about working in psychology, then I needed 'to pull out all the stops'. I thought at that time, I had tried many conventional and unconventional attempts to seek employment as a psychologist and over many years. Further, there was no explanation as to what 'pulling out of the stops' meant. Now I see it as a valueless comment.

Conclusion

One of my concerns is the speed of change in attitudes, if they are in fact changing. I have research and academic literature calling for a change in public and professionals' attitudes towards disabled people written in the 1960s and 1970s. The same points are being made some 40 years later. Disabled people, just like others, need to make life decisions at the appropriate time. It is of little use receiving good careers advice in one's 50s when the disabled person would have benefited from it in their teens or 20s. Even after two decades, I do not believe that I have received good advice. My belief, and it is only a belief, is that employers and advisors are complying with legislation, but underneath they would rather not have the inconvenience of accommodating disabled people.

I would like to see the entire employment application process be made more transparent. For example, if I have a medical examination I need to know that all applicants receive the same treatment and that practitioners are able to assess disabled and non-disabled people with equal competence. Some enlightened employers do give constructive feedback on applications and performance at assessment centres. This allows one to judge to a degree of certainty whether any failure was legitimate or whether it was disability-related. This approach I think should be made mandatory.

Passive advice is not enough – opportunities need to be created and support provided. Given the enormous resistance to disabled people in the workplace and more so, in some areas, active advice, planned approaches, should be given. However, some may not actively assist, believing that there should be an internal locus of control. Although theories of perceived control are not universally accepted, a 'helping hand' may really help. It would be beneficial for some kind of centre of excellence where disabled people could receive good quality careers advice, and if and only if a medical examination is needed, that consultation could be offered in the form of a collaborative exercise with the applicant and be co-signed.

With over 20 years experience of looking for work with all the constraints a physical impairment brings, plus being qualified to an extent in psychology, I would have thought I would be well placed to work in an environment to assist/support other disabled people into work. Yet it seems that employers who provide such a service disagree. In addition, having sought careers advice for approximately 25 years, there appears to be a distinct absence of competence, let alone excellent services for disabled people. As for the future, I think the Disability Discrimination Act needs to be strengthened and it should cover any pre-employment medical examinations, and the fines imposed need to be of a sufficient size to be a deterrent whereas currently they are not. I also think it would be of great benefit to look at disability in a wider context. Is, for example, prejudice towards disability and the judgements made on physical appearance innate or socially constructed? If innate, there is not much that can be done. If it is socially/culturally defined, then there is a possibility for change but this foundation needs to be established.

Chapter 6

Disability and Old Age: Or Why It Isn't All in the Mind

Mark Priestley

Introduction

In industrialized societies, the majority of disabled people are over retirement age and impairment is often considered as a social norm of ageing. Despite this, or perhaps because of it, older people with impairments are rarely regarded as 'disabled' in quite the same way as children, or younger adults, and disability activism has tended to focus on issues affecting those of working age or below. There has been much recent debate about the rights of older people, yet their voices and experiences are under-represented in the literature and disability politics. This chapter addresses some of the key relationships between disability and old age with reference to the body, identity, culture and social structure. Generation is an increasingly important concept in social theory and research. Thus, Alanen (1994) argues that we can think of a 'generational system', functioning in a similar way to the gender system, and that we can see its impacts on all aspects of the everyday social world and social relations. When we examine how disability is understood and regulated within modern societies there are some very important generational dimensions – disability is understood and managed very differently at different points in the life course (Priestley, 2001, 2003a). This argument is exemplified when we consider the situation of older disabled people.

There is little doubt that the global population is rapidly ageing (United Nations Secretariat, 1998) and that there are close links between ageing and impairment. An increasing number of older people acquire impairments in later life, while technological and social developments have led to a dramatic increase in the number of younger disabled adults surviving into old age. The UN International Strategy for Action on Ageing 2002 draws specific attention to the growing number of older people with impairments throughout the world. The relationship between ageing and impairment is also highly gendered. Women are likely to live longer than men and to spend a larger proportion of their ageing lives with impairment (Kinsella, 2000; Leveille *et al.*, 2000). In addition, older women are relatively disadvantaged due to the gendered nature of disabling barriers – for example in housing, transport, widowhood and institutional care (Gibson, 1996). In developing countries, poor older women also experience additional disadvantage due to massive gender inequalities in literacy, education, employment and nutrition (Prakash, 1997).

In Britain, the incidence of impairment is closely linked to advanced age (Martin *et al.*, 1988; Craig and Greenslade, 1998; Disability Rights Commission, 2000) and the majority of disabled people in Britain are older people (including a majority of those regarded as 'severely disabled'). Similar trends are apparent in Europe more generally (Eurolink Age, 1995; McLellan, 1997; Walker and Maltby, 1997). Yet, despite this demographic weighting of impairment towards old age, professional interventions and policies have consistently focused on the needs of younger disabled people (Walker and Naegele, 1999; Priestley, 2000). Historically, there has been a tendency to construct the challenge of disability and ageing in terms of 'health' and 'functioning'. However, this largely ignores concerns about the extent to which the growing population of older disabled people are included in discussions of disability equality. In this context, it is important to consider whether the meaning and experience of disability in old age can, or should, be considered as in any way different from disability in younger adulthood or childhood (Breitenbach, 2001).

Ageing bodies

Bodily ageing is closely associated with the onset of impairment. Broadly speaking, we can identify two important trends. First, medical, technological and social developments mean that there has been a dramatic increase in the number of younger disabled adults who survive into old age (e.g. Zarb and Oliver, 1993; Salvatori *et al.*, 1998). Second, the general trend of population ageing means that the number of previously non-disabled adults who acquire impairments in later life is also increasing. Indeed, we are witnessing a kind of demographic convergence in later life, between those who have grown older as disabled people, and those who become disabled later in life. For example, Holland (2000) and Janicki *et al.* (1999) draw attention to parallel increases in the numbers of people with learning difficulties surviving into old age and the number of previously non-disabled people acquiring cognitive impairments in later life (resulting from dementia or stroke, for example). Similar arguments could be made about convergence in the acquisition of physical or sensory impairments (particularly, partial sight and partial hearing).

Surprisingly, social theories of ageing have often overlooked the embodied connection between ageing and disability (e.g. Öberg, 1996; Gilleard and Higgs, 1998). The normalcy of impaired bodies in old age, and particularly in advanced old age, may help to explain why older people with impairments are rarely regarded as 'disabled' in quite the same way as younger adults or children. In this sense, there is an important contrast between the position of the impaired body in old age and in other generational locations. While impairment characteristics at birth and in childhood have long been constructed as particularly aberrant or untimely, impairments and functional limitations in old age have been constructed as something of a generational norm, if not a defining characteristic of becoming old. So, we might argue that impaired bodies cease to be 'out of place' or 'special' in old age when compared to other generational locations (Zola, 1989).

As an example, this kind of reasoning was used as a justification for differences in disability policy affecting older and younger adults during a major policy review of long-term care in the UK:

> Younger people must try to negotiate their lives while disabled and when the vast majority of their peers, who set the standards of normal behaviour, are able-bodied. By comparison, as 7 in 10 people aged 80 or over have some level of disability, being unable to do some things or needing help with others is a common and anticipated experience. This perception may be behind the differences in the policy approach to supporting younger and older disabled people, both in service terms and financially. (Sutherland, 1999: para. 9.7)

Similarly, in research at Leeds, we found that local service providers and advocacy groups did not think of the older people they worked with as 'disabled' when they were still able to do 'what *a normal elderly person* could do' (Priestley, 2003b). Many age-related impairments were thus viewed as quite consistent with normal bio-graphies of ageing, as an everyday part of the embodied generational habitus of old age (Turner, 1989). In this way, the same impairment characteristics that were regarded as aberrant in younger bodies are often viewed as 'normal' in ageing bodies. This suggests that constructions of bodily impairment and disability status are generationally situated. If disability is perceived as a transgression of embodied norms, then generation plays a big part in defining what those norms are. Thus, people with similar kinds of impairment characteristics may be viewed as 'disabled' or 'not disabled' by comparison with their generational peers (rather than with people of different generations who share the same impairments).

Ageing identities

A second connection is to think about the relationship between disability identities and ageing identities. Here, the onset of age-related impairment is often viewed as an important factor in triggering identity transitions from adulthood to old age. This view has been widely employed in medical sociology, where impairment has been characterized as a form of 'biographical disruption' (Bury, 1982). From this perspective, the onset of impairment is seen to interrupt previous life-course assumptions and narratives, forcing the renegotiation of new biographical identities. However, Williams (2000) contests this view, arguing that the onset of impairment is widely accepted in normal narratives of ageing. Thus, he suggests that the biographical disruption model is adult-centred and has little relevance to the experience of older dis-abled people. Indeed, it could be argued that the onset of impairment in later life *reinforces* the biographical identity of older people rather than disrupting it (see, Carricaburu and Pierret, 1995).

Pound *et al.* (1998) also question the biographical emphasis on 'shattered lives'. Their research leads them to conclude that the generational context of impairment is a very significant factor; one that has been consistently overlooked in research. They suggest two reasons why late life impairment may appear less disruptive to older people than to younger people:

By the time people have survived into their 70s, 80s and 90s, their experiences may have equipped them with considerable skills which enable them to deal with crises and successfully adapt to new situations such as chronic illness. Alternatively, older people, particularly older working class people, may have lower expectations of health ... and may anticipate illness as inevitable in old age, or meet it with a greater sense of acceptance ... (Pound *et al.*, 1998, p. 502)

As with the earlier discussion of embodiment, we might conclude that the reduced biographical disruption of impairment and disability in old age might explain why older people have been left out of disability debates. However, there are some problems with this view. Postmodern identity theories suggest that people can increasingly 'choose' not to be old (Biggs, 1997). For Featherstone and Hepworth (1991) this theme is particularly important in understanding the position of the body in generational identity and the postmodern life course. Thus, they argue that the surface capacities of the ageing body can be seen as a kind of 'mask' that hides a more youthful or ageless self within. The identity tension for older people is then constructed as the problem of maintaining a youthful sense of self in the face of daily conflicts with the limitations and appearance of the ageing body (see also Öberg and Tornstam, 2001).

Linked to this, new cultural challenges to traditional ageing identities have focused increasingly on the concepts of 'successful' and 'active' ageing. Older people and their pressure groups have been drawn to this imagery as a way to assert and maintain more positive identities in later life. However, we have to note that these new narratives and identities are premised upon a view of successful ageing that has no place for impairment and disability. Ageing with disability is implicitly defined as 'unsuccessful' ageing and adopting a positive identity of ageing means distancing oneself from a disabled identity for as long as possible.

Cultural otherness

Turning away from individual biography and embodied identities, there are also parallels in the cultural construction of disability and old age. In particular, older and disabled people have been subject to similar discourses of dependency and otherness that distinguish and distance them from the ideals of an independent and autonomous adulthood. The cultural and spatial distancing of older and disabled people from the mainstream of society go hand in hand – physical segregation from family and work reinforces perceptions of cultural difference (Finkelstein, 1991). In this way the apparent 'disengagement' or the perceived 'strangeness' of older people with impairments (e.g. Cumming and Henry, 1961; Maddox, 1994) has been underpinned by their systematic removal from families and communities into segregated residential institutions.

> Just as theories of disability identify cultural fears of distance from the able-bodied ideal, so perceptions of 'the elderly' from this ideal generate cultural ambivalence, if not hostility from other age groups. Relatively trivial physical manifestations of difference turn into markers of otherness. (Irwin, 1999, p. 694)

Similar arguments have been made about the cultural and physical distancing of younger disabled people. For example, in their study of institutional lives, Miller and Gwynne (1972) pointed to the 'social death' of those segregated from the mainstream. Thus, they argued:

> by the very fact of committing people to institutions of this type, society is defining them as, in effect, socially dead, then the essential task to be carried out is to help the inmates make their transition from social death to physical death. (1972, p. 89)

Picking up this commentary, Finkelstein (1991) argues that institutional segregation is only the final stage in a 'social death model of disability', and that this process begins with the wider construction of disabled people as dependent upon others for permanent care. So it is with old age too. Modernist discourses of adulthood (emphasizing values like independence, productivity, youth and progress) have devalued both older people and disabled people as non-adult dependants.

Cultural resistance to these negative constructions has emphasized the potential for greater independence in later life. 'Sustained personal autonomy' is increasingly viewed as the measure of 'successful ageing' (Maddox, 1994; Ford *et al.*, 2000) and this has been expressed in the growing movement for 'active ageing' (Blaikie, 1999; Vincent, 1999). Claims to active ageing have been less concerned with older people's continued participation in adult labour markets (longer working lives) than with participation in new forms of generational consumption (leisured retirement). Indeed, for older people with access to consumption opportunities, the advent of a leisured 'Third Age' offers more in common with the ideals of independent adulthood than with the presumed dependency and physical decline of traditional ageing (Laslett, 1989). However, such developments also suggest an increasing status divide between older people with and without such opportunities.

Thus, while the phase of active adulthood expands to embrace many more seniors, stronger taboos form around those in poverty, those whose pastimes lack positive cultural resonances, and those suffering from disability and diseases... (Blaikie, 1999)

Social structure

Critical theorists have also drawn attention to similarities in the structural location of disability and old age, as parallel social categories defined by enforced dependency on adult labour. Oliver (1993) summarizes the connection:

both ageing and disability are produced as an economic problem because of the changes that result in the nature of work and the needs of the labour market within capitalism. The political economy perspective points to the structural dependency of the aged arising from conditions in the labour market and the stratification and organisation of work and society... In other words, old people no longer play a key role in the process of production and no longer participate in the labour market. The same is true of disabled people and has been so, except in times of severe labour shortage, since the time of the industrial revolution.

From a structural perspective then, old age has been widely viewed as a category produced through the historic regulation of adult labour in capitalist economies (Phillipson, 1982; Phillipson *et al.*, 1986; Minkler and Estes, 1991). Defining old age as a stage of permanent exit from labour raises questions about the generational location of younger disabled adults who have already been excluded from adult working roles. For example, although increasing numbers of adults with learning difficulties survive into old age, many have been excluded from valued adult labour during their younger lives:

for most of the population life is structured into infancy, childhood, working adult life and retirement. For people with learning disabilities, many of the expectations that people have of life are not available. The most striking example is work.... Without work or its equivalent there can be no retirement. (Holland, 2000, p. 30)

To summarize, there are some important similarities in the way that disability and old age have been produced and regulated within modern societies. In particular, both have been defined by the work–welfare divide of exemption from adult labour (Irwin, 1999). Both have emerged in response to social claims and the changing labour demands of capitalist economies (Irwin, 2001). Consequently, disability and old age are parallel structural locations, perceived as 'dependent' and ultimately as *non-adult* social categories.

Politics

Disability politics and equal rights are relevant to people throughout the life course, and would seem to be particularly significant for the large numbers of people who experience impairment in advanced old age. However, when we look at the politics of older people's rights there has been a failure to engage with critical thinking on disability. Similarly, when we look at the disabled people's movement, and its actions against disability discrimination, there is little reference to older disabled people.

Despite the fact that the majority of disabled people in Western societies are over retirement age, older people remain under-represented, while disability policy making remains focused on the needs of younger adults (and to a lesser extent, children). It is certainly evident that many services treat older people very differently to younger adults, and that older people with impairments have been excluded from some of the more progressive developments in services for 'younger disabled people'. Kennedy and Minkler (1998) conclude that high expectations about disability rights are not being applied equally to older disabled people. At the same time, advances in rights for older people are failing to recognize or include those who are also disabled.

There is a growing appreciation of the potential for reaching goals of autonomy, growth, participation and high life satisfaction on the part of the non-disabled elderly, but these goals tend to be recalibrated dramatically downward for those elders who become disabled. Where 'access' and 'full participation' have become key concepts for the younger disabled population, the sights of families and professionals, and of older disabled persons themselves, tend to be far more circumscribed. In this way, aging professionals [*sic*], elders, and society in general appear to have traded earlier, limited views of aging for an even more limited view of what it means to be old and disabled. (Kennedy and Minkler, 1998, p. 768–9)

It is tempting to suggest that greater alliances and understanding could strengthen the claims of both older people and disabled people. However, while these two movements have many concerns in common, there are obstacles. In particular, there will always be conflicting issues of identity politics so long as claims to rights are based on a narrow view of what it means to be an 'adult' in society. There is a particular danger in the lure to discourses of individual rights that rely on narrow notions of 'independence' and 'autonomy' as the basis of citizenship and personhood.

Conclusions

To summarize, it is possible to think about old age in a number of different ways, all of which have some relevance to understanding disability. Collectively, old age may be viewed as a structural or administrative category deployed to control adult labour supply, and maintained through discourses of 'ability to work'. In this way, old age has been produced and regulated in very similar ways to the category of disability in modern societies. Both have involved categorical exemption from competitive adult markets, resulting in the enforced dependency of both older and disabled people on adult labour. Old age may equally be viewed as a cultural category, constructed in relation to other generational locations (such as adulthood or childhood). In this context, both older and disabled people have been viewed as non-adult 'others', a construction reproduced through institutional segregation and disciplining forms of care.

It is also possible to think about ageing in terms of the impaired body, and its significance in defining old age, since certain impairments are closely associated with advanced ageing and may become normalized as part of the 'generational habitus' or trappings of old age. Perceptions of appearance and physical functioning are therefore generationally situated. Whereas disability in young adulthood is commonly viewed as disruptive to the normative life course, disability in old age is not. This has consequences for the negotiation of embodied generational identities and for thinking about disability. So, in order to explain why older people with impairments are rarely seen as 'disabled' it is necessary to think about *both* their structural–cultural dislocation from modern adulthood *and* the relative normalcy of impairment in biographical identities of later life.

The politics of disability in later life is also important, and organizations representing older and disabled people have become increasingly active, challenging past assumptions and policies. However, despite the fact that both movements have campaigned on similar issues, their strategies highlight differences. Movements for 'independent living' and 'active ageing' have made successful claims at the margins of traditional adult citizenship, but have distanced themselves further and further from the negative imagery of dependency in deep old age. Developments in rights for older people and disabled people have brought benefits for many but there is a risk that those who are already the oldest, the poorest and the most marginalized are also those that are being left behind in the struggle for disability equality.

Chapter 7

Towards a Psychology of Disability: The Emotional Effects of Living in a Disabling Society

Donna Reeve

Introduction

The relationship between the disciplines of psychology and disability studies has been a troubled one at best. The proliferation of loss and stage models about how people with impairments 'adjust' to disability through a mourning process have been extensively criticised within disability studies for failing to reflect the lived experience of disabled people and instead providing a 'psychopathology of disability' (Finkelstein, 1990). This approach to understanding the experience of disability is not surprising given that psychology generally views disability as being the domain of rehabilitation psychology rather than part of mainstream psychology training (Olkin and Pledger, 2003). This skewing of psychology research and theory is also problematic because most disabled people who seek psychological or psychotherapeutic help, for whatever reason, are seen in the community and not in a rehabilitation unit. However, there are consequences to this rejection of the rehabilitation-based models as a way of explaining how people with impairments 'come to terms' with disability. There appears to have been an avoidance of engaging with *anything* psychological within disability studies lest the individual tragedy model be re-invoked through suggesting that disabled people *need* some form of psychological help.

In a recent review of the literature looking at the mental health support needs of people with physical impairments, Morris (2004) suggests that more research is needed to consider how the experience of disabling attitudes and environments affect the emotional well-being of disabled people. Whilst many disabled people have written about their experiences of disabling attitudes (such as Morris, 1991; Keith, 1996) there has been less discussion about the psychological consequences of being on the receiving end of prejudice and discrimination. Therefore there is still a need for a *psychology of disability*, which is based on how '*we make sense of our world according to the way we experience it*' (Finkelstein, 1990, p. 1; emphasis in original), rather than prioritising the imagination of non-disabled people about what it could be like to experience impairment (Oliver, 1996a). This chapter will explore the contribution that an understanding of the *psycho-emotional dimensions* of disability can make towards a psychology of disability which is underpinned by a social model understanding of disability, rather than an individual model approach as reflected in the loss and stage models within psychology.

The psycho-emotional dimensions of disability

Recasting disability as a form of social oppression has been tremendously important in highlighting the social and economic disadvantage faced by disabled people. However, feminist writers in particular have pointed out that the focus of the social model has been on the 'public' experiences of oppression, such as inaccessible environments, at the expense of the more 'personal' experiences of oppression which operate at the emotional level (Thomas, 1999). Consequently, an extended social relational definition of disability has been proposed which attempts to address this criticism by explicitly including both the barriers 'out there' and those that operate 'in here':

> Disability is a form of social oppression involving the social imposition of restrictions of activity on people with impairments *and the socially engendered undermining of their psycho-emotional well-being.* (Thomas, 1999, p. 60; my emphasis)

For example, someone may be disabled by a flight of steps or by being given information in an inaccessible format – these are examples of the structural dimensions of disability which restrict activity. On the other hand, psycho-emotional dimensions of disability would include being stared at or patronised by strangers, actions which can leave disabled people feeling worthless and ashamed, and may end up preventing them from participating in society as effectively as physically inaccessible environments (Reeve, 2004b).

This particular dimension of disability which operates along emotional pathways is highly influenced by cultural representations and disabling images. Disabled people are rarely seen on television or in films as part of everyday situations and when they are part of the story-line, the focus is generally on their impairment. Negative cultural images and the rejection of impaired bodies from mainstream society have an effect on not only how disabled people see themselves, but also how they are perceived by others. Thus psycho-emotional disablism can be found in the ways that some disabled people internalise the negative social values about disability, or within their relationships with family, friends, professionals or strangers (Thomas, 1999). However, it is important to note that the experience of psycho-emotional disablism is not inevitable or fixed. Not all disabled people will experience this form of disability and it will be affected by time and place; whether it is more or less disabling than their experience of structural disability will vary and, as I will show, sometimes the two dimensions reinforce each other. Disabled people often find ways of resisting this particular form of disablism, although this may have additional emotional costs. The experience of psycho-emotional disablism can also be affected by how visible impairment effects are and have an interaction with other aspects of identity such as gender, ethnicity, age and class (Thomas, 1999).

The specific inclusion of both structural and psycho-emotional dimensions of disability within an extended social model definition of disability contributes to the development of a psychology, rather than a psychopathology, of disability. Over a decade ago, a new approach to a psychology of disability was advocated because:

> With the growth of new (social) approaches to disability, there is a need to develop fresh insights into the way disabled people, and others, make sense of, cope with, manage and overcome disabling social and physical barriers. (Finkelstein and French, 1993, p. 32)

In other words, it was acknowledged that there is a need to take account of the personal effects of living with disability in a manner which differs from the traditional psychological models of loss and adjustment. This psychology of disability (rather than impairment) focuses on the psychological anxiety and distress caused by the social relations of disability and is therefore very closely related to the psycho-emotional dimensions of disability.

Examples of psycho-emotional disablism

I will now illustrate several different forms of the psycho-emotional dimensions of disability by drawing on research which explored the ways that people with physical impairments negotiate disability within everyday life (Reeve, 2005). This PhD research used the free-association narrative interview method described by Hollway and Jefferson (2000) to generate narratives of people's 'disability experiences'. As well as indicating some of the forms that resistance took, I will show the longevity and cumulative nature of psycho-emotional disablism and consequent effects on the emotional well-being of these research participants. The pseudonyms used in the rest of this chapter are those chosen by participants.

The experience of structural disability

For many disabled people, the experience of being excluded from physical environments reminds them that they are different and can leave them feeling that they do not belong in the places where non-disabled people spend their lives (Morris, 1991). Robert talked at length about his experience of inaccessible environments, in particular, shops and pubs. As a wheelchair user he finds it difficult to negotiate the doors to most shops on his own and so is forced to rely on the help of strangers to gain access.

> A lot of people see you want to go in, and they just walk past you. Or you ask them to hold the door and they just go on straight into the premises. You know, you just [pauses] how can I put it? Just feel like you're not wanted. They just look, everybody just looks down [their] nose at you. (Robert)

This experience of moving within what Kitchin (1998, p. 351) calls 'landscapes of exclusion' reminds Robert that he is 'out of place' and that he somehow should not be shopping with everyone else. Consequently he finds himself apologising all the time:

> You say, 'Oh sorry for doing this', or, 'Sorry for doing that'. By the time you get home you think, 'Why should I say sorry?' But it upsets you that much – what do you do? You come home, you pop your pills, what you've got to take, and then you go and have a lie-down for an hour and it's still there, you know. (Robert)

I asked him if he felt he had to present himself in a particular light in order to get help in shops and he agreed saying:

> [Y]ou've always got to put that false smile on, say, 'Oh thank you very much. Can you please pass me that? Can you do this please? Can you do that? Oh excuse me, can you move out of the way?'
> (Robert)

So Robert is aware that he is deliberately performing the 'grateful disabled person' role, simply to overcome the physical obstacles within the shop (a structural dimension of disability) and to deal with the reactions of others who look down on him (a psycho-emotional dimension of disability). This is an example of how structural disability can be compounded by the experience of psycho-emotional disablism because the inaccessible shop forces him to ask people for help and the way that these people ignore his request leaves him feeling unwanted and worthless. On top of this he is apologising for bothering people at the same time as feeling angry that he is being forced to ask for help in this manner – the result is considerable emotional distress. Additionally it may be more difficult for Robert to ask and receive help from strangers than for a disabled woman, because of the dissonance between the cultural representations of masculinity (strength and independence) and disability (weakness and dependence) (Robertson, 2004). This illustrates the manner in which the psycho-emotional dimensions of disability can be intersected by other identities such as gender.

Social interactions with others
An important source of psycho-emotional disablism comes from interactions with other people in society, relationships which can be affected by prejudice and myths about disability. One of the prevailing themes that Adinuf (so called because he had 'had enough') talked about was the way that friends and strangers avoided him once he became disabled – even crossing the road when they saw him coming in his wheelchair. This example of psycho-emotional disablism, being regarded by others as someone to be feared and avoided, left Adinuf feeling isolated and unwanted.

This avoidance was exemplified by the story he told about attending a computing course at the local college. When the tutor suggested that they all gather round to watch her demonstrate something on the computer, Adinuf found that no one was willing to sit near him.

I don't even know them and straight away they sort of identified me, 'Ah, stay away from him, he's got a disability, he's got a wheelchair – mustn't go anywhere near him'. [edit] Because people just don't understand disability. They think that, 'Oh, maybe he's going to ask me to do something for him'. (Adinuf)

Adinuf felt that the source of people's avoidance of him was not only due to vague fears of contagion, but also because they were frightened that they might be called upon to help in unspecified ways. Social encounters are usually governed by culturally 'agreed' rules of engagement (Keith, 1996, p. 72), but the lack of such cultural rules for the interactions between disabled and non-disabled people can lead to anxiety and confusion about how one 'ought' to behave, with the result being avoidance rather than engagement as seen here. Adinuf's reaction to this behaviour is to take on the role of educator, to try and prove that people like him are not contagious, that there is nothing for them to be frightened of. Adinuf recognised that generally he took on this role of educating people about 'disability', feeling that much of the rejection he had experienced was simply due to ignorance and people not taking the trouble to talk to him over a cup of coffee, to see Adinuf rather than the wheelchair.

Another problem which many disabled people with visible impairments face is the issue of how to deal with the curiosity of others (Morris, 1991). Rose, as a child, had surgery on her leg following polio and her father's job meant she changed schools frequently. She was always planning how to answer the inevitable 'What happened to your leg?' question.

> Rose: I would go through scenes in my head where I would think, 'What can I say? How can I deal with this? I know, I'll say, 'It was an accident'. Or I'll say, I'll just tell them. Or I'll tell – I won't say anything. Or, and – and, you know, I tried all these things and none of them worked. I would go prepared to say such and such a thing, and nobody would say anything.
> Donna: [Laughs quietly]
> Rose: And I would think, 'Oh, A, they don't mind, B, they haven't noticed, anyway it's alright'. And then a bit later on they might say something, and it might be really unkind [hesitates] and all sorts of things.

Rose is attempting to retain control over what people know about her, which is difficult when impairment is visible. Like Adinuf, she is 'working' to manage the information which others have about her. Once she started dating men she became acutely conscious of how her status would change when they noticed her impairment.

'What did you do to your leg?' And you think, 'Oh, shit!' And immediately it reduces you, it takes you down to a different level – they've noticed that you're not perfect. Because when you're dealing with the opposite sex, you do put your best foot forward and you want to present as attractive a package as possible. And when that major flaw is the first thing, or one of the first things that they notice, it weakens your position. You feel that you have to apologise or make up for it in some way. (Rose)

Rose's story makes explicit reference to the cultural representation of femininity (women as pretty and physically perfect) and the way in which she feels that she fails to meet the required standard because of her 'flawed' leg. Thus, like Robert, understanding how gender and disability intersect provides additional insight into how psycho-emotional disablism affects self-esteem.

In addition to direct questions or avoidance, people with visible impairments also experience being stared at by others. This action is not a value-neutral event, but is an act of invalidation based on public narratives of 'normality, truth, beauty and perfection' (Hughes, 1999, p. 164). Rose hated the way that people had stared at her since childhood:

People would stare, they'd look and their eyes would drop and you knew – and they wouldn't even pretend to hide it and they would just sort of follow you round. And you'd turn round and you knew that they were turned round as well. And I just wanted to kill them, I can't tell you the anger I had inside me, all my childhood, for so long. I really wanted to kill them. I really wished I had a machine gun and I would blow them away. (Rose)

Whilst disabled people are increasingly refusing to accept this invalidating gaze from society (Reeve, 2002), nonetheless the experience of being stared at can seriously affect someone's emotional well-being and self-worth as illustrated by Rose, and its effects should not be underestimated. This is particularly true of an extreme form of medical gaze known as 'public stripping' (French, 1994).

I had periodic reviews at Manchester. Mr G [consultant] was very nice, but I mean, I used to go and strip down to knickers and vest and have to parade in front of a group of students [pause] which got increasingly embarrassing, the older I got. (Rose)

This form of institutional abuse can leave a disabled person feeling vulnerable, exposed and humiliated and is an example of psycho-emotional disablism.

So far I have discussed social interactions which adversely affect the emotional well-being of a person with visible impairments – both Rose and Adinuf are identified by others as disabled because of visible difference. However, whilst people with hidden impairments are much less likely to be avoided, feared or stared at, there is always the risk that their disability status will be revealed and this forms the basis for the 'negative psycho-emotional aspects of concealment' (Thomas, 1999, p. 55). This is probably most marked for disabled people who have some form of incontinence, especially given the powerful social expectation that children and adults should be in control of bladder and bowels (Cavet, 1998). Finally, people with hidden impairments can also face difficulties when they attempt to use facilities which are reserved for disabled people. People who do not match the stereotyp-ical image of someone who is elderly and/or a wheelchair user can result in their right to use facilities, such as accessible toilets or disabled parking spaces, being challenged by others. Consequently someone may choose to use a stick, to adopt a visible marker of impairment, in order to be able to use these facilities without harassment – but this may also have an emotional cost in publicly identifying as disabled (Reeve, 2002).

Internalised oppression
The final example of psycho-emotional disablism I want to describe is that of internalised oppression, which is a feature of any marginalised group in society. In this form of oppression, which acts at the uncon-scious level, individuals within the marginalised group internalise the prejudices held by the dominant group – the acceptance and incorpor-ation of '*their* values about *our* lives' (Morris, 1991, p. 29; emphasis in original). Cultural representations of disability reinforce the myths and stereotypes which underpin prejudices experienced by disabled people on a daily basis; for example the increasing calls for voluntary euthanasia to be legalised and the current debates around bioethics give strong messages to disabled people about the value of their lives.

Thus it is not surprising that internalised oppression can leave some disabled people feeling devalued and disempowered (Reeve, 2004b). This form of psycho-emotional disablism also has a very direct effect on the decisions which disabled people take about their lives; for example someone may decide not to become involved in a sexual relationship because they have internalised the prejudice that people 'like them' are sexually undesirable to others.

The starkest examples of internalised oppression were recounted by Rhodri who had been born with cerebral palsy and was marked out from the day he was born as 'useless' and a 'burden'. The consultant at the hospital told his parents that they should leave Rhodri in the hospital and go home and forget about their baby because there was no future for someone with his condition.

> All my life, call it insecurity, or whatever you like to put on it, right, is that, 'What's the difference with me then? Why was I given up so early?' I hadn't had any chance to prove myself in any form and yet somebody in authority could say I was useless. [edit] I've got the tendency of going too negative-wards, I have, because 'I'm no good', going back to being a kid again. 'Nothing is going to become of this gentleman'. (Rhodri)

This internalisation that he was worthless was made worse by the public humiliation he experienced at the hands of staff at a residential school.

> I was put out in front of the whole school when I was coming up to a teenager, and said, 'This will happen to you, if you wet your clothes'. And I had to go round in a dressing gown and pants and they were spares – so I was a spare person, wasn't I. Only by having a fragment of my life, you can see why I haven't got a lot of confidence. (Rhodri)

Rhodri's impairment meant that he couldn't help having 'accidents' – but when he did, he was publicly humiliated by being made to go around in a spare set of clothes. For someone who already felt worthless, this reinforced to Rhodri that he was just a spare person, someone of no value, a message he carried throughout the rest of his adult life. The effects on Rhodri of the way his school handled his incontinence have also had a direct effect on his physical well-being. Because of the way that he was regarded as 'the dirtiest boy in the school', he is reluctant to seek medical help for current continence problems which prevent him from leaving the house. So this childhood label has lasted 40 years and now directly prevents him from participating in society as well as jeopardising his health. Thus the experience of past psycho-emotional disablism can have an impact on present-day impairment.

Another example of internalised oppression was seen in the way that Rose internalised the view that she was not valued as someone with an impairment. Her parents would not allow her to talk about bullying at school or even how she felt about being disabled – thus Rose became a 'supercrip', someone who works hard to pass as more than 'normal', in an attempt to make her parents proud of her.

> So I grew up trying to excel and pretend that there was nothing actually wrong. And I strove, as I got older, I worked harder and harder to try and hide this defect. I was very, very conscious of it – the older I got, the worse it got. (Rose)

However, this can be a lonely place to be – because she is then neither disabled nor non-disabled, but inhabits a twilight world in between. If Rose's parents had been more able to listen to their daughter and value her for the person she was, her childhood and adulthood would have been much easier and she would have had more confidence and self-respect.

Discussion

I have described different aspects of the psycho-emotional dimensions of disability and shown how they can adversely affect the emotional well-being of disabled people. I have also illustrated the complex nature of this form of disablism, its longevity, as well as indicating the additional emotional costs paid when people did find ways of resisting its effects. Whilst I have presented accounts of people with physical impairments, this dimension of disability can affect any group of disabled people (see for example Marks, 1999). I now want to consider the implications this has for psychology, in particular for psychologists working with disabled people.

Professional responses to disability are not simply about making services accessible to disabled people by putting in a ramp. It is about understanding disability from a cultural, political, social and historical perspective and being aware of the complicated effects of this particular form of social oppression which operates at both conscious and unconscious levels. An important issue, which is discussed elsewhere in this book, is that the psychologist needs to be aware of *their* attitudes and prejudices about disability, otherwise these will be acted out within the therapeutic relationship which can have disabling consequences for the disabled client (Reeve, 2000, 2004a).

The preceding discussion of the psycho-emotional dimensions of disability reveals important aspects of the disability experience which psychologists need to be aware of. Disabled people may seek help with emotional difficulties for a range of reasons which may or may not be disability-related. However, it is important that psychologists remain alert to the *possibility* that there may be interactions between presented difficulties and past/present experiences of psycho-emotional disablism. For example, someone might want help with issues of self-esteem and confidence which stem from problems in childhood. But, if this person has also grown up with impairment it is important that effects of societal/familial prejudice are not ignored. For example, in Rhodri's case, being part of a society with few positive role models and a legacy of negative expectations about his value as a person clearly contributed significantly to his lack of self-worth and confidence. Unfortunately, many of the professionals Rhodri currently deals with do not know his 'history' and accuse him of over-reacting in ways that are quite understandable if one considers his childhood. It is also vital that emotional reactions to the experiences of exclusion and discrimination are not pathologised (Olkin, 1999); for example, Robert's anger with inaccessible shops is a reasonable response to the experience of being excluded rather than an indication that he has failed to adjust to his disability as predicted by the loss and stage models.

Psychologists also need to take account of the strategies people employ to counteract this 'personal' experience of oppression which can involve 'emotion work' either to hide their own true emotions in line with cultural 'feeling rules', or to manage the emotions of others (Lupton, 1998). For example, Adinuf feels that he needs to patiently reassure, explain and educate others who are actively avoiding him, using *suitable* language so that they understand more about disability and are not so afraid of him. Thus he is carrying out emotional labour in order to deal with *their* fears and prejudices about him, as a disabled man. Similarly Rose works to devise a story about what happened to her leg, a story which gives her some control over what the other children know about her, but also in order to deal with the curiosity of others about what is 'wrong' with her leg. In Robert's case, his adoption of the 'false smile' and fake expressions of gratitude means he is behaving in the ways that society expects disabled people to behave. This act may well be conscious and gets him the help he needs (the alternative being to remain excluded), but it has emotional costs because the projected behaviour is at odds with his very real anger at being forced to behave in this manner. This 'emotional dissonance' is a recognised aspect of emotional labour which can lead to emotional exhaustion (Ashforth and Tomiuk, 2000). It could also be expected that such dissonance could have an adverse effect on the physical as well as emotional health of a disabled person. Thus it is important that psychologists consider the emotional and physical effects of resistance to these psycho-emotional dimensions of disability.

The case of psycho-emotional disablism and disabled children is worthy of particular consideration. The definition of emotional abuse is the

> persistent emotional ill-treatment of a child such as to cause severe and persistent adverse effects on the child's emotional development. It may involve conveying to children that they are worthless or unloved, inadequate, or valued only insofar as they meet the needs of another person. (Department of Health, 2001a, p. 43)

The consequences of psycho-emotional disablism on the self-esteem and self-worth of disabled children are potentially very similar to those resulting from emotional abuse – children who believe they are worthless, inadequate and useless. Thus psycho-emotional disablism could be viewed as a form of emotional abuse. In the example of Rhodri who ended up feeling like a 'spare person', it is clear that this was caused by institutional practices in which disabled children were not valued as human beings. Disabled children's experience of internalised oppression with its impact on self-esteem may render them more vulnerable to being abused than non-disabled children. Given the negative social values which are placed on disabled children, it is not surprising that some children accept abuse because they believe they are 'defective' and abusers feel it is all right to abuse a child who is already deemed 'worthless' (Kennedy, 1996). This same author also quotes the experiences of one disabled adult who points out that the experience of 'public stripping' described earlier could be seen as 'grooming' for future sexual abuse – how, as a disabled child, do you draw the line between what a doctor asks you to do, or the porter?

The levels of abuse of disabled children are significantly higher than for non-disabled children and yet this issue rarely receives the attention it deserves from professionals (NWGCPD, 2003).

Finally, it is imperative that there is more training about disability on psychology courses, especially given the scarcity of disabled psychologists, teachers and students (Olkin and Pledger, 2003). However, this training has to cover more than basic Disability Equality Training, an introduction to disability as an equal opportunities issue; it is vital that it also includes information about the psycho-emotional dimensions of disability if the full impact of the experience of living in a disabling world is to be understood (Reeve, 2004a). The impasse that has existed between psychology and disability studies is one contributory factor to the lack of such training – a situation that needs urgent redress.

Conclusions

For many disabled people, it is the barriers which operate at the psycho-emotional level which have the most disabling consequences on their lives. I have indicated how the experience of exclusion, prejudice and the reactions of others can adversely affect someone's emotional well-being, a situation which can be exacerbated by the emotion work which some disabled people undertake as a way of resisting psycho-emotional disablism. The application of individualistic models as a means of understanding how people respond to disability ignore these psycho-emotional dimensions of disability, fail to take account of their long-lived and cumulative effects and additionally risk pathologising justifiable emotional responses to being excluded and discriminated against.

Consideration of the psycho-emotional dimensions of disability as part of a psychology, rather than a psychopathology, of disability would help bridge the existing gap between psychology and disability studies. Recognising the social, cultural, political and historical aspects of disability is vital if psychology is to stop being 'part of the problem', yet another disabling barrier created by the viewing of disability as an individual deficit (Finkelstein, 1990). There is an urgent need for mainstream psychology courses to include disability as part of their diversity training. Given the nature of the emotional level at which psychologists work, this has to include reference to the psycho-emotional dimensions of disability, recognising the pervasive and long-lasting effects this can have on the emotional well-being of disabled people, affecting who they are and what they choose to do. Rhoda Olkin concludes:

> Disability studies and psychology can join hands, but they haven't yet. (Olkin and Pledger, 2003, p. 303)

Recognising the impact of the psycho-emotional dimensions of disability on the everyday lives of disabled people goes some way to helping this happen, whilst maintaining the vital connection to disability as a social construction rather than as individual tragedy.

Acknowledgements

This chapter was written as part of my PhD which is supported by an ESRC studentship (R42200034345).

Part II

Disability, Psychology and Practice: From a Disabling to an Enabling Psychology

Chapter 8

Against Stereotypes: Experiences of Disabled Psychologists

Freda Levinson and Simon Parritt

Introduction

The authors have been requested to reflect upon what it was like to train and work as disabled psychologists. In a sense we were fortunate in being able to obtain established appointments, as disabled graduates have long had problems in obtaining *relevant* work; and the representation of professional psychologists was then very low. Further, as we will demonstrate in this chapter, psychologists face specific difficulties because of the nature of the work setting. Much of our account will focus on our actual experiences. We realised, however, that it was necessary to relate these to the explanations offered by mainstream psychological studies in disability, and to consider how disability is viewed in the training and practice of other psychologists. It is not possible to do this without employing a framework to examine the reactions we have encountered, or by ignoring the wider context in which our experiences took place. This must, of necessity, include the current legislation, that is, Disability Discrimination Act (DDA) 1995 and how the British Psychological Society (BPS) has responded to this. To date, the BPS has paid little overt attention to accommodating trainees and qualified psychologists who are disabled, and has not yet produced any specific guidelines to advise its subsidiary bodies. Not surprisingly, we have noted much confusion over the DDA and its relevance for both the BPS and individual psychologists. The dominant approaches to disability in clinical and health psychology are reflected in their mainstream publication, a high proportion of which are concerned with developing models focussing only on individual responses to being disabled. The influences of environmental factors – physical, social, cultural and financial – are largely ignored. In social psychology and related social science studies, there is an awareness of the relevance of environmental factors, but these are invoked mainly at a theoretical level and seldom related directly to studies of disabled populations. We would like to attempt an integration of our personal experience and observations with the prevailing approaches to disability, and to suggest how the BPS could foster more positive training, practice and research in the relevant applied disciplines of clinical, health and counselling psychology.

Work settings

As practising psychologists, who are disabled, holding appointments within the NHS and in the voluntary and private sectors, we are able to view our position from both sides of the fence. A primary concern was access to most areas of the institutions, in which we worked. Gaining access to meeting places, clinical areas, libraries, and to the cafeterias and other social amenities, required prior awareness of all the barriers to be negotiated (e.g. steps, fire-doors) for each location. Once we completed these internal inventories, which were usually implicit, access could become a routine. However, some of our most discomforting experiences arose when attending other institutions for professional purposes, for example supervising, lecturing and attending meetings. Arrivals, already complicated by the parking lottery, could be rendered more stressful by receptionists, who, assuming we must be patients, tried to direct us accordingly. One learns various strategies to combat this stereotyping, but the hassle entailed was an unwelcome distraction. Freda recalls arriving with a colleague, to attend a meeting at a large district general hospital:

> As we entered the crowded lift for the administrative section, we were interrupted in our discussion, on the forthcoming meeting, by a staff member who asked 'Are you in the correct lift?' 'Yes,' we assured her. 'But are you sure?' was the response, repeated twice and loudly despite our confirmation. Finally, exasperated, I snubbed her (unkindly). 'You should not assume that someone disabled must be attending this hospital as a patient.' Confused and flushed she got out at the next floor.

What do these experiences illustrate? (Apart from the obvious fact that the NHS accords a low priority to access issues.) First, that disabled practitioners in any of the health professions (not just psychologists) are comparatively rare. Within any social grouping, the recognition of a particular sub-group depends upon the number of individuals sharing defining characteristics. The point we wish to make here is that the number of disabled professionally qualified psychologists, and those in training, is so small, and that any influence they may have can make only a minimal impact on stereotypes and policy. Secondly, it is known that the health professions, notably the medical faculty, do discriminate against colleagues who become ill or disabled. There is much anecdotal evidence, which reveals that disabled practitioners and decide against making their condition known because they fear reprisals (Steinberg *et al.*, 2002). It is likely that psychologists are not immune to these attitudes; and find it hard to cope with disabled colleagues, especially in a hospital setting where a sharp distinction is drawn between patients and staff. Since the role of psychologists in health care settings is still not as clearly defined as the more traditional professions, these negative reactions may be intensified.

Colleagues' reactions

We both have long experience working as disabled psychologists. Freda had completed her training, but was disabled for most of her working life. Simon was disabled from childhood; and first had to overcome many problems in obtaining basic qualifications and training for an appropriate profession (see also Chapter 5 by Stannett, this book). Along the way, we have encountered all the reactions listed below; not all the time; by no means from all colleagues; but often enough to make life difficult.

• *Stereotyping* – Most stereotypes of disability are negative and lead, all too readily, to prejudice and discrimination, since those holding them are unable to perceive the disabled person as an individual. They bring a host of limiting assumptions regarding skills and competence, which may restrict severely the disabled individual's capacity to perform (Goffman, 1963). Further, any shortcoming may then be ascribed to the 'disability', for example preconceptions of a 'sick' role for disabled people. Psychologists and sociologists have devoted much study and research to the concept of stereotyping (Kurzban and Leary, 2001);

and it is well known that it is very difficult to combat entrenched stereotypes, even when using well-reasoned knowledge-based arguments. Further, research has demonstrated that expressed attitudes and observed behaviour do not necessarily correlate well. Disabled psychologists may challenge the underlying perceptions of clinical and health psychologists and members of other health professions. The professional role of a disabled colleague clashes with stereotypes of disability which are firmly linked to patients.

• *Rejection* – Made to feel a thorough nuisance, even when making a minor disability-related request: At least the reaction is clear; one is viewed as demanding, expecting too much consideration. However, it can result in discomfort, embarrassment or even exclusion from some activities. We should note that current attitudes towards disability have evolved from earlier responses, which linked disability with contamination and frequently evoked feelings of fear and disgust. This could lead to avoidance and outright rejection. Such reactions are rooted deeply within society and can create a pervading sense of discomfort without the full awareness of the individuals concerned. As it is hard to persist in the face of rejection, disabled psychologists may be marginalised easily and directed towards working with disabled clients only.

• *Inappropriate concern and sympathy* – It can be very tiresome to be asked, repeatedly, 'do you want this or that?', 'Are you comfortable?', or to hear 'poor you!' intoned many times. Even when you realise that these expressions may serve to mask uncertainty, or anxiety, which may be mixed with genuine concern, the embarrassment, often on both sides, does not make for easy relationships. Further, one can be inhibited from asking for something really needed. The current practice of medicine still concerns itself largely with 'acute' conditions and corresponding interventions. Chronic and long-term conditions are left to care staff, with a low hierarchical status and a limited budget. Therefore, the provision of facilities relies heavily upon charitable and voluntary resources. Historically, charity advertising has portrayed disabled people as either sad and helpless or courageous. It is this charity/victim model of disability which probably underlies expressions of excessive concern. It also harks back to early psychological models, which perceive disabled people as victims and assume their dominant reactions are bereavement and loss (Salzberger-Wittenberg, 1970; Berger, 1988).

• *Denial* – Refusal to acknowledge disability. Denial includes a variety of responses, not just on the part of colleagues but disabled individuals as well. Once more we need to consider the problems posed by the patient/professional boundary. Denial is a means of reducing the role confusion, which may arise in the relationship of a disabled professional with other colleagues. At its most direct it is a way of dealing with unresolved feelings, when a disabled associate requires help. A more complex situation is when a disabled psychologist holds a senior position, since disabled people are expected to assume only subservient or marginalised roles. The need for denial is even greater to reduce this role confusion. It is particularly hard to modify such reactions when disabled people themselves collude or even invoke denial themselves.

• *Projected anxiety* – Concern expressed on behalf of others, for example students, patients: It is an uncomfortable experience to be told that your very presence may be awkward for other people. And, to hear misgivings about your competence to deal with patients may be quite undermining. There is a strong element of stereotyping underlying this response, together with a subtle form of rejection (Gething, 1992). These colleagues are asking how a 'patient' can be a provider of therapy. Before demolishing this argument we need to know how patients react. We believe the following section gives the lie to this assumption.

Interactions with patients and clients

On the whole, we can report favourably on our interactions with patients and clients as neither of us encountered any overt adverse reactions. Between us we span a wide age range of clients, from infancy to old age, and an equally diverse range of presenting problems in a host of different settings. Almost without exception, we found that providing patients/clients perceived that they were receiving adequate attention to their problems, and that the interaction and therapy appeared to benefit them, so they were apparently unconcerned by disability. This suggests that the patients'/clients' expectations and their stereotypes of professional status override any initial concern – that may be present – when meeting a disabled practitioner, providing, as noted earlier, they are receiving a satisfactory service.

Indeed, patients usually are very compliant and co-operative, although it has to be accepted that they may harbour doubts, which they do not express. This does appear to be the view of some colleagues who expressed misgivings concerning therapy. We would suggest that these individuals react adversely to disability and project their discomfort onto patients. In established work settings where we held recognised treatment roles, referrals from a range of other professional colleagues did not appear to be affected by disability concerns. Nor were there any problems with professional interactions, providing the necessary boundaries and etiquette were maintained.

We conclude that any problems in this area are more likely to stem from colleagues than patients themselves. After all, we know that patients could feel uneasy regarding the race, gender or age of any professional. There is no reason to assume that they would be any more or less prejudiced regarding disabled professionals.

Models

How meaningful were models in understanding our experiences? And which were the most relevant? Psychology has traditionally used models in order to make sense of the world in which human behaviour operates. It has also largely focussed upon the individual, especially when working with, or researching, clinical populations. However, whilst the value of models cannot be dismissed when it comes to understanding some aspects of impairment, the reliance on individual models has led to a poor understanding of how psychology can be of use to a disabled person. This is probably no more evident than in the area of rehabilitation where coping models are often used to assist in understanding how the individual can 'cope' and 'adjust' to the situations in which they find themselves. This is often irrespective of the disabling socio-political and economic aspects of acquiring or being born with impairment.

At this stage, we do not wish to contrast the 'medical' and 'social' models or any others, rather to invoke them to gain more understanding of our observations. It's unlikely that our colleagues (or ourselves, for that matter) had such concepts directly in mind, but they would be incorporated into all our thinking and inform the responses. On reflection, it seems that many of the reactions could be predicated on the 'medical model'. This was seldom made explicit, but was manifest as a pervasive influence, which related all problems to individual impairment. Therefore, the solutions were viewed primarily as the responsibility of the individual. It was up to each of us to identify a difficulty (e.g. steps, heavy books), maybe wait to see if a realistic solution was proffered; then to outline our own solutions. Responses varied according to how well one could enlist the understanding and support of the colleagues – and administrators – concerned. It was important to gauge which people were most ready to engage in mutual problem solving and join in identifying barriers. In other words, view the situation from the standpoint of the social model.

It's worth considering at this point how clinical psychologists are trained, and how much they have in common with the newer professions of counselling and health psychology. There is no doubt that the focus is on the individual (or familial) problems, and their identification and treatment regardless of therapeutic orientation. Thus, practitioners tend to think in terms of any dysfunction being located in the individual and/or the family. Whilst training does take account of cultural, ethnic and possibly economic factors in formulating problems, treatment remains focussed on the individual; particularly as attempts to modify environmental factors are usually beyond the scope of most psychologists. Counselling psychology as a newer branch of psychology in the UK has been more diverse in its training and recruitment and is moving towards a more unitary professional path. This has offered more freedom to incorporate and be aware of social and environmental factors, but again, therapeutic models tend to dictate an individualistic approach. So it should not be surprising if our colleagues reacted in ways described earlier.

As previously noted, people usually react without any direct awareness of their internal models. It is also far from clear how making these explicit may modify attitudes let alone behaviour. This requires a lengthy programme of learning and repetition; even then we cannot expect appropriate action as this depends heavily upon suitable resources and funding being available.

Successful functioning?

It would appear that many psychologists see disability in negative terms, and that disabled people can be viewed comfortably only as patients. And they are more acceptable as students than colleagues. Of course, we have met colleagues, who are good psychologists, in the sense that they are able to form positive work relationships with disabled co-workers without feeling threatened, or even uncomfortable. They clearly believe in empowering others (and not just in invoking these principles in publications). We would like to see an increase in their ranks, since negative attitudes lie at the roots of discrimination.

A positive outlook enables physical, as well as social, barriers to be overcome more readily. There is great scope here for Disability Equality Training (DET), providing this is undertaken systematically on a wide-ranging basis. Perhaps DET should form a component in all professional training courses. But even well-organised training is not sufficient: much discrimination arises simply from ignorance. It is, therefore, essential that the psychological organisations familiarise themselves with the DDA (1995) and how this applies in different situations.

Leaving aside the theoretical and conceptual issues, how a disabled psychologist may function successfully? The sections listed below indicate, ironically, only by embracing one's impairment and by becoming one's own agent in overcoming barriers.

The necessity of establishing one's own openings

In common with other minorities we observe the importance of creating our own opportunities. It seems appropriate at this point to refer to our own endeavours in this respect. Freda was able to take the opportunity to set up a new postgraduate in-service training course in clinical psychology, which she developed and managed for over 20 years. It flourished and enjoyed the support of the regional health authority and the BPS and, most importantly, her colleagues. Simon, partly by spotting opportunities and establishing professional contacts, offered counselling psychology where little or none was previously available. Building on this to embark on other enterprises, he was helped by counselling psychology offering a more flexible training path and a different philosophical approach.

Anticipating barriers

It is important to anticipate barriers and enlist support in advance in order to arrange or negotiate designated assistance when required. Never rely on organisers of events to do this – they won't. And that, regrettably, applies also to disabled organisations. While some events and organisations now routinely include opportunities to register 'special needs', it is unwise to depend on this being noted accurately or to be acted upon appropriately. It has to be accepted that organisers often have difficulty in understanding what is required. We recognise that overcoming barriers requires patient and lengthy negotiation with the organiser concerned, and that it can make all the difference if an individual is designated specifically to deal with such requirements and requests.

Using legislation to support requests whenever possible
This is a controversial area and some people would claim it is irrelevant
to their needs. Nevertheless, we maintain that it forms the essential
foundation for progress, and Barnes (1994) has presented cogent arguments for this. Even though at this stage many organisations remain
unaware of the DDA, let alone what it means and its implications, it
is still possible to call on this legislation at an individual level to satisfy a
need. It is helpful to point out that any modifications will benefit
others in the future. We would therefore counsel persistence despite
what can be a protracted and tedious process.

Keeping one's temper and sense of humour
All situations, where anyone is faced with lack of understanding or
co-operation, benefit from a good-humoured stance. As disabled
psychologists we can be put easily in a no-win situation rather than
make a fuss. One alternative is to suffer in silence, and fail to participate
fully with one's fellow professionals, or, even worse, to withdraw on
some spurious pretext, hiding the true reason, and so to marginalise
oneself completely whilst protecting colleagues from the 'problem'. To
avoid these unattractive options, another course is to adopt a
light-hearted and non-threatening approach, realising these risks-
endorsing stereotypes of being 'brave'.

Facing up to the extra financial costs
Functioning as a disabled professional inevitably incurs extra costs. It
may take longer to train or the competition may be greater for both
jobs and promotion. One should also be aware of the extra day-to-day
costs of just keeping going. Having a job and an income may make it
worthwhile, but we should not ignore the financial realities.

*Drawing a sharp distinction between one's professional activities
and skills and the 'adjustments' needed, before one can practise them*
It is necessary to get oneself *in situ* before assuming one's professional
role, whether in a meeting, lecture room or clinic. It also separates our
professional and disabled identities in a way we see as constructive in
establishing our professional credentials in the eyes of colleagues and
relevant organisations. Respecting the professional contribution of disabled people is possible only when unnecessary barriers, both physical
and social, are recognised and addressed. However, without an organisational lead and framework the onus remains on disabled individuals
and a few enlightened colleagues to come to *ad hoc* arrangements.

Why open up? Advantages for the psychology Profession

What advantage is there to opening up the psychological professions to disabled people? We believe that the BPS, throughout its entire organisation, would benefit from a positive and systematic approach to the inclusion of disabled individuals, and should use its influence to promote their training and employment opportunities. This is not just a matter of the BPS waking up to the requirements of the DDA, of which it seems barely aware, but of recognising, explicitly, the considerable potential contribution that disabled psychologists may bring to all aspects of psychology, both theoretical and applied. There are many areas of investigation which could develop from the involvement of disabled people (just as the study of racial and gender issues have benefited from the contribution of individuals directly concerned). Some of these areas are listed below:

Generally:

- A better understanding and insight into disability from both the theoretical and practical standpoint
- Less stereotyping and a more humane and effective therapeutic response to disabled people and those with chronic illnesses
- Demonstrate that the psychological professions can be more diverse and representative.

Specifically:

- Increase choice in the recruitment pool
- Disabled psychologists make good employees
- Generally cost less than having to recruit and train new staff
- Adjustments and adaptions can bring benefits to other employees and patients.

There is already a large body of research, conducted by disabled people and organisations, and numerous publications (Swain *et al.*, 1993; Hales, 1996) of which the majority of psychologists in every field remain largely unaware, to the detriment of their professions. It would be a sad commentary on psychology if there is a failure to recognise that personal experience can illuminate many areas of study, and that the usual requirements of research can also be respected. In fact, a considerable contribution to the study of individuals with learning difficulties, and to our understanding of learning processes, was made by psychologists with direct experience as parents and relatives. The efforts of blind psychologists in USA to make the APA more receptive is of relevance here.

Employers also need to change the way they see disability... Instead of viewing people with disabilities as liabilities, they should realize that blind psychologists' empathy, resourcefulness and ability to raise others' awareness of minority, disability and accommodation issues make them assets. (Clay, 1999)

Currently, the initial employment prospects of disabled graduates, in general, are certainly improving, as reported by Farrar (2003); though she notes that employment opportunities, in health and education, are lagging behind graduate entry to other professions and management. Since her data is based only upon the first year after graduation there is scanty evidence concerning postgraduate training. And to date there is no information available on postgraduate training in psychology. (Winter personal communication, 2004) suggests that the barriers to clinical training are being breached gradually. Also there have been a few studies reported recently which offer some encouragement (e.g. Dent and Atherton, 2004). However, without the BPS developing a systematic policy with regard to disability, progress will remain sporadic and slow. The following outlines how this may be done.

It is more than time for the BPS to join other professions and produce its own Equal Opportunities and Procedures Statement in accordance with the DDA, such as those published by the Royal College of Physicians (1998) and the Employers Forum (1994). We know, from personal contact, that tentative moves were made in 1998; on request we prepared a draft Statement, as indicated, but there was no follow-up. Such a document should be based on an initial audit, and should be comprehensive, covering training, employment and service provision. There should be consultation with students and qualified graduates. And the final document should be disseminated throughout the entire organisation. Naturally, this will take time and suitable resources, though financial support could be obtained for the audit. In the meantime the BPS should engage in less formal activities. Implementing the following recommendations could make a world of difference to disabled psychologists and clients:

- The inclusion of DET in all professional training courses;
- The introduction of a mentoring programme, taking into account the approach adopted by the American Psychological Association (APA, 2003);

• Encouragement to broaden the scope of psychology studies in disability to take account of the social context (Craig, 2003), and to recognise the contribution of disabled investigators.

Conclusions

We have tried to convey what it has been like to work as disabled psychologists. We have also attempted to relate our experiences to psychological interpretation. Further, we have outlined how the prospects of disabled psychologists could be improved. Writing this chapter has made us realise that the reality is very different from what might be suggested by theories and much research. For much of the time, we were not thinking of ourselves as disabled psychologists, just 'psychologists', though the barriers were real and we faced many problems. At present, it remains essential to seize opportunities as they arise. The future depends on how much the BPS is prepared to play a lead role.

Chapter 9

Understanding Intellectually Disabled Clients in Clinical Psychology

Jennifer Clegg

Introduction

The field of intellectual disability has been isolationist long enough. Having asserted its independence from mental health, because it had been confused with mental health and dominated by it for too long, it needs new allies. Yet perhaps intellectual disability should be wary of unquestioning incorporation into a disability agenda that originates in concerns and experiences of people with physical impairments. This chapter contributes to that debate by exploring how clinical psychologists attempt to understand their clients, to what purposes that understanding is put, and whether these are relevant to a critical psychology of disability. These are not straightforward questions for me (a social constructionist aware of the deep suspicions that arise from Foucault's questioning of the 'psy' professions as a group, and of psychology as an academic discipline in particular). Suspicions concern a focus on individual change when many problems arise from interactions between people and society; and growing numbers and types of professionals, whose apparent support to the marginalised actually enhances their own status. There are tensions and legitimate questions to ask about clinical practice: but for me acting with as much reflection and care as possible seems preferable to doing nothing but criticise.

In order to understand how clinicians as opposed to critics perceive their practice, this chapter starts with contexts. It describes briefly a clinical psychology service within a contemporary UK NHS service, how and why people have described adults with intellectual disability, and ways that intellectual disability affects human interaction. These descriptions support the body of the chapter, which considers who and what needs to change, in four situations: abuse, empowerment, bereavement and aggression.

Contexts

A *clinical psychology service*
An urban environment of 650,000 people employs 3.4 clinical psychologists to support adults with intellectual disability who have psychological needs, neither the best nor the worst-staffed service in the region. Three men are referred for every woman; most clients are aged between 20 and 45 years, and live in different types of residential or family homes. A very small number spend time in a specialist assessment and treatment unit with 12 beds, or a hospital day centre with 25 places, both managed by the NHS. Psychologists do most of their clinical work in community settings. Some of this is individualised, much of it privatised, but congregate care exists: day centres can contain 200 people, hostels 25.

The health service has no properties in the community: psychologists negotiate with other agencies to access rooms near clients. Spare rooms in day centres, mental health centres and GP surgeries are lent, but reclaimed when lenders experience space pressures. Other staff vacate their offices in order to allow people to speak with us in some degree of confidence. There is rarely any reception, rooms are not sound-proof, and sessions are often interrupted. Sometimes we work with people in their own homes, aiming to avoid all of the intrusions and compromises that accompany sessions held in people's bedrooms, although occasionally that is the only option. Our specialist hospital base has appropriate rooms which we sometimes use, particularly if the person referred may pose a risk to the clinician. They are not chosen lightly, because clients usually dislike attending an institutional site. A few take buses to see us; most cannot travel independently and are brought by family or staff.

Almost constant organisational change obscures a focus on clients. In the last decade we have left the NHS to become a Trust; experienced radical overhaul of service commissioning when the local health authority was disbanded and Primary Care Trusts (PCTs) created that ensure GPs control secondary health services; and were affected by major re-organisation of our most significant partner, Social Services.

Subsequent merger with other Trusts four years ago continues to have implications, as sectors lower down the organisation merge. The region within which the Trust sits has also been re-organised, changing effective working alliances concerning training. Cutting across this, the national learning disability service was reviewed in a policy document *Valuing People* (Department of Health, 2001b), which specified organisational changes. This was part of a general review of mental health services. However, government National Service Frameworks specified changes in services for child and adult mental health, and the elderly, providing additional resource to achieve it. Only intellectual disability services had a white paper, requiring change with very limited resource.

While management changes are endemic, the psychologists and other professional colleagues create a relatively stable clinical environment, working to minimise the inter-professional jealousies fed by reorganisations. People often remark on the lively exchange of ideas, evidence and practices: each psychologist researching their particular area of expertise probably helps.

Recognising people who need help

I meet the minority of adults with intellectual disability whose needs are sufficiently complex to require the support of health service staff. A constructionist critique of professional knowledge is that a large group becomes defined by the limited knowledge professionals hold about a minority who use clinical services. This is an appropriate warning, so the information should be placed alongside accounts from advocacy groups, but these are also partial: they represent the most vocal and able while making little mention of people with no speech and/or complex needs. Continual revision of ways to describe this group reveals important facets of their relationship with society. Here history is important because confusion reigns if synonyms and differences are misunderstood. The first Royal Commission for England and Wales (1908, cited by Thomson, 1998) crystallised a medical conception of mentally defective people as a category with three types: feeble-minded (IQ 50–70), imbeciles (IQ 50–20) and idiots (IQ <20). By 1913 the passage of the Mental Deficiency Act altered this from a medical to a medico-legal category, by introducing responsibility for control: the public were to be protected from the mentally defective, and the mentally defective from the public. Terms for the condition itself differ across time and countries, moving through mental deficiency, mental handicap, mental retardation, learning disability and intellectual disability. These can become confused with terms for specific types of physical conditions associated with intellectual disability: those with known genetic causes such as Down's syndrome, or syndromes with genetic linkages but no specific marker such as autism, which affects people with and without intellectual disability.

Terms that describe degrees of impairment have varied, including cretin, moron, trainable versus educable people, and mild, moderate, severe and profound intelligence. Current recommendations from the British Psychological Society (BPS, 2001) are that only two distinctions between impaired intellectual functioning should be made: Significant (IQ 55–69) and Severe (IQ <55).

BPS (2001) core criteria of 'learning disability'

- Significant impairment of intellectual functioning,
- Significant impairment of social functioning and
- Age of onset before adulthood.

'Borderline' people whose IQs are above 70 lie outside any formal definition of intellectual disability. In practice, most services include some, particularly when there are social implications such as failure to acquire minimally effective parenting skills, or when people offend. Xenitidis *et al.* (1999) describe a service for people with 'mild intellectual disability and challenging behaviour' which includes people with IQs up to 84; Palmer and Hart (1996) cited a court of appeal as having no interest in which side of IQ 70 the person falls. Population data reveal the reason for debate: while 2 per cent of the population have IQs under 70, 9 per cent lie under IQ 80 (Wechsler Adult Intelligence Scale-III, 1998). Accepting people with borderline abilities has major implications for services.

Another set of terms describe a broader set of individuals. These encompass everybody whose compromised development requires additional service support, and are more commonly used in services for children. The USA term is *developmental disability*, in the UK children with *special needs* or *learning difficulties*. This broader approach is reflected in the International Classification of Functioning, Disability and Health (World Health Organization, 2001). This International Classification of Functioning (ICF) system is relevant to people with and without disabilities: it analyses environments with the intention of reducing gaps in functioning between performance and capacity, although ICF tools to address physical disability are the most well developed.

Both ICF and the American Association on Mental Retardation (AAMR, 2002) systems attempt to integrate medical, psychological and social models of disability, by assessing five domains: intellect, health, adaptive activities, participation and context. Both documents have strengths as well as limitations, and accept there can be changes in functioning over time, particularly if the right support is in place. The AAMR system has a three-stage framework: diagnosis establishes eligibility for services, benefits and legal protection; classification concerns intensity of needs; then support planning specifies types and levels of assistance required. These classification systems respond to criticisms of identification based on the single criterion of IQ, and their analysis of need has been particularly welcomed. However, they are cumbersome to use, and their lack of a single criterion creates difficulties for research. Since the only justification for classification is that additional resources support the people so categorised, it is also of some concern that Chapireau (2004) considered the universality of the ICF insufficient to identify all those who need specialist support.

Reforming legislation can also bring unexpected disadvantages. Considering intellectual disability as something that varies according to environment and levels of support can create perverse disincentives for clinical intervention. For example, a man became agoraphobic following the sudden collapse and death of his sister when they were out together. Following intervention he started to go out again, then his Disability Living Allowance was stopped; many reports and a tribunal were required to reinstate appropriate levels of financial support. Six months of worsening poverty taught him an unhelpful lesson about the consequences of retrieving his independence.

Classification has increasingly focused on support, while the medical model continues to be criticised for listing deficits and problems. Nevertheless, secondary disabilities commonly found among people with intellectual disability do have a major impact on their lives: blindness, deafness, physical disability or epilepsy. Other difficulties or behaviours include incontinence, movement disorders, self-harm or assaults on others. The person may also have socially disconcerting features: dysmorphic faces, baldness, drooling, stereotyped behaviours, or they may make strange noises. The social model glosses over such matters, focusing on environments and behaviour. This has generated many revealing accounts of the lives of intellectually disabled people (e.g. Edgerton, 1984). Research following this tradition has described the way that boys who use respite care services imagine they must have done something wrong since their siblings do not stay away; how people who have been physically restrained feel it was an arbitrary decision; how much intellectually disabled people fear community harassment. The social model tends to consider people with significant rather than severe intellectual disability, and those at the lower end of the statistically normal range whose impairment has been exacerbated by accumulated physical and social deprivation. Considerable 'early intervention' research and practice in psychology focuses on diverting as many children as possible away from such accumulated disadvantage. *Valuing People* (Department of Health, 2001b) reinforced a user group's assertion that people with intellectual disability can speak for themselves. Yet there is growing concern among even radical social scientists (Hanlon, 1998; Gleeson, 1999, 2003) that such user involvement results in disproportionate resource going to people most able to state their case. This develops Hart's (1971) *inverse care law*: the availability of good medical care tends to vary inversely with the need for it. Hubert's (1991) finding that the least help went to young people with the most difficult behaviour and/or profound intellectual disability extends Hart from health to social care.

The term now coming into use, *intellectual disability*, harmonises across nationalities. It is used by the major international research conference, and by some academic journals. It replaces *learning disability*, used for the past decade in the UK and still widespread, because in the USA learning disability describes specific problems such as dyslexia that exist within an otherwise normal intelligence. The USA alone uses the term *mental retardation*. Constant revision of terms led a psychoanalyst (Sinason, 1992) to argue that a process of euphemism is occurring because of cultural inability to confront realities of the condition. By contrast, Gleeson (1999) argued that definitional confusion originates in theoretical underdevelopment of disability studies, and in awareness by disabled people that definitions carry political weight. He rejects humanist preference for 'people with disabilities' because it depoliticises the social discrimination they experience, favouring a return to 'disabled people'.

Relating to people with intellectual disability

Neither medical nor social models give much insight into the way intellectual disability affects interaction. Students struggling to understand a person often ask how old they are, even when they are looking at a videotape. Apparently the questioner feels this would provide solid ground: it is hard to accept solid ground may not exist. When first meeting an adult with intellectual disability you do not know whether they will speak to you and, if not, whether their silence indicates shyness or inability. Some speak with such poor articulation that you cannot understand; or the omission of a crucial piece of information means you understand the words but not their meaning (Beveridge *et al.*, 1997). You may find it hard to look at the person because of unusual features. The person may be warm if somewhat over-friendly as they hug you; equally, they may be suspicious, distressed or rejecting. Small wonder that many find this interactional space disconcerting.

Reinders (2000) argued that the rights agenda and subsequent legislation has created enormous change for people with intellectual disability, but that legislation can only open doors. What happens when people with intellectual disability walk through those doors requires not more legislation, but social change. Meininger (2004) considers the encounter with difference in intellectual disability is profoundly disturbing for most people in the community. Patterns of behaviour and communication that people take for granted turn out to be useless, creating feelings of estrangement and uncertainty. Meininger suggests that parents of disabled children are forced to come to grips with this strangeness; communities also have to discover the right relation towards their own ambiguous feelings and attitudes towards people with intellectual disabilities. Interactional skill can reduce some awkwardness, but it is our own ability to tolerate and accommodate the stranger that is the real issue.

What and who needs to change

Clinical psychologists who wish to avoid blaming the individual by changing the human systems with which they interact nevertheless work within the NHS, whose remit is to respond directly to distressed individuals. Clinicians who engage with both the person and key carer have been criticised for giving too much credence to 'gatekeepers', disempowering the disabled person, but in general I follow Brown *et al.* (1992) in assuming that splitting people with intellectual disability from their carers creates unnecessary difficulty for both. When people with intellectual disability do object to carers being involved in an intervention they usually make that clear by refusing to speak. Most of the time, including carers is consistent with a constructionist valuing of lay knowledge alongside professional knowledge.

The realities of the NHS require that clinical work with care systems ('systemic interventions') and services link to a client somehow. The four situations that follow have been developed to illustrate different issues and types of work. No real individual is discussed, names merely make stories easier to read: brief illustrations and vignettes combine aspects of different people and situations encountered in 25 years of practice, omitting and changing as many irrelevant details as possible. Abuse, cognitive limitations, bereavement and aggression are considered: deep human experiences that clinical psychologists frequently encounter, although knowing that women often hurt themselves to counteract painful memories does not equate to an understanding of how somebody can pull their own toe-nail off. In all cases I hope the purpose is not voyeurism but some understanding of people in distress, and ways to create change with them.

Responding to self-harm

Increasing numbers of people with intellectual disability who use specialist health services disclose sexual or physical abuse, but if they have therapy before the trial they risk the accusation of having been 'coached'. Many prefer to take the abuser to court and seek psychological support later, as they struggle to make a relationship with new carers and their post-abuse selves. Sleep disturbed by nightmares is common, in both men and women. Men may drink or gamble to excess. Women wash their bodies and clothes many times a day, or spend money on clothes they cannot afford. Some go back to self-harm when reminders, such as a well-meaning GP who suggests they have a cervical smear, re-evoke the experience.

Let us imagine Helga. Neglected when young, she moved into a foster-home where she was financially abused as a domestic servant with no resource or freedoms, and perhaps sexually abused too. Recently she moved into a type of adult fostering with Audrey, who knows the abuse history, but finds it painful knowledge to hold in mind. She wants to provide a new start, a safe home; but Helga still self-harms. Audrey gets angry about the injuries, Helga conceals, Audrey gets angry about the lies, Helga feels everything wrong is her fault, making her more vulnerable to the upsets that prompt self-harm. They have created an impasse: Audrey makes Helga promise never to self-harm again, so Helga lies next time she hurts herself.

A systemic psychologist meets them together, asking questions that help them see the impasse for themselves: what happened then, how did that affect others in the house, what did they do, how did each person experience this response? The aim is to stay with the conversation until it becomes possible to generate new ways to interrupt the cycle: to help people find their own way out. Within the context of a therapeutic discussion that explores and respects people's resourcefulness, rank-ordering questions can open up nuances if discussion becomes stuck: which is worse, the injuries or the concealment? Which types of self-harm are most/least distressing? Which cover-ups are most/least distressing? Which of Audrey's responses are most/least difficult for Helga to handle? Recognising differences creates a basis for developing alternative responses, starting a process of change.

Some carers find their own difficulty comprehending self-harm is part of the frustration, and ask for information about it. In agreeing to provide a summary at the next session, psychologists emphasise it would not be expert knowledge about the client herself, only what other people had said. Clients would be disempowered by expert knowledge: it is vital that they agree to say which, if any, of the ideas reflect their experience, and reject those that do not. Discussion of such research findings can enable people to reveal details of the urge to self-harm for the first time. In one of those surprising flashes of insight that sometimes happen, one woman compared her compulsion to hurt herself to that of becoming an alcoholic. Following this discussion, the carer understood the chronic effects of abuse and the necessity to live in the knowledge of those effects. She felt less anguish when injury occurred, so responded more coolly; soon the injuries became less frequent and less severe.

Reflection
This shows the importance of thinking who needs to understand: individual work without the carer could not have succeeded on its own, although it is sometimes a useful adjunct. Many carers feel the person's self-harm is a 'slap in the face', rejection that often provokes unhelpful responses. Understanding builds a meta-perspective, a position from which clients and carers can put the issue into proportion, allowing them to create different ways to respond to one another.

Empowerment and cognitive limitation
Disability activists prefer to empower people to direct their own lives, and to transform socially oppressive structures, opposing this to the 'reformist' aim of lessening disability through increased support. Yet Gleeson (1999) and Reinders (2000) argue empowerment imposes the liberal value of autonomy onto intellectually disabled people inappropriately: unattainable for most, autonomy erases mutuality and relationships from their lives. Concern to empower also sometimes pushes

people beyond what they can tolerate (Thomas, 2001; Skelly, 2002). Pressurising people with intellectual disability to perform at peak capacity too much of the time loses sight of the way intellectual disability affects lives.

Other problems occur when considering the empowerment of people with severe and multiple disabilities. Imagine Janet, a woman in her late 20s with severe intellectual disability and total blindness: she frequently self-injures by banging her head. Recently, Janet moved into a small private home where the manager Sue, supported by Janet's father, demanded that the speech therapist provide an electronic communication aid. They wanted something that would reduce what they believed to be Janet's 'frustration', by speaking for her at the touch of a button. The therapist, Joe, had exhausted all explanations about why this was impossible: it was not a problem of expression, but Janet did not have the cognitive ability to construct opinions in the first place. After a staff training session about communication had failed to shift Sue's demand for the communication aid, Joe referred to the psychologist.

This care system expressed a common wish: 'if only she could speak, we would give her what she wants'. Janet's communication during the previous three years had been limited to occasional names and one-word labels. Even without the complexity of her blindness (communication aids operate with keys or screens covered in pictograms), basic naming is a long way short of forming and expressing opinions. Yet Janet's father reported she had used complex speech as a child, so could again. Accounts of skilled past behaviour are common in adult intellectual disability services: impossible to verify, they establish the importance attached to that particular attribute by the narrator. Stuck systems need new perspectives, which sometimes emerge from considering different levels of the organisation. Further checking revealed that Sue had been promoted internally following only a few months' knowledge of intellectual disability: with no previous management experience, she was effectively on probation for the manager's post. Rapid expansion of their organisation meant that a completely new staff team had been appointed to this home during the previous two months. Sue was a sensitive carer, but currently a defensive and somewhat dogmatic manager.

Joe met the psychologist to find ways out of this stalemate. Noting Sue's pride in her positive relationship with Janet, Joe realised that suggesting alternative communication strategies may have challenged Sue's main source of confidence. He had also not realised that his staff training session, which aimed to engender reflection and inter-actional change, had been carried out with staff who had met their first person with intellectual disability only a few weeks before. Hindsight suggested he had expected too much. Other hypotheses about the origins of the 'stuckness' were that Sue might have wanted to estab-lish her authority by teaching the new staff about communication strategies herself; and that since Janet's father had complained about staff before, Sue found it especially difficult to resist pressure from him that she obtain a communication aid. Her insistence on the aid started to make more sense.

Systems often show repeating patterns. The staff appeared to be expecting too much of Janet, which Joe mirrored unknowingly by expecting too much from them. The staff responded defensively that it was not their actions that should change, nor their disputed inter-pretations of Janet's cognitive ability: Joe should provide the aid. A solution was devised to side-step this dominant discourse of high expectations and demand. Joe agreed to reduce staff defensiveness by re-assessing Janet's communication skills, documenting the huge increases in ability and quality of life she had made since moving into this individualised environment. Rather than expecting the staff to change, Joe changed, by expressing uncertainties about his own communication with Janet and with other people who have severe intellectual disability. This introduction of doubt made it more permissible for staff to be uncertain, to question their beliefs about what Janet needed. Joe sketched out stages towards Janet becoming able to use a communication aid, and empowered the staff by suggesting Sue should contact him when they were ready for some new ideas that would encourage Janet to move to the next level.

Meanwhile the psychologist introduced a different way of thinking about self-injury. While it may communicate a need, self-injury can be the result of both too little and too much stimulation. The staff were invited to gather information about Janet's pattern of self-injury for a month, which clearly showed that it worsened with too much novelty. The psychologist supported Sue to develop a care plan that limited the amount of new people or activities Janet experienced in any given week. The psychologist negotiated its content in detail with Janet's father, ensuring he understood the reasoning. He was worried this might limit Janet's new life, but agreed to co-operate with a six-month trial while data was analysed about its effect upon her well-being. With these interventions, the heat went out of demands for a communication aid and Janet's self-injury decreased.

Reflections
This example illustrates the narrative force generated by a culture that places such disproportionate value on the self-determining individual; complex dynamics between different members of a care system readily become hooked onto it. While they moved away from complete deadlock with Joe, neither Sue nor father was wholly satisfied by this outcome. Accepting Janet's severe limitations, and keeping her arousal within safe boundaries, was counter-cultural: what they sought was an increase in Janet's self-determination through technology. Difficulty witnessing Janet's self-injury was never made explicit, but reducing it probably released some of the force of their feeling. Staff were empowered by gaining control over when and why they worked with Joe, perhaps too by designing a plan that managed Janet's level of arousal better. Gaining father's agreement to it may also have helped to improve their relationship. Since over-controlled staff are more likely to be coercive towards clients, this intervention assumed that empowering the staff was the best way to empower Janet.

Meeting tragedy
The ambivalence, dependency and guilt that complicate many family relationships make it more likely that people with intellectual disability will be severely affected when parents or siblings die (Clegg and Lansdall-Welfare, 2003). Yet Reinders observed that 'clinical intervention, whether in medicine or psychology, does not have much patience with the notion of the tragic. But it is precisely the notion of the tragic that allows for the expression of powerlessness that is experienced in bereavement and loss' (2003, p. 92). Saetersdal (1997) complained that services have swung so far away from medicine's deficit model that they seem unable to connect with the distress people experience at all. In similar vein though in a different field, Frank (1992) reviewed first-person accounts of illness which showed people want affirmation: the space and time to suffer, for others to join and bear witness.

Loss through death is often a component of complex problems with which psychology can help, but these observations suggest that clinical psychologists need to encounter bereavement carefully. Let us imagine John, who lived with his mother. Sufficiently able to travel independently on buses, Down's syndrome affected his articulation badly so his speech was difficult to understand. John had been supported by the psychology service previously for dangerously impulsive behaviour which led to him being suspended from the day centre: he hung around the town centre until a group of children accused John of being a pervert and severely assaulted him. A behavioural contract established consistent expectations and consequences, and his behaviour returned to acceptable limits.

When John's mother became ill he moved in with his sister Paula. He was present when his mother died and attended the funeral, but complained to Paula thereafter that he wished he had not seen mum die because it had changed him. Nevertheless, he settled in well. Two years later impulsive outbursts reappeared, and day centre staff feared his reputation. He responded by describing nightmares about his mother. During a review to consider what was happening, Paula thought John was merely using bereavement as an excuse to get him off the hook; yet she cried while discussing their mother. Both Paula and John agreed to meet the psychologist to explore what should happen next. With Paula's interpretation and John's patience, the psychologist learned how to tune in and understand most of his speech. John wanted to talk about drinking: Paula would not let him have enough alcohol. He wanted to talk about disturbed sleep, not nightmares. Paula put the question of his behaviour at the day centre on the table but did not push for it to take priority. Neither wanted to discuss bereavement. We explored how they both managed alcohol so he did not lose control; and established more effective routines for sleep. In session three their mother's death came up, and John asked to attend the next session alone. Having promised but forgotten to bring the psychologist's sleep charts back to subsequent sessions, he found it easy to remember to bring his short homily in remembrance of mother. It had been written by the vicar from their conversation, and read out at the funeral. This much-thumbed and treasured speech was discussed for the whole session, using reflexive questioning (Tomm, 1987) to help John talk about it.

Subsequent sessions with them both unfolded further stories of their mother: her love of parties, the way she ate crisps, her death and funeral, the siblings' sense of continuing bonds with her. John's complaints about having been persuaded to be with mum as she died ameliorated: he accepted Paula had to guess what would be best for him in new situations, and could not always be right. What had started as one story became two: Paula's ongoing connections through remembrance, John's mixed feelings about moving into independence. The nightmares subsided and behaviour problems at the day centre stopped. They were 'inoculated' to future problems by discussing how angry feelings sometimes return during changes, such as John moving out; if they wished to when the time came, they were invited to return and talk about that transition before problems occurred.

Reflection

Paula's sensitive facilitation and her openness were keys to the successful outcome. It would not have been appropriate for psychological intervention to occur at the point of bereavement: culturally normative support from friends, family and their vicar were what was needed. However, changes at home and in the day centre had destabilised John's equilibrium, generating behaviour intertwined with bereavement that was too risky for friends and family to manage. Then psychological intervention needs to stay alongside people and witness their grief, while looking out for signs of movement that will support changes the people themselves seek.

Systemic issues in aggression

Goldner (1998) summarises a lifetime's experience of holding various frames of reference in mind while working with couples who have a history of violence. Such couples think in strong polarities: love and hate, remorse and cynicism, blame and over-responsibility, exaggerating or minimising danger. Such powerful messages invite professionals and researchers to mirror that polarising process; the field of domestic violence has been chronically burdened by ideological divisions. Goldner argues that the therapist must be able 'to recognise the value of competing and contradictory perspectives, and to negotiate the emotional demands...without splitting ideas and people into good and bad' (1998, p. 268). In similar vein, Miller has written about the educational psychologist's task when addressing difficult behaviour in disabled and non-disabled pupils, a vexed area so 'suffused with notions of blame, that people are stuck, demoralized and set against each other as a result of it' (2003, p. 101).

Aggression certainly has the power to split intellectual disability care systems. Parents who have been quite unable to cope complain their relative is not active enough when admitted to a special unit; care staff respond by freely admitting they fear engaging the person. Some direct care staff believe safety lies in establishing firm boundaries that contain the person, others seek to avoid unnecessary confrontations that may provoke aggression. Psychiatrists may be accused of applying a 'chemical cosh' to people who have no psychiatric diagnosis, but psychologists can also be accused of designing interactional programmes that require unsustainable amounts of staff time. The effective clinician refuses to adopt any of these polarities: a key task is to keep people engaged with each other and negotiating a shared way forward. It is tempting to imagine that a radical psychology of disability has no business in such situations. Better environments with increased staff numbers and individualised living spaces have removed many situations that prompt aggressive behaviour; some contemporary radicals believe that is all that is needed. At a recent international conference I attended, a delegate exemplified this position by asserting that adults with intellectual disability show difficult behaviour solely because they have experienced the malign paternalism of services: empowerment not treatment is needed. As Foucault observed in *The Birth of the Asylum* (Rabinow, 1984), myths about nineteenth-century philanthropists such as Pinel remain foundational. Pinel had expressed the romantic notion that 'raging madmen' were only intractable because they had been deprived of air and liberty: many were reported to show no problems once released. On this reasoning, there is no need for any special services for people who display risky and chaotic behaviour: they just need freedom and empowerment.

Most clinicians do not believe that all people with intellectual disability can escape the emotionally distressing experiences that underpin risky or chaotic behaviour. Of course treating people well makes a difference, but the belief that better environments and kindness dissolve all problems is unsustainable. Caseloads of clinical psychologists working in intellectual disability include increasing numbers of individuals whose behaviour inspires fear in others. Some have had long histories within various care systems and probably have been damaged by them, but the insecure relationships, neglect and abuse that usually result in children being taken into care are not likely to disappear in the immediate future.

My response to aggression follows Goldner (1998) in drawing on multiple sources and shifting between levels and domains. The goal is engaging with the person and all members of their care systems, exploring differences while avoiding polarities in order to develop and keep an intervention in motion. Informal relationship-building is essential, but psychological assessment may have a place too. While there are many appropriate criticisms of psychological assessment, a focus on risk analysis and reduction often distracts people from finding out enough about the person. Assessments not only help others to attune their interaction, they also provide a structure that some clients find safer than open conversation.

I assessed a man who refused all invitations to explore his feelings about a bereavement that precipitated his admission to hospital: during a verbal comprehension test he defined words at the edge of his knowledge in terms of the death that was on his mind. Acknowledging this with a gently reflective comment opened a conversation he clearly needed but had dreaded. Another man with sophisticated verbal abilities could not sequence pictures: it became clear that his sight was much poorer than anybody had realised, reducing his ability to pick up cues and engage with the world. The provision of glasses started new possibilities for action.

While individual understanding is crucial, so is supporting staff and minimising turnover. Hatton (1999) summarises research on stress and turnover. Turnover rates of intellectual disability staff in Britain vary between 10 and 50 per cent per annum. On a standard measure, 33 per cent intellectual disability staff report high stress compared to 27 per cent of general health service staff and 16 per cent of the general population. Challenging behaviour in residents is associated with higher turnover rates, but organisational factors are more relevant than client characteristics: overload, low pay, lack of job security, poor promotion prospects, role ambiguity and lack of participation in decision-making are the main problems. These need attention. Miller's (2003) observations about staff cultures also need to be tackled. When staff regard problems as component parts of somebody's personality they exchange horror rather than success stories, inculcating hopelessness rather than creativity. These contribute to staff demoralisation and high sickness rates, making it even less likely they will have the personal resources to create change.

The policy context of service delivery is also relevant. An inquiry into a fire that killed nine men with intellectual disability in Australia 'found that a decade of official neglect of public facilities for disabled people had contributed to the deaths' (Gleeson, 1999, p. 155). Yet community care, once considered the solution to such problems, is itself coming under scrutiny. Gleeson criticises privatised services in Australia, Britain, Canada and the USA because of staff problems: poor training, high turnover and low morale. In the USA, community care for people with intellectual disability has been criticised for lethal neglect and poor monitoring of privatised services. Brindle (2004) recently criticised *Valuing People* for allowing commissioners to leave people languishing in private facilities. Poor services create increased burdens on informal carers, usually women. 'Throughout the Western world, the failure of many governments to resource and manage community care programmes adequately has diminished popular support for deinstitutionalisation and has even encouraged some disability advocacy groups to call for the establishment of new and enhanced institutional facilities' (Gleeson, 1999, p. 167). The current model of community care, welfare pluralism, has also been criticised for competitiveness that undermines the long-term collaboration necessary for effective human service delivery. It seems the ideal pattern of service has yet to be established and maintained for people who show aggression. In the meantime, broad-mindedness and flexibility bring the best results.

Reflections
Finding ways to work with and around aggression requires the ability to think about multiple realities. If the staff team are burned out, there is no point urging them to new heights of bravery and creativity: the smallest effort they make needs to be noticed and affirmed. It is important to argue for conditions of service which encourage staff to stay, and to act in ways that maintain morale and good practice. However, psychologists earn the right to be listened to by spending time with difficult and chaotic people themselves, using the understanding that assessment yields to co-construct some intervention that makes some difference.

Summary and conclusions

Clinical psychologists attempt to understand clients with intellectual disability by spending time with them, by talking with them and often with their carers, by taking their history seriously, by offering research findings for people to accept or reject, and by using formal psychological assessments judiciously. Our frequent failure to understand, and limitations to the amount that the person can understand, comes with the territory and need to be acknowledged too. Whenever possible, interventions enable clients and carers to recognise and unravel their own knots. Clinical psychologists also aim to understand and intervene in clients' immediate and wider contexts: the blame and polarisation that split care systems, the staff stress and turnover that make effective care impossible, the constant changes that allow no service to bed in and become efficient.

Including people with significant and severe intellectual disabilities into a critical psychology of disability requires accommodation on both sides. If commonalities with people who have different types of disabilities are to be adequately theorised, answers will need to be found to the following questions:

- What difficulties do people without disabilities experience when they first encounter somebody with significant disabilities? Condemning or ignoring those who struggle impedes the growth of tolerance and acceptance.
- How can empowerment move away from unrealistic hopes of autonomy, towards a new focus on enabling justice which avoids amplifying unhelpful or dangerous beliefs?
- How can a psychology of disability address the knots that develop between people and their carers, and include the most profoundly disabled people, if carers are always excluded from the picture?
- Can a psychology of disability graduate beyond opposition to the medical model, to develop a distinctive position that rests on an agreed theoretical base?

Acknowledgements

Some family therapy alluded to briefly here derives from clinical work done with Susan King; valuable comments came from Catherine Blair, Alinda Gillott and Naz Wagle.

Chapter 10

Enabling Practice for Professionals: The Need for Practical Post-Structuralist Theory

Liz Todd

Introduction

I have several roles that have led me to take a broad view of the way professionals work with parents and children. I work as an educational researcher looking at how different professional roles are developing in extended schools. I deliver training sessions to various different professional groups working with children – on narrative practices and how to include children and young people in service delivery. I also work as an educational psychologist and I train educational psychologists at Newcastle University. This chapter introduces the reader to ways that all professionals can promote a critical approach to their work in order to develop enabling practice. An enabling practice here is defined as an involving one, working alongside parents and children in ways that engage with an agenda for inclusion. The reader is encouraged to brave theory – particularly post-structuralist theory and related narrative practices.

The context

Working as a professional in the 21st century for those whose roles aim to facilitate the inclusion of society for children and young people with special needs and disabilities has become a very complex endeavour. The range of professional titles has increased – with a number of different kinds of roles in each of health, education and social services. In education, newer roles have included Connexions service workers (advice and support for young people to transfer from school to adulthood), and in schools there are now a range of new titles for senior staff (inclusion manager, business manager, full-service school co-ordinator). In an effort to solve some of society's deep-seated problems such as area regeneration or social exclusion, a range of partnerships are being encouraged in addition to the joining up of funding streams and the changing of old professional roles. New organisations of services in the form of SureStart, Children's Centres, and Full-Service Extended Schools (or New Community Schools in Scotland) are being developed to bring about new ways of solving problems and – as a key to it all – multi-agency working. Community involvement and consultation are high on the written formal agenda of each but more variable in practice. All the existing statutory work of different services continues – primary care delivery, disability teams, mental health services, child protection and statutory educational assessment. Some of these are now delivered on multi-agency sites with newly constituted teams if they happen to become part of one of the initiatives. The following quotes illustrate some of the challenges for an enabling practice.

A young person talking about experiences in a mainstream school:

> I feel a bit more independent than at the other school... There's not always someone looking after you here – you're a bit more free to do what you want... I didn't hate it at the other school, I liked it, but there were physios, doctors and that. Here you feel a bit more normal I suppose.
>
> When I move in a handicapped school I really feel handicapped. When I've been in a normal school I feel like I'm like the rest of them. Just counting myself like them. (Madge and Fassam, 1982, p. 43)

Parents talk of their perspectives on professional practice:

> Stephen is my son and I love him very much. He came to live with us when he was nearly three and we are now adopted. We are determined that Stephen would be included in the mainstream of our community. We knew the system was one that:

- Moves children and adults with disabilities from one segregated setting to another, kept apart from the ordinary world
- Perceives people with learning disabilities as its clients – and in doing so feels it somehow owns these people and can make decisions for them and their families
- Portrays people with learning difficulties as recipients of sympathy and charity not as friends, neighbours, workers, colleagues, parents, sons and daughters, brothers, sisters, lovers, not as ordinary Graham Jones, Pippa Penman. (Murray and Penman, 1996, pp. 48–49)

How one educational psychologist sees her role:

if there is blame involved, you are never going to establish any sort of parent partnership. So bleaching the arena from blame, as it were, is very, very important. But certainly, amongst teachers, I think, there is often a need to blame somebody else, because they are under stress. So the psychologist's job is often to tackle that blame game and represent the views of all the professionals to each other and to the parent... it's about making a fertile ground for change and for movement, for the child,... I think a lot of the defensiveness and aggressive reactions do stem from people feeling under attack.... So I would say that my job as a psychologist is very much in clearing up any of these contaminating things. (E. S. Todd, 2000)

What is enabling practice?

One of the key aspects of an enabling practice with disabled children and young people is that of working alongside, and encouraging an appropriate degree of involvement. There is little evidence of any real or extensive participation of children and parents in services. When parents engage with services for their children they often experience a confusing array of different agendas which require much stress, effort and the development of new skills and roles in order to interact with those services (Duncan, 2003; Swain and Walker, 2003). They may also experience themselves as looked upon in a way that involves some kind of blame. There are parent partnership schemes (PPSs) in all local authorities who train independent parent supporters, but there is little evidence of widespread take-up. PPSs also give support and advice to those parents unhappy with local authority actions.

Parents are assisted by PPSs in the provision of parent advice, their own report, as part of a statutory assessment of special needs. There is, however, some suggestion from parents that PPSs take parents one stage further away from the real centre of decision-making (Todd, 2003b). In some areas there are now key or link worker schemes for the parents of disabled children to assist in co-ordinating services for the child and parents. Once again these are not widespread (Sloper, 1999) and parent involvement in the delivery of such schemes varies (Greco and Sloper, 2004; Halliday and Asthana, 2004). Some professionals see themselves as advocates for parents (E. S. Todd, 2000) but professional agendas make this very unlikely for most (Galloway *et al.*, 1994). Children are often the 'absent special guest' in the reports and meetings that form professional practice (E. S. Todd, 2000; Todd, 2000). The selected aspects of children and their situations presented by professionals may not be those preferred by the children themselves or their parents (Murray and Penman, 1996). There is evidence of greater attempts to ask children and young people their views, for example, but little authentic or extensive involvement in the services used by children and young people (Cutler and Taylor, 2003). There is evidence that young people have been involved in the development of a small number of medical services for children, some for disabled children (Sloper and Lightfoot, 2002; Lightfoot and Sloper, 2003). Some educational psychologists have been trying to encourage the development of methods to involve children more in assessments (Roller, 1998; Hobbs *et al.*, 2000; Todd, 2003a, 2003c). They have produced some very useful tools, but there is little evidence of widespread use by the profession. Young people, children and parents are looking for a professional practice that enables greater inclusion in society via more involvement in services. What needs to happen to professional practice to bring this about?

The need for change

There is no shortage of professional commitment. Professionals are trying hard to do a good job for their particular 'client' group. However, despite best intentions, there is a mismatch between aims and outcomes. For example, many educational psychologists have a commitment to see the child as the main client (Lucas, 1989; Dowling and Leibowitz, 1994) to look at the system rather than look only for in-child solutions (Wagner, 1995), and to focus on ways that privilege the child's voice (Hobbs *et al.*, 2000). However, it is often very hard to find practice that goes beyond the individual. Where this is found it shows itself as moving 'blame' from the child to others, such as the school, the family or an unspecified 'culture'. One group of practices developed to look beyond the individual is that of consultation, where a model is developed of teacher–psychologist consultations to facilitate teacher-led solutions to problems. Whilst these have been helpful in moving the focus away from the child as the problem, it has also distanced the child and parent from involvement in the early stages of any problem-solving. In general, and looking at the practice of a variety of professionals working with disabled children, it is hard to find more complex or challenging systemic practice that goes further than an analysis resting on some kind of assumption of deficit or blame.

The need for change now in professional practice to develop more systemic 'enabling' practice is particularly important. We know something of what might be described as a 'non-enabling' practice. It excludes children and young people and their parents from professional processes. It focuses on the child as the source for change rather than taking a systemic approach. And professional solutions and labels are adopted rather than solutions that come from children and young people, enabled by parents and professionals. However, the development of change away from this picture is arguably harder to achieve than at any other time. Indeed, non-enabling practice could become even more widespread with the growth of multi-agency teams in the multiple new developments within statutory services. The complexity of the changes happening in the different services – changes in management structure, changes in funding arrangements, different teams for different purposes – makes it very difficult to reflect critically on one's role at a time when this is urgently required. At a time of transition, it may be more likely that professionals will try to hold on to what is historically distinctive about ways of working rather than look to develop new practices. However, without considering carefully role and purpose there is a real possibility that practices will become less involving of children and parents (Stead *et al.*, 2004). Moreover, there is a danger that the joining up of services is likely to lead to a less inclusive outcome for children, one that favours professional labels and solutions for children. Arguably, child protection and the need to develop effective tracking procedures for individual children is the driving force for many of the changes. Both focus on the individual child, and on matching a child to an intervention. Consequently, some professionals involved in these changes in service organisation find little focus on ways children's problems may have resulted from the system – for example from aspects of the school or from the ways professionals work together. The focus on early intervention is double edged – problems get dealt with before they become too difficult and complex to solve – but it can also mean that children become labelled early by the system, grow into a label, and problems multiply (Tomlinson, 1982; Fulcher, 1989). In one study of children defined as having behavioural problems, one boy, on hearing he was going to a mainstream school rather than to a special resource for behaviour difficulties, said to the professionals:

> Now I'm not going to be naughty because I'm not going to the unit. They said I don't have to go to the unit any more. Then I can start being good. (Galloway *et al.*, 1994)

The outcomes of some of the new partnerships from current initiatives in education could, therefore, be children and young people who are less not more included in society. Once again this would be contrary to the espoused aims of most of these developments, which is around a broadly articulated social inclusion, and usually includes an aim to involve users.

Why an enabling practice needs theory

Many professionals do not seem to like talking about or thinking about theory. They like to act, to do something that will help further meet the needs of clients. However, theory is always there somewhere – underlying role and purpose is an implicit and usually unarticulated theory of practice. People making changes in practice, or trying to develop practice, seem to find some theory helpful. This is because it allows reflection on why change should happen and on why certain actions could most reasonably lead to the desired changes. Theory can be simply seen as a set of logical ideas that connect issues in an area of practice. This can be very useful to practitioners where it helps understanding and informs actions. Theory is particularly important in complex areas where easy solutions seem illusive and hard thinking is needed to work out how to move forward – and inclusive education is one such area. It is also particularly important in the current situation where busy committed professionals find a mismatch between what they want to achieve and what happens in practice. In fact, 'theory' can be another word for 'hard thinking'. We therefore need tools – theory tools – to help to inform understanding and action. For me, theory is essential to how I develop what I do in the messy real world. This chapter aims to provide some of these tools – 'practical theory tools' for changing practice.

Post-structuralism

Changing practice in the face of strong professional agendas is not easy. I have found several theoretical frameworks helpful, including post-structuralism, socio-cultural activity theory and personal construct theory. This chapter focuses on the first of these. Post-structural theory encounters individual perspectives and critically analyses the themes or discourses which underlie and attempt to govern actions. Post-structuralism understands society as both constructing of and constructed by people. Post-structuralist thinking encourages professionals to see professional practice, as all social life, as constructed, and to deconstruct in order to reflect on how to develop enabling practice. We can think of society as a text, like a book, that can be read. What we would look for in order to read society would be constructed ideas – the themes, narratives, discourses – that come to be given the status of 'truths' that are around us, in the 'ether'. They are beliefs we may not even really realise we have about how things are and how things should be. They are simple and complex; they are contradictory and change all the time, yet they are ever present. These truths construct norms around which persons are incited to shape or constitute their lives. Therefore these are 'truths' that actually specify persons' lives (White and Epston, 1990, p. 21). This is a different understanding of what power is about – as, 'Power is actively (re)produced in discourse' (Billington, 2000, p. 59).

The discourses of professional practice, of the language used, of the models of practice, and the assumptions of the roles being adopted all help to shape the people professionals work with. Language is not passive but is active in helping to construct identities. Language does not passively stand in for objective realities. Post-structuralism gives us a way to reflect upon the terms and processes we have constructed around disabled children in order to see how this can help or hinder the development of an enabling and inclusive practice. In this light, all the terms – such as 'disabled', 'special needs', 'difficulty', 'differentiation', 'assessment', 'consultation', 'inclusion', 'enabling' and even 'disability' itself – become constructed terms. They have developed over time, responding to a complex set of needs. If we unravel these terms we find out things useful to an enabling practice, assuming this to be a practice that is effective for children, young people and their parents.

What can be particularly important and helpful is to investigate discourses – to interrogate them about what their purposes are, whose interests do they serve, how have they come into being, and who are their bed-fellows. But first the discourses need to be identified. Many of these are discourses that operate in and define professional practice. This process of identifying discourses, of reading life as texts, is referred to as deconstruction:

> A deconstruction is a process of critical reading and unravelling of terms, loaded terms and tensions between terms that construct how we read our place in culture and in our families and in our relationships, and how we think about who we are and what it might be possible for us to be. (Parker, 1999, pp. 6–7)

I have worked with many different professionals in workshops encouraging them to investigate the words, terms and ideas around their own professional practice. They have said this has been a fascinating, challenging and fun process. I encourage them to work in pairs. One person takes on the identity of, and pretends to be and speak for, one term from their practice such as 'behaviour', 'problem', 'inclusion', 'need' and so on. The other acts as a detective in asking questions to explore the way this term, this idea, operates in the world. The detective interviews the person who has taken on the identity of, say, 'disability'. The latter pretends to be 'disability' by imagining disability as an entity and answering questions as if the person was 'disability'. This is not the same as pretending to be a disabled person. If the term chosen was 'need', the person would pretend to be 'need', and if the term was 'inclusion', the person would pretend to be 'inclusion'. The following are some of the directions for this activity:

Imagine 'ADHD' is a thing.

Imagine it could speak about what it is doing in the world.
Imagine it could tell us all about what it is up to, its successes, its intentions, its friends, how it achieves its goals, and what stops it from having influence...
Is it particularly in evidence, active, at the moment – is there a lot of it about? – if so why? If not why not?
Does it help us to become the kind of people we want to become? How does it help...how does it limit...our relational identity...?

If we deconstruct professional practice we are likely to find the key discourses of scientific objectivity and rationality. These are given a high level of value in Western capitalist societies. Psychology and medicine are both based on the assumptions underlying scientific enquiry, enabling professions based on such disciplines to claim authority. In other words, practitioners can claim to be scientists using objective tools, with findings that can be very difficult to challenge. This calls some practitioners into the use of certain tools in order to bring forth discourses of objectivity, rationality and the certainty of science, as in the case of the use of psychometrics by psychologists:

> Given that objectivity was not possible about another human being, she (the acting Principal Educational Psychologist) indicated that the educational psychologists' psychometric tools were the best EPs had for bringing greater objectivity into the process. (E. S. Todd, 2000)

To continue the deconstruction, I can also suggest professionals are more like artists than scientists, fashioning identities from their particular professional perspectives. Professionals can be understood as all operating through different frameworks, using different ways of seeing. What is found by chiselling at clay is different according to who is doing the chiselling, what tools are used, and how the artist goes about the task. Thus constructing is power. There is no 'real' shape of the person, no objectively defined needs, hidden in the clay to be discovered. However, professionals often act as if people, adults and children, can be defined in fairly absolute terms, labels that can become fixed. Multi-professional assessment can be seen as combining discourses of rationality, objectivity, bureaucracy and control into 'totalising identities'. Professionals can decide that there is a problem, can decide what that problem is, and can define the child in relation to that problem.

> The psychological language gained its authority from the mastery and control of a technical vocabulary, grounded in a quasi-scientific authority that contributes to the stratification of languages of representation and thereby the construction of children's identities. (Mehan, 1996, p. 261)

Most parents of children with special educational needs are required, by the need to liaise with teachers and other professionals over the assessment and education of their child, to have a relationship with schools that is different to that of other parents, and one they may not wish to have:

Disabled children and their parents become the objects of scrutiny and separation from the moment impairment is identified, and identification leads to separation in terms of policy and practice. Irrespective of grand claims to inclusion. (Corker and Davis, 2002, p. 88)

The identities fashioned for children and young people by the processes of schools and professional practice may not be those wanted by the children and young people themselves. We seem to be creating educational landscapes that do not recognise the nuanced lives of children. From the rich variety of ways in which children are very different from each other, certain differences become constructed as more important and notable than others. These include the differences of ability, special need, low achievement, Emotional behavioural difficulties (EBD) – and disability. These labels, these discourses, can become the main ways in which a child is understood, the only available story about that child. In other words, these discourses can have a totalising effect. The categorisation of children as disabled 'involved disability as a dominant status, where other differences or similarities remain muted or unattended to, and everything related to a child being explained by their impairment' (Watson *et al.*, 1999). The way this effect is resisted by children has been widely demonstrated (Madge and Fassam, 1982; Allen, 1999; Watson *et al.*, 1999). In the research by Watson *et al.* (1999):

The young people in the study identified with disability in many different ways. Sometimes they saw themselves as the same as others with their impairment, or indeed the wider group of disabled children. Sometimes they saw disability as something which marked their difference from other children. They saw disability as a term with different meanings, and contested boundaries; some children disavowed the label for themselves, whilst ascribing it to others. Children displayed fluidity in claiming disability as an identity: they described how they were not always disabled in every situation. They also resisted adult discourses which gave primacy to disability when dealing with disabled children.

Narrative practice
Narrative practices draw heavily on social constructionism (Burr, 1995) and demonstrate that professionals need to understand the role they have in shaping totalising identities. An alternative for professionals is to adopt practices that assist people to develop their own preferred

identities (Morgan, 2000). This is crucial for inclusion, since it suggests that there are many other stories about a child or young person that are available but often pass unnoticed in the interactions teachers and other pupils have with disabled children, with other stories with different people outside these interactions. Many of these are stories that connect disabled children with all children, and therefore make inclusive education more likely. There are a range of narrative strategies that professionals can use in schools, with individuals and in meetings with children and in team meetings with other professionals – all to help develop more inclusive practice (White and Epston, 1990; Smith and Nylund, 1997; Winslade and Monk, 1999). Narrative ways for structuring conversations and for positioning the disabled person as expert in his or her own life can help to develop what are known as 'thick' rather than 'thin' identities – more complex stories of people's lives where disability is just one aspect. Narrative conversations with groups of children and teachers can help explore what certain thin identities – such as 'special needs', 'gifted', 'bully', 'behaviour problem' and 'disabled' – are doing in classrooms and schools, and to help develop a more 'thick', complex identity of the classroom or the school. The process of 'externalisation' might be part of this.

Externalising locates problems, not within individuals, but as products of culture and history. Problems are understood to have been socially constructed and created over time (Carey and Russell, 2002).

Externalisations could involve a conversation with the child that, placing the child's perspectives and ideas as central, by careful use of language, separates the child from the problem, names the problem and perhaps draws it as an object. The child can be assisted to talk about their relationship to the problem, what effect it has had, what the child thinks of this, and why they take any particular stand on the problem. This gives the problem a story-line, and allows other story-lines to become known. When there is a history to a problem there is a possibility of re-claiming one's life from the problem and the effects of the problem. Unique outcomes, times when the influence of the problem has not been strong, can be explored. Ways these unique outcomes have been possible can be explored and they can be placed into alternative story-lines. The problem story is thought of as a 'thin' identity, and the alternative story-lines as 'thick' identities. Such ways of talking are not just linguistic techniques, but they are linked to post-structuralism, to a way of thinking about identity. A key element of externalising conversations involves the particular beliefs, ideas and practices that sustain the problem.

Narrative conversations can also be used to explore what is happening in groups and communities. By externalising bullying, for example, a group of children can look at what 'name calling' or 'leaving someone out' is doing in the class. A new space is created that avoids blaming particular pupils, or going down the structuralist route of defining 'bullies' and 'bullied'. The latter imprisons people in thin identities, whilst externalised conversations open up possibilities for new story-lines on class and school relationships.

How discourses make inclusion or participation more or less possible

The narratives professionals tell themselves about their role – the discourses of professional practice – are also crucial to the possibilities for inclusive education. It is likely that professionals will consider themselves 'neutral' advocates for the child and fail to notice discourses that define practice. If the narratives of professionals run counter to those of inclusive education, professionals are unlikely to find themselves in a position where they facilitate inclusive education. Professional discourses can also make it very difficult to fashion processes that involve children and parents as most discourses run counter to collaboration. Such discourses include being the expert and being the one who defines the problem using objectivity and rationality. Professional practice is also influenced by discourses of 'the child' circulating in society: of the child as different to the adult, as not yet mature enough to have a voice, or the child to be protected, or a wild beast to be contained.... Once again, such discourses make collaboration with a child unlikely.

Galloway *et al.* (1994) suggest that even if professionals aim to involve a child in an assessment, it may not be poor professional practice that leads to a lack of involvement. They found some professionals genuinely wanted to involve the child, but 'a complex situation of competing clients which determine the extent to which a child's perspectives are "allowed to be relevant"' (Galloway *et al.*, 1994, p. 66). It is difficult for the professional to hear what the child has to say when account has to be taken of the needs of other participants in the process.

> [I]t (the starting point for assessment) reflects a particular view of the child's needs which then becomes the starting point for subsequent negotiations, may itself lead to the disempowerment of the child. (Armstrong, 1995, p. 119)

The 'needs' of children are also presented as objective, unquestioned 'oughts', but they have origins – are constructed – and certain interests are served in the construction of these needs. The ways children's needs as defined by professionals meet the needs of professionals are complex, but one example is that of the preference of teachers for one label for a child rather than another:

> The Head's and the class teacher's insistence on a behavioural label and refusal to accept a learning difficulty or to relate his difficulties to his 'ability' can be seen as an attempt to maintain their professional identity... Teachers can maintain their sense of themselves as skilled professionals if they are able to have challenging pupils legitimately identified as the responsibility of others and if they can 'redefine their role in terms of the skills associated with teaching "normal" children' (Armstrong, Galloway and Tomlinson, 1993). (E. S. Todd, 2000, p. 400)

Towards an enabling inclusive participative practice

This chapter has suggested that post-structuralist thinking can assist professionals in the development of an inclusive participative practice. The key is to interrogate and be aware of professional discourses, the models, ideas, terms... around the systems, institutions and people with whom we work. Reflection on what discourses are doing, and whose interests they are serving, at the same time as bringing to the fore professional hopes for one's work and one's values, can bring to light possibilities for change. Greater 'political' literacy is needed. Allen (1999, p. 119) also suggests 'refusing the other', refusing to gaze, and allowing the 'cannibal desire to know the other give way to the act of hearing what the speaker says'. In the process, professionals may find themselves challenging their own 'Professional Thought Disorder' (PTD):

> a compulsion to analyse and categorise the experience of others, disordered cognition – rigidly held beliefs, delusions of grandeur, negative transference and projection in which sufferers cannot distinguish their own wishes and impulses from those of the people they wish to be helping. (Defined by Allen, 1999, p. 119)

A questioning of the current accepted dynamics of power relations, of expectations for client identity and of professional actions and behaviour is likely to be part of an enabling practice. This would allow professionals to take part in working alongside children, young people, parents – and each other – opening further spaces for people to fashion their own identities. Professionals should refuse to offer promises of rescue or escape routes to the 'grounds of certainty' (Allen, 1999) but instead allow competing accounts of practice and identity. Roles as experts may be abandoned to those of facilitators, advocates and consultants. Narrative conversations with individuals or in groups, with children, parents and professionals, can separate people from problems and from 'thin' identities and help them to see other story-lines. In this way, instead of the constant search for 'best', 'most effective', 'good', 'functional'...family, way of learning, new community school, model of inclusion, communities could work together to build their own story of family, learning, extended school of inclusion. Professionals – as members of communities – may find themselves creating new ways of being a professional at the same time as children and parents create new ways of being included.

Chapter 11

Counselling with the Social Model: Challenging Therapy's Pathologies

John Swain, Carol Griffiths and Sally French

Introduction

To address the topic of counselling and disability is to step into the individual–society divide that lies at the heart of this book. Essentially, it would seem that counselling individualises problems and solutions while, within a social model, disability is a social problem generated by a disablist society and overcome through social change. Nevertheless, counselling has been a service long associated with disability. It is generally recognised by disabled people as a valuable service and is provided by Centres for Integrated Living, managed by disabled people themselves (Priestley, 1999). Furthermore, the British Association for Counselling and Psychotherapy (BACP), who see disability issues as an important topic, instigated a 'Disability Issues' committee to promote awareness of disability to all counsellors and to facilitate BACP furthering its Equal Opportunities Policies with respect to these issues. To illustrate and inform our analysis we shall draw on a research project that explored the provision of counselling for disabled people in primary health care and a further education (FE) college, through open-ended interviews with both counsellors and disabled clients (Swain *et al.*, 2003b). In the following section, to set the scene, we provide a brief summary of the research methodology. In the section 'What's your problem?' we then explore understandings of disability emanating from the disability studies and counselling literature and as embedded in counselling practice. From this foundation we move on to 'What's your solution?' to engage with counselling as a process of personal and social change. To conclude we tentatively suggest some principles for an approach to counselling that is compatible with a social model of disability.

The research project

The methodology of the research project at Northumbria University was grounded in the general philosophy of qualitative research (McLeod, 2001). The research team (including Swain and Griffiths) aimed to explore understandings of disability within the context of counselling from the viewpoints of counsellors and disabled clients in primary health care and also in a FE college. For the former, the first stage consisted of unstructured, conversation-type interviews (Rubin and Rubin, 1995) with 11 counsellors working in primary health care. The counsellors were invited to participate in the research through the regional co-ordinator of the counselling service in primary health care. The interviews attempted to elicit counsellors' definitions and understandings of disability, and then to explore the implications of disability in terms of the provision of counselling. During the second stage an interim report, entitled 'An Holistic Model of Disability' and based on an initial analysis of those interviews, was circulated to the participants. This document argued that the 'story' linking the recurring themes within the interviews was a holistic model of disability. This is neither a medical nor a social/political model (though both were referred to by counsellors). It clearly relates to the theory/philosophy of client-centred counselling and the worldviews of counsellors. Disability was not, it seems, caused by impairments, nor imposed on people with impairments by a disabling society. It is individual, built into his or her self, relationships, lifestyle, as defined by the individual. The participant counsellors then met as a group with the researchers to discuss the findings and collaborate in the design of the next stage of the research.

After discussion it was decided that the counsellors would approach some of their own clients to ascertain whether they would participate in the research. Subsequently twelve clients were interviewed by seven of the counsellors. Participant counsellors did not interview their own clients. These interviews explored clients' views and experiences of counselling. All the interviews were tape-recorded, the tapes were transcribed and the researchers conducted the analysis. For the final stage of the research, a second interim report was prepared from this analysis for presentation back to the disabled clients, entitled ' "A

Ton of Weight off my Head": Counselling from the Viewpoint of Disabled Clients'. This document concentrated on control in the context of the aims of counselling, suggesting that it is directed at emotions and feelings. It also suggested that there is another form of control which, especially in relation to disability, might be thought to be important for a person's well-being and that is control over access to facilities. Not only is counselling itself often physically inaccessible, but clients are not necessarily encouraged by counsellors to view these elements of life as needing control. It is the response to the difficulty which becomes the counselling issue. Six clients were then interviewed again, but this time by one of the researchers, providing an opportunity to explore the issues with an interviewer who was not a service provider.

The research in the FE college followed a less complicated design. Four counsellors working at the college were interviewed. Eight students with disabilities were also interviewed by a member of the research team though they were not contacted via the counsellors themselves, rather through general 'advertising' via tutors. The analysis presented in the research reports provided the foundation for the discussion in this chapter.

What's your problem?

The crucial development in disability theory over at least the past 30 years has been the establishment of the social model of disability. The social model has been significant in a number of ways. First, it stands in direct opposition to the dominant individualistic models of disability, including tragedy and medical models. In particular, the medical model assumes that the difficulties faced by disabled people are a direct result of their individual impairments. The social model of disability, on the other hand, recognises the social origins of disability in a society organised and constructed by and for non-disabled people. The disadvantages or restrictions, often referred to as barriers, experienced by disabled people, permeate every aspect of the physical and social environment: attitudes, institutions, language and culture, organisation and delivery of support services, and the power relations and structures of which society is constructed (Oliver, 1990; Swain *et al.*, 1998).

Second, the social model of disability promotes the personal and political empowerment of disabled people. As Mercer and Barnes state, 'the medical approach concentrates on a set of discrete functional limitations requiring technical intervention and individual adjustment' (2000, p. 85). The social model engenders self-confidence and pride, rather than the guilt and shame associated with the individual tragedy model. The political implications of the social model, often explicitly stated, are to promote the collective struggle by disabled people for social change, equality, social justice and the rights of full participative citizenship. Furthermore, as a collective, dynamic theory, the social model is undergoing continued development. The works of Thomas (1999) and Reeve (2004a) are of particular pertinence to our present discussion. Both have written about 'the psycho-emotional dimensions of disability'. There can be psycho-emotional responses to the restrictions placed on disabled people:

> For example, feeling 'hurt' by the reactions and behaviours of those around us, being made to feel worthless, of lesser value, unattractive, hopeless, stressed or insecure. (Thomas, 1999, p. 47)

Reeve (2004a, see also this book) provides an analysis of three examples of this dimension of disability. These are: responses to experiences of structural disability; social interaction with others, including dealing with the frank curiosity of other people; and internalised oppression. Her analysis does not stem from an individual model:

> Although the psycho-emotional dimensions of disability operate at an emotional level I would not suggest that this form of disablism can be 'fixed' by a visit to a psychologist or counsellor; such professionals generally work within an individual model of disability and are more likely to add to, rather than resolve issues associated with the psycho-emotional dimensions of disability. (Reeve, 2004a, p. 95)

Turning to the research project, we begin with the viewpoint of counsellors in primary health care. Some counsellors were reluctant to label anyone 'disabled' and, by implication, to label everyone (at least potentially) as 'disabled'. One counsellor stated:

> I try not to [label]. If an individual describes themselves to me as having a disability then that's good enough for me. I mean I hate labelling you know. I hate all these sorts of labels that we pin on people, you know, so that we can neatly pigeonhole them for our own convenience. (Counsellor)

The danger of what another counsellor referred to as 'putting people with disabilities into a group' was perceived to be the unexamined presumptions that might be entailed. The disavowal of labels was associated with a broad definition of the term 'disabled'. In a sense, from the viewpoint of the participant counsellors, everyone who seeks counselling may be defined as disabled. The individual, it seems, owns the problem. The findings suggest that some counsellors do not operate either a medical or a social model of disability but one that might be called 'holistic', a term that proved acceptable to all the participant counsellors. Central to these counsellors' images of people is the commitment to regarding, and relating to, individuals holistically. This holistic approach gives equal regard to emotional, mental and physical characteristics and difficulties, and recognises the interrelationship between them:

> They're maybe having difficulty coming to terms with the disability or the loss... it's not just the disability often, it's the loss of the lifestyle that they had before the disability – the friends, the job, all of that that goes with it and how they see themselves as a person. (Counsellor)

Turning to the counsellors working in FE, there seemed to be a broader range of understandings of disability. There was a clear rejection of what was seen as the traditional model, or the individual medical model.

> Things like learning disability is seen as a traditional care model of disability which is at best a remedial model of disability where 'if we do enough these people are going to get better'. Something like that. I find it extraordinary. (Counsellor)

Disability was seen by a couple of counsellors as being primarily socially defined. It is created by a society that discriminates against disabled people.

> It has meanings about a social construct of disability in society that sets disabled people apart. You can identify disability by being unable to access things or finding it difficult or society making it difficult for a disabled person to access in the same way as a so-called able-bodied person. (Counsellor)

As in primary health care, however, all the counsellors resisted the differentiation between groups of people. Non-disabled counsellors can, in this sense, be disabled. Indeed, everyone can be disabled to a degree, as conveyed in the following quotation:

> But the reality is actually that there are a lot of different degrees of ability and disability, however you define disability polarities, and then the greys in between. I think disability makes me aware of my own disability. We're all disabled in some respects. (Counsellor)

The clients in primary health care were also reluctant to use the term 'disabled', but for these participants the problem was one of personal identity rather than possible presumptions about others.

> *Client*: The word 'disabled' horrifies the life out of me.
> *Counsellor*: Right.
> *Client*: Because I haven't always been disabled.
> *Counsellor*: Hmm.
> *Client*: It's only this past two years.

The reasons clients gave for their referral to counselling offered a significant light on their view of 'the problem'. The theme of 'control' repeatedly emerged in relation to clients' experiences of referral for counselling. Although diverse, there seemed to be two types of reasons: long-term reasons, described by one client as 'getting into a bigger and bigger hole', and more immediate crises, such as bereavement. Often clients cited both. The following are two illustrative examples of clients' reasons for referral.

> I went to my GP because I was going through a bereavement. My husband had died. I just felt very, very low and I felt as though I was having a breakdown. You know the stress just got worse and worse over the six months. I tried to pick myself up and carry on and, you know, move on, but I just couldn't. (Disabled client)

> It just was a downhill slope and I was virtually at the bottom of this slope and once you get there you just give up. (Disabled client)

The first of these quotations is from a client with a physical impairment who had been subjected to physical abuse by her late husband. If she was out, when he returned home, he would beat her on her return. Her husband, as she conveyed it, had controlled her life. This, however, does not seem to have been seen by herself, or anyone else who knew, as a reason for seeking counselling. Her feelings of loss of control over herself and her life, particularly over her emotions following his death, were the reasons for referral.

The experience of disability for many students with disabilities at the FE college was characterised, particularly for students with learning difficulties, by separation from the other students and barriers to inclusion. The barriers included physical barriers, particular mention was made of heavy doors. Examples were also given of social barriers, including teasing and name-calling.

> It happens at times. They just say 'oh look at that blind person with a stick', so I just ignore them. I just have to get on with it. (Disabled student)

Such difficulties could be more serious:

> Some times they judge that person 'cos they got disabilities, take the mick. They think you're not as good as them. It sort of puts you off coming to college. (Disabled student)

What's your solution?

Joy Oliver discussing the implications of the social model of disability for counselling, emphasises that 'distress and psychological problems' experienced by disabled people are caused by the disabling environment, rather than by impairments. On the basis of her research she found that 'many' of the counsellors she interviewed talked about the social model of disability and stated:

> It is evident that, in many cases, by removing the disabilities caused by the practical and social environment, the physically impaired person would have no more need of counselling than any other person. (1995, p. 277)

It is questionable, however, whether the findings in her research can be generalised to the beliefs of counsellors and the provision of counselling in primary health care. Three of the eight participants in Oliver's study were themselves disabled. All but one had worked with physically disabled people for at least three years, and they were contacted through disability organisations and disability resource centres.

From her review of the literature, her own experiences and those of her friends as disabled clients, Reeve suggests that counsellor-disabled client relationships are problematic. She argues that counsellors can further oppress disabled clients:

> examples of oppression include assumptions by the counsellor that relationship problems are totally caused by the presence of impairment, disbelief that a disabled client would consider refusing surgical intervention to be 'normalised', as well as relocating a counselling session to an inaccessible room. (2000, p. 672)

She explains this in terms of counsellors' prejudices and disablist attitudes arising from exposure to the dominant disablist culture.

A search through the counselling literature reveals few moves to address the social model of disability. Individual models, including the tragedy model and the medical model, predominate. If we take the *Handbook of Counselling* (Palmer and McMahon, 1997) as a typical example, disability and chronic illness are dealt with in the same chapter (Segal, 1997). Whereas the chapters on gender and race both take a political perspective with issues of sexism and racism taking centre stage, Segal's approach is evident from the first paragraph in which she says of disabled people:

> Some have physical disabilities, some intellectual, and some emotional. Some were born with disabling conditions; some developed them in later life...(2000, p. 402)

There are examples of recent literature that recognise the social model of disability, such as Parritt (2000, see also this book). Nevertheless, the starting point for understanding disability is predominantly as a condition of the individual, caused by their impairment, not as social oppression caused by a disabling society. We would suggest that the perspective adopted by Segal, who has published quite widely, remains largely unchallenged in the counselling literature.

McLeod (1998) argues that counselling has emerged within a social, historical and cultural context dominated by an ideology of self-contained individualism and he refers to the 'profoundly individualistic nature' (p. 28) of counselling. The over-individualised response to what are seen as 'personal problems' has ignored the social origins and conditions that ultimately produce these problems. Smail (1993, 1996) has developed a similar critique over a number of years. He states:

I have become less and less able to see the people who consult me as having anything 'wrong' with them, and more and more aware of the constraints which are placed on their ability to escape the distress they experience. (1993, p. 3)

In McLeod's (1998) view there is now a second wave of counselling approaches, including feminist, multicultural and narrative, that addresses questions of power in counselling, and the notion that counselling is a social and political act. Disability as a political issue, however, is rarely specifically addressed. Pilgrim (1997), for instance, presents a comprehensive critical analysis of counselling and psychotherapy that is close to that of Smail. His analysis covers arenas of class, gender, race and age, but not disability. Even in debates around the politics of counselling, it seems that disability remains marginalised.

It would seem that there is now some recognition of the social model in more specialised counselling literature. In the field of rehabilitation counselling, for instance, the social model is mentioned in at least a couple of the chapters in Etherington's (2002a) edited book. Etherington herself explores a narrative approach to counselling suggesting that:

New stories are continually emerging and increasingly disability is understood in terms of the relationship between impairment and physical and social environments. (2002b, p. 226)

In pursuing new models of practice, however, she still wishes to define disability as an individual problem as well as a social creation.

Turning to the practice of counselling as illustrated within the research project, though a social model was sometimes evident in the views of counsellors in the FE college, the practice of counselling seemed to be defined in relation to purpose and process. Purpose was nebulous, though this in itself was part of the definition. In both purpose and process, counselling was held to be something of a 'shared enterprise'. Though there is recognition of power in the relationship, for counsellors there can be mutuality. The following are two typical quotations:

Well I'm not sure what it is. I think it's a process and I think it's about two people. I think both people, ideally, can grow through the process of counselling. And I think I understand that growth as perhaps becoming more of ourselves in some ways. Perhaps use the word 'authentic' or having good faith rather than bad faith in an existential way. Understand yourself. (Counsellor)

I've been trained in the person-centred tradition and therefore I would see counselling very much as a listening but, in that process, helping the client to reflect on their own material. It's very important to live eventually in a more fulfilled way. That would be how to define outcome. . . . But in terms of counselling I try and see everyone as an individual regardless of any either obvious physical disability or mental disability of some kind. (Counsellor)

The individualistic nature of counselling, as defined through the process, was clearly evident. It is a process that is seen as being defined and constructed in, by and for itself, rather than any broader structures or relations. Not surprisingly, the need for a counselling service was seen to derive from the student, and in particular the student's view of themselves and disability.

Part of the work for the student is in terms of accepting and living with and maybe seeing in more positive terms whatever their difficulty or disability is. That it's the whole sort of mix of defining disability either there's some kind of deficit, you know, there's something wrong, there's something missing, or at the more positive end of things, the differently abled concept where what you're looking at is what they can do and not what they can't do. (Counsellor)

This individualistic conception was also apparent in the students' thinking about counselling. A students' union representative stated:

I will try and promote the counselling service in a way which isn't a place for loonies or isn't a place that you've got to be mad or insane . . . I think most young people think counselling is for loonies, I mean you know you've got to have some major drug habit, some kind of marital problem or be, you know, a bit crazy. (Student)

When asked what 'might you talk to a counsellor about', a student with disabilities who had used, valued and advocated the counselling service answered:

People when they've got problems. When they are going to hang themselves and that. (Disabled student)

In primary health care, the counsellors' views of the nature and process of counselling emphasised the fact that they regard their role as an enabling one. Clients are seen as being able to act and make decisions for themselves, as having 'agency', or the capacity for control over themselves and their lives, if facilitated in a non-judgemental way, within a supportive context. One counsellor summarised this view as follows and could have been quoting from a textbook on humanistic counselling:

> Well, I regard it as an opportunity for clients with a range of problems, to have time that's dedicated to them, for them to talk through their problems and the issues that are facing them, and for that to happen with somebody who values them, who is non-judgemental, who can empathise with them and who can help them to untangle their problems and perhaps find solutions, solutions that work for them. (Counsellor)

Again the individualistic nature of counselling practice is apparent. In the process of counselling, as constructed in the interviews between counsellors and disabled clients, 'acceptance and control' emerged, in different guises, as key concepts. These concepts clearly reflect the holistic model of disability as adhered to by counsellors as, in general terms, they refer to acceptance of and control over the self and lifestyle.

In person-centred models of counselling, an acceptance, by the counsellor, of the client is paramount. This is, indeed, an aspect of counselling that is appreciated, and commented upon, by most clients. One stated:

> Nothing I say has ever, you know, made her think, you know. Sometimes I thought, 'oh my goodness I must be batty', you know, not wanting to go shopping on my own but D [the counsellor] has always filled me with confidence, helped me to talk about things and I've always felt better when I've come out. (Disabled client)

Acceptance and control were not just themes in reasons for referral, but were also applied to the process of counselling itself. Inherent in the clients' experiences of counselling was the need to accept the 'rules' of counselling. These include an obligation to talk and reveal feelings, leading to recognition of the 'problem'. Acceptance of the rules of counselling is not, though, an end in itself. It is the preliminary step on the road that may encourage acceptance, by the client, of their circumstances and limitations. One client said:

> You should listen to what your body's telling you. If you feel tired it means it's your body saying to you, 'You can't do that'. You have to think what well maybe I could do it tomorrow, or get someone else to do it for me, or you know, just learning to sort of to cool down a bit. (Disabled client)

Constraints that are to be accepted may include not only family and social circumstances but also restricted lifestyles. This may occur especially in cases where the effects of disabling barriers are particularly frustrating or upsetting. One client, in expressing the anger she felt at the limitations placed on her when she developed physical impairments, was encouraged to see her anger, not the limitations, as the problem. The 'problem' thus becomes a personal failure, of the emotions, to be remedied. Despite identifying a social problem, she saw the frustration as a personal failure and the ideal as acceptance, and was encouraged by her counsellor to take this view.

> *Client*: At the very beginning of this, I used to go out on a Friday and a Sunday. But I've actually found I cannot do it anymore, 'cause of Saturday morning. And I don't drink alcohol because of the medication I take and I find on a Saturday morning I'm absolutely exhausted and cannot do anything. I can hardly get up. I can hardly walk about – and, I mean, I suppose disabled people are entitled to enjoyment, you know.
> *Counsellor*: Why of course, yes.
> *Client*: But it's just had to go by the board.
> *Counsellor*: You had to accept really what you cannot do.

Control, as constructed between the counsellor and the client, is directed at emotions and feelings, as indicated by the following example in which a client is describing her response to the delivery of incontinence pads. Embarrassment is reinforced as the problem, rather than focusing on the treatment to which this client has been subjected or on questioning social attitudes towards incontinence.

> *Client*: I feel very ashamed of having, there's a man comes once a fortnight with a big rental truck and I get pads delivered and I am so embarrassed. In bags and it's wrote on what they are.

Counsellor: Yeah.

Client: You can see them and, as it happens, I'm at the doctors or the hospital and they leave them with my mam and my dad, 'cause they carry them along.

Counsellor: Right.

Client: Which I find absolutely horrendous. I really do.

Counsellor: Yeah, well that all adds to the embarrassment doesn't it?

The next example concerns access to facilities for counselling. The focus, or the problem, is the client's personal difficulty rather than the physical environment and possibilities for changing access.

Client: But, it's very slow, but I do, I manage to get up the stairs with my stick.

Counsellor: So, you go up the steps to the counselling room.

Client: To the counselling room.

Counsellor: A couple of flights up.

Client: Two very long flights of stairs.

Counsellor: Right, so that must be difficult for you.

Client: It's an effort, yeah. It is an effort.

Essentially, then, counselling is orientated towards empowering the individual in controlling emotions and accepting 'themselves'. The research suggests that, from the clients' viewpoint, this has much to offer. Gaining control was the main theme in clients' responses:

I've found since I've had counselling, you can hardly recognise the signs (of depression) 'cause I found before I was having the counselling, you wouldn't realise you were getting down and down and down until it was too late. (Disabled client)

I got a lot more ease from the counselling through this. You know it was very very beneficial. It has a very knock-on effect, which for me is very good. It is very liberating. I've found I can do lots of things now that I couldn't do before. I was never allowed to go out at all. I was very frightened. And I always used to think, even though he was dead and he wasn't here, if I went out I always used to think he would still be here and I would get a hiding when I came in. It opened a lot of avenues, a lot of doors for me. It's very rewarding. I would advise anybody to try. (Disabled client)

Towards counselling with the social model

The implications of the social model of disability, in terms of counselling for disabled people, is summarised by Oliver and Sapey as follows:

> From the perspective of the social model, what is required is to evaluate the usefulness of counselling in the struggle to remove disabling barriers. (1999, p. 182)

There seems to be a tension between the social model of disability and 'seeking social change through a medium which individualizes and "psychologizes" social problems' (McLeod, 1998, p. 26). We conclude by summarising some tentative thoughts about the implications of the analysis in this chapter. As McLeod (1999, p. 221) suggests, a social perspective does not prescribe any specific techniques or counselling interventions, but offers a set of principles that may be of value both to clients and practitioners of counselling. Swain *et al.* (2004) present a similar set of principles as a foundation for the work of professionals in health and social care.

Perhaps the first principle, indeed requirement, for counselling with the social model is accessible counselling services. Reeve (2004a) outlines some of the barriers faced in accessing counselling, such as counselling rooms at the top of flights of stairs (as in the example mentioned in p. 167). In relation to this, Alexander (2003), exploring the implications of the Disability Discrimination Act (1995), points out that counselling agencies will need to provide access to a sign language interpreter, as well as making 'reasonable adjustments' to their premises.

Second, we would suggest that the challenges to practice should engage with the counsellor–client relationship. The social model was borne out of contexts in which groups of disabled people shared their experiences and found commonalities in the discrimination they faced and questioned disability as personal tragedy. Transposing this to counselling practice suggests models of practice that include group experiences. Without going into detail, it is possible for the group to provide support of various kinds and for people to role-play the issues they want to confront (as for instance in assertiveness training).

Third, building on the previous point, it needs to be recognised that the struggle to remove disabling barriers can have its own costs for individual disabled people. People may need support to deal with their emotions after such events. The recognition of barriers may mean that the disabled person needs to change (at a personal level) to do anything about them. This may be a particularly difficult issue for disabled women and for people who have been to special schools and other institutions that have disempowered them over many years. This again raises the notion of collective action in removing disabling barriers.

Fourth, moving towards counselling with the social model is clearly about the inclusion of disabled counsellors as well as disabled clients. This is parallel to the view that inclusion in education is about disabled teachers and tutors, as well as students with disabilities and pupils. Though there are no clear figures, the number of disabled counsellors, disabled people training as counsellors, and disabled supervisors and tutors is low (Alexander, 2003; Reeve, 2004a).

Finally, the establishment of different models of counselling practice must address the provision of training for counsellors. One strategy proposed by Reeve (2000, 2004a) is the inclusion of Disability Equality Training (DET) within counselling courses. She states:

> It is vital that Disability Equality Training becomes a mandatory part of all counselling courses so that students (and tutors) learn about the social model of disability and understand how disability is socially constructed rather than being caused by a person's impairment. (2004a, p. 236)

We would suggest, too, that this needs to be part of critical reflection on the dominant ideology of individualism and the pathologising of social problems.

Chapter 12

Doing Community Psychology with Disabled People

Carolyn Kagan, Rebecca Lawthom, Paul Duckett and Mark Burton

Introduction

In this chapter, we show ways in which a particular form of psychology, community psychology, can enable and facilitate alternative ways of working with disabled people. The focus of the work, the doing of community psychology outlined here, is with people labelled as having learning difficulties. We first present a brief overview of community psychological practice, showing how it differs from traditional psychological understandings. We then show, using case studies, how community psychological practices can differ in the ways that work is conceptualised, enacted and followed up. The case studies are drawn from authors' experiences.

What is community psychology?

Dalton *et al.* (2001, p. 5) argue that community psychology concerns the relationships of the individual to communities and society. Through collaborative research and action, community psychologists seek to understand and enhance quality of life for individuals, communities and society. At this time, the links between community psychology and learning difficulties (Kagan and Burton, 2005) and community psychology and disability studies (Goodley and Lawthom, 2005) are beginning to be mapped out. The landscape is an interesting one as both community psychology and disability studies (and learning diffi-culties) are themselves extraordinary non-dominant ways of thinking. Alternative psychological models of disability and learning difficulties have already been thoughtfully theorised within this book (within the spheres of personal experience, education, counselling, etc.). What can a community psychology approach bring to the table?

Community psychology has a growing presence in the UK (Burton and Kagan, 2003; www.compsy.org.uk), and whilst it is not possible to write about a homogenous community psychology, there are common features. There is perhaps consensus on the following:

- Context: A focus which places individuals within their historical, cultural, environmental and political contexts (Rappaport, 1977; Sarason, 1977; Orford, 1992; Levine and Perkins, 1997) so as to counter the individualistic bias and victim-blaming ideology of mainstream psychology.
- Vision: a commitment to improving the human condition and promoting psychological well-being (Pretorius-Heuchert and Ahmed, 2001; Prilleltensky, 2001).
- Multilevel practice: A focus on long-term projects and collaboration, working within the complexity of people's natural environments rather than laboratory settings (Rappaport, 1977; Bishop *et al.*, 2001).

Central to most definitions of community psychology is an explicit commitment to social change and transformation (Montero, 1998, 2004; Nelson and Prilleltensky, 2004) as well as to continual reflec-tion (Gregory, 2001; Kagan and Burton, 2001). Enhanced well-being, social inclusion and empowerment of non-dominant groups who are marginalised by social systems are components of a vision for a more just society. A community psychological perspective would encourage us, and the people with whom we work to have such vision to guide our actions and frame our reflections. This vision unleashes our creativity and criticality, enmeshes our hopes and desires and engages our political values in our work. The idea of a value-based practice will be familiar to many working within the field of learning difficulties (see for example Race, 2002).

As community psychologists, the value we place on social justice leads us towards working in different ways: to ensure resources are available to people labelled with learning difficulties; to enable services and/or families to support people labelled with learning difficulties in ways that promote safety and equality of opportunity; with employers,

and/or the benefits system, so that people labelled with learning difficulties have the same access to work and income as everyone else; and
to explore new and creative ways to enable people labelled with
learning difficulties to make decisions about their lives which are
important to them. Other values such as equality, respect, democracy,
autonomy and peace are linked to justice.

As community psychologists we might include other forms of
work: to create new opportunities for people's skills and qualities to
be recognised and valued; we may work with local communities to
expand ways in which they can include people labelled with learning
difficulties in ordinary community activities; to link different groups
of professionals together with people labelled with learning difficulties and their families so that they might learn from the most
progressive, innovative and creative projects that might be of benefit
to people labelled with learning difficulties; and to ensure that the
interests and views of people labelled with learning difficulties are at
the heart of the ways resources are gained and used to support them,
and that there are continuities of relationships in people's lives. Other
values such as solidarity, collective action, participation, empowerment, well-being and sustainability are at the heart of such work.

As community psychologists we might work on social connections:
to find new ways of enabling people labelled with learning difficulties
to retain friendships and intimate relationships as well as encouraging
people who do not have the label of learning difficulty to meet with
and get to know them; to enable communities – geographical, workplace or communities of interest – to be able to welcome and support
people labelled with learning difficulties in their midst; and to create
opportunities for people labelled with learning difficulties to
contribute to the social life of their communities and enable services
and other social institutions to identify and celebrate the contributions made by different groups within them. Such workplaces value
concepts such as friendship, solidarity, diversity, commitment, and
inter-dependence and community.

Being explicit about the value base of our work enables us to question continually *how* we work and on *what issues* we work – ethical
considerations (Sánchez Vidal *et al.*, 2004). This is important, given
that there is no single, homogenous model of community psychology.
Community psychology is not formulaic, and its practice emerges in
response to particular issues. It is not only values that serve to guide
us in how and on what issues to work. Within the field of community
psychology, there are also some shared principles that help define its

practice and priorities, and help distinguish it from other forms of psychological work.

The paradigm and principles of community psychology

Montero (2004) integrates community psychological perspectives from North America, Europe and Latin America to argue that community psychology constitutes a psychological paradigm characterised by a distinct ontology, epistemology, methodology, ethics and politics. It is a paradigm that presents a strong critique of other psychological paradigms, whilst at the same time offering an alternative way of doing psychology. Within a community psychological paradigm there is no separation of psychologists and community members in the way there is in other paradigms (for example, of experts and clients, researchers and research participants). Instead, both are active producers of knowledge and understanding, being one and the same time authors and owners of knowledge and experience. It follows, then, that community psychology is a fundamentally socially constructed and relational discipline that is politically reflective.

Thus, community psychology differs from traditional psychological models that often individualise problems and solutions, and from disability studies, where the focus is on disabled people. A number of principles can be identified, which help to clarify these differences, although there is again no agreement on exactly what these principles are. For example, Orford (1992), citing Rappaport (1977), notes eight principles, whereas Thomas and Veno (1996) identify four key themes and Montero (1998) eleven characteristics of the discipline. In part these different views reflect different contexts (UK/USA, New Zealand and Australia, Latin America respectively). We have synthesised these different views to suggest the following principles.

An ecological approach
An ecological approach recognises the importance of the historical, cultural, political, economic, environmental and situational context of people's lives. This context might be linked to the roles that other people play, the actual physical environment, the legislation and policies framing a particular issue or the discourses and representations of people or problems in society at large. An ecological perspective locates psychosocial problems not in the individual but more often in cultural, economic, political and social relationships that encircle the individual. Community psychologists problematise the

medical model when it is used to explain the causes rather than effects of broader social problems. The strategies for intervention promoted by community psychologists will usually operate at multiple levels, sometimes simultaneously, including the individual, group, organisation and broader social systems. Furthermore, an ecological approach also enables community psychologists to anticipate the impact of change more widely. By taking an ecological approach, community psychologists are adopting a systems perspective in their work. Knowledge about how social systems operate helps community psychologists understand the multiple causes of social problems, at different levels, from global to individual levels. Multilevel, complex analyses and interventions enable a holistic approach to be adopted, which inevitably means community psychologists are interested in the perspectives of different stakeholders, and in analysing and using power in all its manifestations at different points in the social system.

Diversity, power and action
Community psychology adopts a particular ideological orientation towards the concept of diversity (see for example Trickett *et al.*, 1993, 1994). Diversity occupies an important place in the history and future of community psychology and in this regard demarcates it from much of mainstream psychology. While psychology has spawned a range of specialised sub-disciplines, each of these sub-disciplines is typically founded on a common ideology – a white, male, heterosexual, non-disabled way of thinking. Trickett *et al.* (1994) detail the challenge made to this common ideology in psychology that has come from the ethnic psychologies, psychology of women, gay/lesbian psychologies and, the most recent academic development, a psychology of disabled people. Each of these critiques views difference positively and finds a valued place for the 'other' that has been marginalised in the past. Each of these critiques points to the need for diversity to be explored both through the nature of the questions psychologists ask (multilevel analysis), and the people with whom psychologists work (multidisciplinary approach). Thus, community psychologists recognise the artificial boundaries between different professional and academic disciplines as well as the limitations of psychological perspectives (Smail, 2001). They bring to their work a commitment to understand problems in different ways and to work with others for better understanding and better use of resources at a local level. Furthermore, they recognise that there are many other community practitioners who share some or all of the values and principles of community psychology.

It is, therefore, not necessary to be a psychologist to work community psychologically. Through engaging with a power analysis of diversity, community psychologists seek to facilitate the empowerment of economically and politically non-dominant groups through inclusive individual, group and collective action. Resources and capacities are restored, developed or improved through the organisation and maintenance of networks for the interchange of knowledge, goods and services and psychological resources. In our work, community psychologists explore the nature of oppression, in partnership with people marginalised by the social system. A community psychological goal is to address social and individual change, both of the internal agents (people of the community) and the external agents (psychologists or other professionals) of transformation. Crucially, it is for communities to decide their destinies – psychologists may help to catalyse change whilst challenging prejudice, as external agents.

As community psychologists we will often work with individuals and groups, not just on individual interventions for immediate problems, but rather in ways that divert resources towards the promotion of well-being or prevention of problems, at any or all of the different levels of the social system. So, we may be working with individuals developing self-help strategies, or in terms of changing some aspect of the immediate environment that contributes to a problem. Alternatively or simultaneously, we may work at policy levels, be these local or national. Throughout our work, we endeavour to work in ways that are more likely to promote well-being, lead to the empowerment of economically and politically marginalised groups or individuals, and wider scale social change, as well as to prevent problems occurring (Albee, 1982). The types of work we may do include helping people develop information campaigns, supporting self-help organisations or training for professionals so that institutional practices change. Working with the explicit value base outlined above, we may also support individuals or groups and lend both our expertise and our time to working alongside economically and politically non-dominant groups in direct social action. Sometimes we will get involved in ways of helping those from different backgrounds, come to a shared understanding of a problem and work together for effective solutions. Wherever possible, we will look for strategies of working that maximise the joint resources different professionals or interest groups can bring to a problem. Relationships with community members, groups and organisations are viewed as partnerships, where each partner makes important contributions, but where the concerns and interests of the community are paramount. There is no assumption that communities are homogenous and one task is to identify and include different interest groups in the process of change. As community psychologists we listen to local people about their concerns and viewpoints, contribute our 'scientific' knowledge and resources, and together negotiate a way of working towards shared goals. The work that we do as community psychologists is not neutral. We work with those members of communities who share a commitment to greater social justice.

Why community psychology and learning difficulties?

Historically, people labelled with learning difficulties have been socially marginalised and disempowered in a number of different ways (Wolfensberger, 1992; Ramcharan *et al.*, 1997; Race, 2002; Kagan and Burton, 2004). This social position stems from the way Western societies are historically organised (Burton, 1983). All too frequently people labelled with learning difficulties have poorly satisfying social opportunities (Burton and Kagan, 1995). Ongoing debates in service provision ask: 'should clients mix with people without or with learning difficulties?' The latter is viewed as creating ghettos, the former as a form of 'divide and rule' – circumventing shared experiences and identities (see discussion in Meyerson, 1988). The very existence of the debate further impoverishes the social lives of people labelled with learning difficulties, as whichever is preferred by people themselves, the preference is made for rather than by people labelled with learning difficulties.

Until recently, people labelled with learning difficulties also had a disempowered role in the services they used. The service system (health or social care, public or independent sector) decided what services to provide and how and to whom they would be delivered. Eligibility criteria, strictly applied, are based on the ability of professionals to assess need, and may or may not correspond to people's preferences or desires. People labelled with learning difficulties may have little say over where they live and with whom. If they live in residential accommodation (a hostel) or supported living, they may not even get to decide what to eat and when. Even in services designed to promote independent living it will often be the staff that decide what this means and what is important to spend time on. People labelled with learning difficulties themselves may have little or no say about the running of the hostel where they live or about activities at the resource centre they attend. This is slowly changing. In terms of housing, for example, the trend is towards tenancy agreements and away from passive service recipient relationships. Furthermore, committees of those using services are increasingly in evidence. The publication of the White Paper *Valuing People* in 2001 (DoH, 2001b) stipulates requirements on services to take the views of people who use them into account and to find ways of supporting self and other forms of advocacy. Even so, disempowerment is still a feature of the relationship between people labelled with learning difficulties and the organisations that plan and deliver their services.

People labelled with learning difficulties are generally excluded from gainful economic activity. They are more likely to be unemployed than any other disabled group or any other non-dominant group. If in employment, they are more likely to be in poor quality employment. If in training, they are more likely to be in poor quality training. People labelled with learning difficulties frequently live on inadequate welfare benefits and are thus poor, or have whatever money they are entitled to controlled by family members or professionals.

Culturally, people labelled with learning difficulties have their adulthood denied. Many are denied the right to form intimate relationships or to have children (Booth and Booth, 1994; McCarthy, 1999). A 'Peter Pan' ideology entraps people into lives dependent (rather than interdependent) upon others, exacerbated by the hegemony of the medical model of disability that constructs identities of pathology and passivity on those so labelled.

People labelled with learning disabilities are politically disempowered, having an unclear role in the Disability Movement and little visibility in other political processes. Stories of their ill-treatment and past incarceration are used to highlight disablism and oppression yet when it comes to inclusion in political movements, they are more often overlooked. Recent consultations on the new Disability Rights Commission have led some commentators to be concerned that people labelled with learning difficulties will be further excluded from political activism (Aspis, 1997).

In the field of learning difficulty people's communicative abilities are often underestimated, and frequently misattributed. For example, where people labelled with learning difficulties are able to communicate their preferences, their positive choices can be pathologised as aberrations called 'acquiescence' (compliance). Their negative choices can be reinterpreted as 'challenging behaviours' requiring rehabilitation and correction. These medical reinterpretations of what are essentially social acts are common place (Rapley and Antaki, 1996; Duckett, 2001). Thus, people's impairments are often judged as more relevant that the broader socio-political context in which communication is embedded. Indeed, the extraordinary contexts in which people live must be fully understood, in order to understand the meanings of people's behaviour (Duckett, 2001).

Having contextualised elements of community psychological practice and briefly touched upon the experience of individuals labelled with learning difficulties, we now show how community psychological thinking can be used. There is a rich body of work in this area. For example, Burton and Kagan (1995) provide varied case studies of community psychological practice with people labelled with learning disabilities; Kagan and Burton (2005) point out the different emphasis of community psychology (as a social phenomenon) when working with people labelled with learning difficulties; and Duckett (2001) explores issues around user involvement. Work in this area in the UK has been further stimulated by a recent White Paper (DoH, 2001b) which prioritises the participation of people labelled with learning difficulties and their families in both practice and policy. One strategy used in this movement towards greater social inclusion is Person Centred Planning (PCP). PCP has some resonance in a number of fields in psychology (for example, through person centred theories that have informed counselling theory and practice). Whilst PCP has limits as strategy for social and service reform (Burton, 2004; Mansell and Beadle-Brown, 2004), its influence extends far beyond the disciplinary boundaries of psychology. It is part of a movement in social service provision towards user involvement. User involvement has become a popular and progressive concept that has been employed in the practice of service provision for people labelled with learning difficulties in particular (Carnaby, 1997), and disability more generally (Beresford and Campbell, 1994). The question of whether service users *should* be involved in service planning and delivery is now fully rhetorical. The question is *how* should service users be involved. Here, we turn to a couple of case studies that will elucidate some of the characteristics of community psychological thinking.

Sarah and Ted

Sarah lives with Ted in a staffed house within a service that is keen to support person centred planning. Sarah and Ted communicate well with their key workers although neither of them use verbal communication. They have both been labelled as having profound and multiple learning difficulties. Working community psychologically involved training the staff to find meaningful ways of finding out what Sarah and Ted's preferences were. Very quickly it became clear that the difficulties staff had in thinking about Sarah and Ted's interests being central were a problem with the whole service and a process of cultural change in the organisation was required. Before any person-centred planning could be introduced with people using the service, therefore, a programme of awareness raising and skills development was introduced. During the planning of this programme, it became clear that if only service staff took part, family members and other people labelled with learning difficulties would be at a disadvantage when the person-centred planning was introduced. So the training and cultural change programme involved family members and people labelled with learning difficulties too. Some family members and some people labelled with learning difficulties became particularly interested in the ideas behind person-centred planning and wanted to do more in the way of raising awareness about it more generally. They established a mentoring scheme across the service and more widely to include people living in other parts of the region. The mentoring scheme, over a period of two years, became widespread. When person-centred planning was finally introduced, people labelled with learning difficulties and family members were, indeed, central to the process and could participate on an equal basis with professionals using any one of a range of creative ways of participating, including drama, life story work, advocates and 'circles of friends'. Furthermore, some family members had developed skills not held by professionals in how to work with all interested parties around person-centred planning, training on person-centred planning and mentoring other parents and people labelled with learning difficulties. This is a composite case study based on work undertaken by Helen Sanderson, Alison Short and colleagues (see for example, Sanderson, 2001, 2002; Kilbane and Sanderson, 2004; Short, 2004; Towell and Sanderson, 2004), and Paul Duckett (2002).

The work with Sarah and Ted quickly moved from work with them as individuals, to work at the level of the culture of the service organisation supporting them, to work with parents of people labelled with learning difficulties more widely and the establishment of a new and innovative process of raising awareness of PCP and enhancing the skills of the non-professionals participating in PCP.

As part of its ecological perspective, community psychology looks at people's behaviours and experiences as being part of a complex system of relationships. A popular way to think about this is in terms of 'nested systems' (Bronfenbrenner, 1979). People are situated within a micro-system, a meso-system, an exo-system and a macro-system, each level encompassing the others. The micro-level encompasses all those relationships with which a person has direct contact. In Sarah and Ted's case it is each other, their families and the staff working with them. The meso-level points to the connections between parts of the micro-system, for example the relationship between staff and families, or staff and other professionals and so on. The exo-system is those parts of the context that do not affect people directly but that have an indirect effect on both the meso- and micro-levels. In this case it is the wider service system, other community resources affecting the services and the families. The macro-system is the level in which all other levels are embedded, and includes cultural values, customs and legislation. Parts of the macro-system at work in our example is the requirement within the White Paper to undertake PCP and cultural values and attitudes affecting attempts to involve Sarah and Ted and those close to them in decisions about their lives. Our example shows how working community psychologically requires us to understand the different levels and to work at levels beyond the micro-level. Dealing with organisational culture is an exo-level activity; involving families in PCP is a meso-level activity; supporting parents in defining new ways of working with PCP is an exo-level activity. Our work here was multilevel, concerned with empowerment and had the position of marginalised people at its heart.

Another example of work at different levels can be seen in the case of Anthony. Here we were centrally concerned to ensure that Anthony was able to live as part of his local community and thus inclusion was central. However, to ensure that he could be included in ordinary activities and get to know a wider range of people, our work was, again, not with Anthony directly, but with those who were to support him. We helped to develop the capacity of staff working with Anthony.

Anthony

Anthony, a young man with a reputation for violent behaviour, was being brought back to his own neighbourhood from a residential facility some 250 miles away. The staff unions of the new facility in which he was to live were about to withdraw their cooperation and refuse to have staff work with him, for health and safety reasons. (The facility was planning 24-hour support for Anthony.) If the staff refused to work with him, Anthony would have to remain in an institution.

We decided to work with the proposed staff team to find ways of getting to know Anthony before he moved and to identify appropriate supports for him, *with* him and for themselves (rather than relying on other people's assessments). The plans for the new support service ended up looking quite different from the existing one and from the original plans for his move. The staff then needed support in arguing for the new service with managers who did not want provision for Anthony to change.

Once Anthony had moved (successfully) staff were given more support and training in thinking through and devising ways for Anthony to become more integrated in his neighbourhood. A big challenge was how to bring more people who were not paid to be with him into Anthony's life. This support went on for three years during which time staff could not always enable Anthony to remain in his own home, and he was moved on two occasions to a more secure setting. This was only ever for short periods of time. Staff were encouraged to link with groups of staff in other authorities who had faced similar challenges. Over this period the staff group stayed working with Anthony – no one refused to continue and for the first time in his life Anthony experienced continuity of relationships with other people. Staff resisted management plans to rotate their time working with Anthony (as a protection against 'burnout') and instead they all got the opportunity to get to know – and like – each other.

Anthony now lives in his own home and participates in lots of local activities. Violent behaviour is extremely rare. (Although Anthony's story is real, names have been changed. The case study was originally reported in Kagan, 1997.)

The community psychological emphasis in Anthony's case, as we have seen, was on inclusion, on the development of social networks and relationships. It is also another example of multilevel work, beyond the individual level, focussing on organisational capacity building. In terms of the training about ways of supporting Anthony so his violent outbursts reduced, we were 'giving psychology away' in the form of training in the understanding and management of aggression and violent behaviour.

A rather different approach was taken to the work with Bill. As with so many examples of work with people labelled with learning difficulties in the UK, our work with Bill was to ensure he retained good supports for living in domestic scale housing in an ordinary neighbourhood where he already knew a lot of people and took part in everyday activities. In Bill's case, there was a dispute between what some members of his family wanted for him and what the services were offering in the way of support. The community psychological work was to ensure, through processes of advocacy that Bill's interests were served and his views could be represented within the decision-making process.

Bill

The future of Bill, a 35-year-old man with no verbal communication was in jeopardy. Bill lived with two other men labelled with learning difficulties in a home in a residential neighbourhood of a town, supported by 24-hour staffing. Professionals in his life wanted him to remain in this ordinary, domestic scale house near his friends and family. His elderly parents wanted him to move to a small institution (catering for 53 people labelled with learning difficulties) 60 miles away from his family, friends and local community. They were convinced staff in the institution had the specialist skills to enable Bill to learn to talk.

An advocate (the community psychologist, with no professional involvement) was appointed to represent Bill's interests in the decision-making process. She spent time with Bill (approx. 50 hours in the different settings in which he spent time). She was able to describe his preferences, likes and dislikes; his life now and what was good about it, and what might improve it, all within a clear value framework. During the process Bill's parents abducted him from the day centre, refusing to let him go home. Instead, they took him to live with them, in unsuitable conditions – a small upstairs flat with lots of ornaments around and little space to move about – Bill liked to pace up and down energetically. They then moved house and managed to get Bill admitted to the institution. In the midst of objections from professionals, a sister and the advocate, the senior managers took what they thought to be the course of least resistance and moved Bill to the institution. The advocate was able to challenge this decision on the basis of its inconsistency with Regional policy. She was also able to support Bill's sister in gaining legal assistance and in monitoring his situation at the institution. Periodically, the advocate was able to write reports, and support the sister in writing reports, highlighting the situation the young man was now in, and its comparison with how he was living before. The senior management in health and social services, as well as the institution, received these reports with hostility. The advocate was able to muster support from senior managers elsewhere in the Region who were trying to adhere to Regional policy. She was able to use her network of contacts to alert other relevant professionals to concerns surrounding his placement. She was able to help the sister compile a case highlighting the deterioration he had undergone. Two-and-a-half years later, a decision was made to bring Bill back to his own neighbourhood. (This is a real story, using pseudonyms, reported in Kagan *et al.*, 1995.)

The work with Bill was direct at the start, offering advocacy and enabling his interests to be heard when he could not voice them himself. As the process became more complex, it moved to being indirect in the form of supporting his sister to advocate on his behalf, whilst at the same time trying to work with the services to enable them to continue to provide good supports for social inclusion. Advocacy on behalf of and with people who cannot speak for themselves is both a skill and strategy of community psychology (Brandon *et al.*, 1995; Kagan, 1997)

Common threads
The case studies so far discussed show how community psychological practice works. Community psychologists in the scenarios discussed are not powerful professionals working to a specified agenda, rather, the work involved a value-based practice aiming to achieve social justice. In their work, community psychologists engage in a constant cycle of doing, learning and critical reflection, and they try to encourage others to adopt a similar approach to change. Thus, doing without understanding or reflection is not enough. As community psychologists we strive to make sense and learn from what it is that we do, and we strive to follow our understanding and knowledge with action. The three components of activity are inseparable and can be summed up as a *critical praxis*. Community psychology creates professional space to engage with inclusive empowerment and socially just working practices in the field of learning difficulty. Community psychology is not new to this field; indeed emancipatory, critically framed ways of working in the disability field exist outside of the field of community psychology. Below, we examine the kinds of roles occupied by community psychologists.

Community psychology roles

As we can see from the case studies, a community psychologist might occupy a number of roles, even though there are few opportunities to be employed as a community psychologist with people labelled with learning difficulties. Not all community psychologists undertake all of these roles, and the roles themselves are not unique to community psychologists.

Figure 12.1 summarises the different roles a community psychologist might take, with those discussed in the case studies highlighted. Whatever the role being undertaken, community psychologists will endeavour to follow the principles outlined below, and work according to the central values of community psychology.

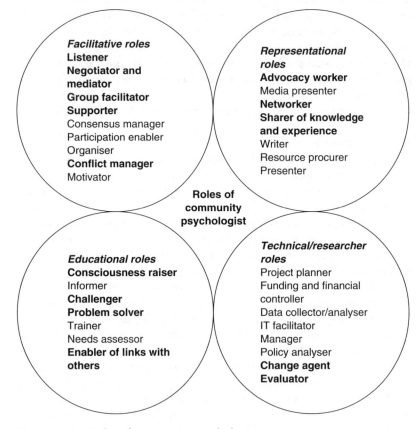

Figure 12.1   Roles of community psychologists

In our work, we engage in a constant cycle of doing, learning and critical reflection, and try to encourage others to adopt a similar approach to change. Thus, doing without understanding or reflection is not enough. As community psychologists we strive to make sense and learn from what it is that we do, and we strive to follow our understanding and knowledge with action. The three components of activity are inseparable and can be summed up as a *critical praxis*. Figure 12.2 summarises the skills that are linked to community psychology roles, with an understanding of the complex context framing these skills, and self-awareness, critical reflection and critical praxis at their core. It makes more sense to view these skills as developing through a constant process of learning, rather than as skills that can be acquired or not.

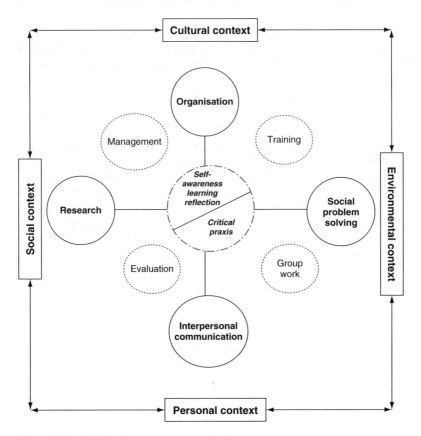

Figure 12.2 Skills of community psychology

Conclusion

In this chapter we have argued that when working with people, inclusion not marginalisation, power sharing not professional diagnosis and so on can change the ways psychologists work. At the heart of this approach is a commitment to a reflexive stance that works with capability not disability. A community psychological approach pushes participation, whilst simultaneously stressing the attitudinal, ideological and legislative contexts that affect lives. Shifting the focus away from individuals with impairment, poor education, low IQ, poor functional abilities or problematic family dynamics, community psychology engages with social systems. We hope to engage others in using principles of community psychology to de-expertise psychology and to encourage professionals to think about the transparency of the relationships they engage in.

These can be summarised as follows: assumptions about causes of problems (malfunction in psychosocial problems does not reside in individuals, but most often in interpersonal, contextual and social relationships, including social settings and systems); multiple levels of analysis (ranging from macro-factors – including environmental, cultural, political and economic factors to micro-factors – including affective, cognitive and motivational factors); pluralistic research methods (with an emphasis on qualitative research and action research); locations of practice (in the real world, based on people's lived experiences); collaborative approaches to planning services (grounded in people's experiences and creating opportunities for inclusion); practice emphasis (prevention rather than treatment); sharing psychology (taking every opportunity to share knowledge and understanding and to learn from others); and working with non-professionals (including community groups).

Chapter 13

Conclusions: Making Enabling Alliances between Disability Studies and Psychology

Rebecca Lawthom and Dan Goodley

Introduction

One of the pioneers of British disability studies, Len Barton (2004), has argued that social exclusion, of which disability/disablement is one element, has many compounding forms of differing exclusions; is not a natural but a socially constructed process; has no single factor that can remove it and is in constant need of conceptual analysis. This book addresses some of these analytical considerations. Part I shed light on the process of disablement from infancy to adulthood: conceptualising these stages not as deviations from normal development stages but as encounters with the social processes of disability and exclusion. Part II took up the challenge of theorising and changing disablement, via forms of psychology, by working alongside rather than on or against disabled people. All contributors capture the inherent contradiction of disablement: where there is oppression, there is also resistance. All are mindful of the ingrained institutionalised discrimination faced by disabled people. All recognise that simply challenging psychological practice will not overturn the exclusion of disabled people. Yet, in making alliances between psychology and disability studies, we feel that some significant ideas and practices can be elicited which chip away at disablement. In this final chapter of the book, we identify some key objectives that need to be addressed by a psychology that aims to promote the analytical qualities and emancipatory aims of disability studies.

Rethink impairment

Psychology's preoccupation with the rehabilitation of impairment is disturbed by the contributions to this book. Instead, a case is made for psychology adopting understandings of impairment that are in direct contrast to the pathological views of current society. We are reminded here of Abberley's (1987) and Hughes and Paterson's (1997) classic texts in which they argued for the development of social theories of impairment. The task for both disability studies and psychology is to unravel the complex social relations that intertwine the perception, moulding and construction of impairment. Tregaskis, Chapter 2, demonstrates the need for a psychology of impairment that locates analysis in family dynamics and the familial discourse of parents and children. This sensitises us to the ways in which environments can work with children with impairments as opposed to fitting in with existing professional discourses on impairment. As Tregaskis points out, having the diagnosis of Cerebral Palsy (CP) allowed her and her family to get on with life. Getting on with life is not the same as adjusting to the 'tragedy' of impairment. It is about learning to know aspects of one's lifeworld and the possibilities of lives to be lived. Todd, Chapter 10, draws attention to the ways in which British society is increasingly caught up in the creation of educational practices that fail to recognise the nuanced lives of children. From the rich variety of ways in which children differ, certain differences become exaggerated and understood as more important than others. Impairment is often over-emphasised and ripped out of its rich relational context. Stannett, Chapter 3, talks about the 'can't do' attitude of psychology in relation to supporting disabled psychologists. This neatly coins a phrase for what has been termed 'deficit thinking': where disabled people are viewed solely in terms of the perceived pathologies of their impairments. Murray, Chapter 3, suggests that if a support worker or educator holds fixed ideas about impairment that deny alternative ways of being, then this can have massive impacts on the person being supported (Goodley, 2001). This is clearly evident in the student case studies provided by Viney, Chapter 4, where students are forced to use their impairment labels in order to access funds for education. Students are compelled by the system to declare their impairment, have it individualised, objectified, assessed and measured in order to receive support. Over-identification with individualised constructs of impairment become compulsory in order for students to participate. Rather than talking of access requirements – which broadens the responsibilities of Higher Education Institutions (HEIs) to all students – the usage of individualistic constructions of impairment continues to separate students with disabilities from their non-disabled peers. It also places responsibilities on individuals, rather than on institutions and the wider net of support practices. Note too the professional coping strategies employed by Levison and Paritt, Chapter 8, in response to the discriminatory thinking of colleagues and clients. Tregaskis, Chapter 2, also alerts us to the ways in which impairment labels hunt in groups. Certain psychological theories and practices are notorious in promoting groupings of pathologies – a phenomenon known as co-morbidity – which further locates understandings of impairment in the deficient individual.

This individualistic thinking about impairment is at odds with the complex meanings of humanity promoted by various branches of psychology. It seems that when impairment is considered then only simplified bio-psychological theories are adopted. But, as any psychology graduate knows, numerous psychological stories can be drawn upon to make sense of humanity. Impairment can be thought of in more relational, familial, social, cultural, historical and political ways. Tregaskis, Chapter 2, remembers a childhood encounter with an orthopaedic surgeon who greeted her as a complex person with typical aspirations (who so happened to have the label of CP). The assumptions at play here appear to resonate with a psycho-emotional vision of impairment and disability, introduced by Reeve in Chapter 7. This raises the question: What psychological theories can be adopted to provide enabling understandings of impairment? We return later to the value of different theories, but there is a question of epistemology to keep in mind. If psychologists only view impairment from an individualistic stance then this not only limits the socio-cultural ambitions of disability studies but also promotes bad psychology – drawing as it does on a simplistic biogenic vision of the individual. This point is taken up, not without controversy, by Clegg in Chapter 9, who argues that simplistic usages of the social model are in danger of downplaying the complex barriers faced by people with 'severe' learning difficulties. Generally, however, the contributions to this book pinpoint a key element of making alliances between psychology and disability studies: refuting the notion that impairment is a naturalised given. As Kagan *et al.* argue, Chapter 12, psychology needs to place individuals within their historical, cultural, environmental and political contexts. In doing so, impairment is not only a phenomenon of social scientific debate but an aspect of social identity that can be celebrated (as one aspect of human diversity) rather than mourned (as a tragic deviation from the human norm).

Recognise and resist the elusive psychological elements of disablement

British disability studies was founded on materialist sociological theories of the social world. These foundations are crucial. They continue to allow disabled activists and researchers to unpick the structural and institutional bases of the social exclusion of people with impairments. The contributions to this book recognise how these structures are implicated in disablement but also add (social) psychological flesh to the materialist bones of disability studies. Reeve, Chapter 7, notes that the psycho-emotional dimensions of disability include being stared at or patronised by strangers. These actions can leave disabled people feeling worthless and ashamed and may end up preventing them from participating in society as effectively as physically inaccessible environments. Indeed, for some disabled people, for example people with learning difficulties or mental health system survivors, disablement is fundamentally built upon the rejection of their very personhood as it is so directly associated with impairment (Goodley, 2001, 2004; Wilson and Beresford, 2002). This is seen in professional encounters (Reeve and Tregaskis) and community and mainstream settings (Murray, Todd, Kagan *et al.*). The psychological consequences of exclusion can be massive.

Disability studies has long understood these consequences in terms of internalised oppression (Swain *et al.*, 1993). This concept has proved useful to the disabled people's movement: particularly in promoting the realisation that psycho-emotional difficulties are less to do with impairment and more to do with living in an unequal society. But what of the subtle forms of oppression that might occur even as a consequence of seemingly inclusive practices? Psychological analysis can be a very useful resource in accounting for the often elusive psychological experiences of disablement. Viney's account, Chapter 4, is not simply an account of HEI's institutional barriers but of young disabled people swimming against a tide of alienating assessment and mind-numbing bureaucracy. Murray, Chapter 3, alerts us to the psychological pain that can be caused by everyday experiences of rejection in schools that purport to be inclusive. Todd's analysis, Chapter 10, highlights subjective experiences of disability discourses that inhabit educational spaces and the assumptions that underpin (some) educational professionals' practice. In Chapter 6, Priestley notes how modernist discourses of adulthood, which emphasising values like independence, productivity, youth and progress, devalue both older people and disabled people as non-adult dependants. Psychological knowledge can be utilised in disability studies to understand *and* challenge the psychological experiences of exclusion. Psychological theories of subjectivity can be drawn upon to display the consequences of, for example, nuanced education (Murray and Todd), gerontology practice (Priestley) and marginalised communities (Kagan *et al.*), which subtly but nonetheless significantly exclude young and old disabled people. Social psychological theories of in/out group processes illuminate those products of mythical 'inclusive school practices' that continue to separate disabled children from their peers via 'empowering' professional mentoring systems. Most significantly, psychological theories can further demonstrate that the shame of exclusion should not be felt by disabled people but by institutions who continue to discriminate. Psychological theory can be a further ally in disability studies' engagement with the social relations of disablement.

Promote socially valued understandings of disabled identities

This book offers an antidote to the dehumanising consequences of psychological reductionism. The representation of disabled scholars parallels the established organic intellectualism of the disability studies (Oliver, 1990). Other non-disabled contributors have attempted throughout to call open the expertise and experience of disabled people. However, not all contributions have been affirming. They have reported on the ways in which personalities of disabled children and adults are framed in terms of spurious concepts of abnormality. Impairment means lacking personalities. Murray, Chapter 3, draws attention to the apartheid within schools which threatens the person-hood of disabled children. The analyses offered by Stannett (Chapter 5) and Levinson and Parritt (Chapter 8) – qualified and practising (disabled) psychologists – display the discrimination that widely exists in the psychology community. Their accounts tell of professional identities being relegated. Their perceived identities as 'tragic people with disabilities' are promoted. Priestley, Chapter 6, reminds us that while disabled identities are as complex as non-disabled identities, disabled people often face further barriers when socially perceived 'weak identities' merge together (old and disabled).

This text also promotes valued understandings. Todd, Chapter 10, highlights the ways in which (disabled) children inhabit a *number* of 'thick' identities. This multiplicity of identity positions is often ignored by professionals and researchers when conceptualising disability. The implications seem to be that disabled people are, well, disabled. Yet, Tregaskis, Chapter 2, makes a crucial point that disabled people do not simply take as given their impairment labels nor the professional interventions that they receive. Indeed, for many disabled people, challenging professional intervention and knowledge is a crucial part of developing a positive identity. Children (in Todd's chapter) articulate a complex sense of disability. Murray, Chapter 3, argues that we can only begin to listen, in any meaningful sense of the word, when we acknowledge the reality of another's internal experience. We need to acknowledge the many identities that are the mark of humanity. Yet, the valuing of different identities should not be reduced to the recognition of individual complexity. Identities are also relational. Swain *et al.*, Chapter 11, associate good practice of counselling in terms of the identities that are formed through the relationships that exist between counsellor and client. Clegg, Chapter 9, advocates the use of systemic interventions in clinical practice, with clients with the label of learning difficulties, in order to consistently view the client as a related being: reliant, as we all are, on family, support and friends. Kagan *et al.*, Chapter 12, pinpoint the raison d'etre of community psychology – working with people and their communities. Identities and their relational components are conceived as resources for the doing of enabling psychological practice. Finally, in valuing disabled identities we also question the values and affiliations of psychologists. The values of social justice, equality, respect, democracy, autonomy and justice seem most readily able to inform an alliance between disability studies and psychology (Kagan *et al.*). Even, within the scope of this text (where a common underpinning framework around disability is assumed) differences emerge in relation to labelling disability and tensions between help and care versus support and advocacy. (Clegg)

Assume an active/activist vision of person

As far back as 1947, Gordon Allport argued that psychology was in danger of creating a victimised view of the individual. This version of the individual as a mindless human subject ready to be controlled by authority and shaped by the irrationality of social groups was exemplified by the classic studies of Asch (1951) and Milgram (1983). Parker (1989) argues that this conception of humanity typifies a psychological stance that conceptualises people as the passive recipients of more powerful social influences. In contrast, much social psychological research has been undertaken to rethink this concept of the individual. As Kagan *et al.* suggest, Chapter 12, individuals are not just products of their environments but also agents of change. Disabled people are recognised in these ways by the contributors. Disabled people and their allies are engaged in resistant practices. Tregaskis and Murray (Chapters 2 and 3) report on how disabled children and their parents devise strategies to cope with the disabling world. Families often collectively challenge disabling discourses. The personal is political and many of the narratives presented in this book display political actions to discrimination and exclusion. Stannett's career biography, Chapter 5, maps periods of repeated rejection but also huge personal resilience. Disability studies emerged not as a consequence of well-meaning academics and practitioners but as a result of the power and potency of the disabled people's movement (Barnes and Mercer, 2003). The Disability Discrimination Act (DDA) legislation identified by Viney (Chapter 4) and Levinson and Parritt (Chapter 5) would not have been produced without the direct action, lobbying and input of organisations of disabled people. Alternative forms to mainstream psychology, such as community and critical perspectives, see the self as potentially transformative through action, language and meaning-making. The person is inherently a social, political and potentially resistant being. Hence, while disabling structures do impact upon the life chances of people, oppression also brings with it resistance. Here, psychology has the potential to promote resistant understandings of personhood which should be the ontological choice of its practitioners. (Disabled) people are not passive recipients of psychological practice. Psychology must work from an assumption of competence, capacity and comrardary. Clegg, Chapter 9, raises some concerns about the promotion of empowerment. Too often self-empowerment is considered as a marker of independence rather than as a product of resilient relationships as described by Kagan *et al.*, Chapter 12. There are real opportunities here for combining the structuralist analyses of disability studies with some of the more agentic commentaries of psychology.

Acknowledge the complex relationship between individual and social worlds

The bringing together of disability studies and psychology opens up ways of addressing the complex dynamics between individual and social worlds. A structuralist view of disability which considers only the public material and structural constraints of the social world is in danger of ignoring the complex construction of private life (Thomas, 2004). A psychological view of disability that emphasises only the individual experiences of people with impairments fails to contend with the troubles of a wider disabling world. Swain *et al.*, Chapter 11, confront these two competing epistemological positions in their discussion of counselling. They note that while counsellors may state an objective of humanistic, holistic interpretation this often sterilises the counselling room of wider social, political and cultural factors. For Olkin and Pledger (2003), too much clinical and counselling practice prescribes a narrowing of perspective to the individual rather than the environment. Tregaskis, Chapter 2, records the ways in which disabled children are treated within the health service. The social unit of the family is given scant regard as the individual child forms the main unit of analysis and assessment. In Chapter 3, Murray's Table 3.1, p. 40, captures some of the effects of exclusion, including depression, feeling useless, lacking confidence, being stressed, expressing anger. These emotions and experiences are the bread and butter of psychological intervention. But they are often theorised as individualised states in need of amelioration rather than the products of living with impairment in exclusionary environments. Similarly, the legislative context around HEIs, explicated in Viney's Chapter 4, highlights the ways in which state support such as the Disabled Student's Allowance tackles individuals' needs. Meanwhile, the wider context of the establishment and their barriers remain intact. It is essential to pitch student experiences in this cocktail of individualistic support and institutional barriers. In Chapter 6, Priestley, we see that these constructions of bodily impairment and aging are generationally situated and experienced individually. Levinson and Parritt, Chapter 8, point out that much training in professional psychology is meted out on an individual level and fails to understand the culturally grounded nature of psychology. In Chapter 9, Clegg argues that most clinicians do not believe that all people with intellectual disability can escape the emotionally distressing experiences that underpin risky or chaotic behaviour. Some have had long histories within various care systems and probably have been damaged by them, but the insecure relationships, neglect and abuse that usually result in children being taken into care are not likely to disappear in the immediate future. Clegg's clinical response to aggression, for example, draws on multiple sources and shifting levels and domains. The complexity of humanity is viewed in relational and person-centred ways recognising that from the outset individual and social worlds collide. Kagan *et al.*, Chapter 12, argue that community psychology aims to address social and individual change, both of the external agents (people of a community) and the external agents (psychologists and other professionals) of transformation. Such a vision of psychology parallels the complex relationship of individual and social worlds as they intersect in challenging disabling society. The disabled people's movement boasts a history of political and personal change (Campbell and Oliver, 1996). How psychology can work alongside disabled people to further enhance such transformative processes is a crucial question raised by the contributors to this text.

Work towards enabling psychological practices

Finkelstein and French (1993) maintain that most people remain confused about defining disability, not least psychologists. The way in which disability is conceptualised determines the intervention of psychologists. The growth of the disability movement and the progress it has made has produced a significant corpus of expert knowledge. Psychological practice therefore needs to be a collaborative activity with this knowledge, disabled people and their communities. Tregaskis, Chapter 2, observes that the parents of disabled babies she worked with gained so much from voluntary parent groups. This reiterates a common practice now of psychological professionals working alongside voluntary groups. Revisioning forms of psychological reality on the part of disabled children appears to be crucial, in the light of the denial of such realities by educational contexts and professionals (Murray, Chapter 3). Professional boundaries and psychology careers need exploring in the light of Stannett's account (Chapter 4) and Levinson and Parritt's reflections (Chapter 8) that 'we have met colleagues, who are good psychologists, in the sense that they are able to form positive work relationships with disabled co-workers without feeling threatened, or even uncomfortable'. For Kagan *et al.*, enabling psychological practice takes place both within professional services and outside of the confines of psychological institutions. Many disabled people's interactions with psychologists will be in service and community settings. In such contexts, disabled people continue to be excluded from decision-making about the services that they receive. It is little wonder why the disability movement, rather than the service setting, has become the preferred place of residence for many disabled people. Yet, the number of psychologists who are involved in the lives of disabled people continues to grow rapidly. For many of the contributors to this book, enabling psychological practice emerges only when community, activist and service settings are transcended together; when disabled people are fully collaborating in the services and practice that they are being offered; when disabled people are represented as psychologists and consultants and when the values of psychologists and disabled people are shared. The wider backdrop to changing practices is a messy landscape where service provision occurs within complex systems. Todd, Clegg and Kagan *et al.* show that health, care and education systems are subject to professional boundaries and institutional, governmental priorities which are shifting and refocusing all the time. Despite this, many authors assert enabling, transformative practices to be the central agenda.

Transform institutions

Institutions that provide psychological training and employment are microcosms of wider disabling society. Stannett, Chapter 5, illuminates the barriers that disabled psychologists face. Choose a field where there is no history of people working in a field and it is much more difficult to enter and therefore apparently support a disabled person (Levinson and Parritt, Chapter 8). The inclusion of disabled people in educational and professional contexts is important, not only because institutions become more inclusive but also because diversity is a professional as well as human resource (Barton, 2004; Rieser, 2004). For Swain *et al.*, Chapter 11, an increase in disabled counsellors would enable attitudes to change. For Levinson and Parritt, Chapter 8, environmental adaptations benefit not only disabled psychologists but clients as well. Stannett's experiences indicate that psychologists (working in clinical or organisational practice) need to look more carefully at their ethical codes. While disability is rarely mentioned in these codes (potential) disabled psychologists face obstacles which are multilayered, personal, political and institutionalised. Todd, Chapter 10, illustrates the complexity of discrimination within the cultures of educational institutions. Todd depicts intra-service contexts in which labelling, classification and assessment abound. Clearly, in aiming to transform psychology into an allied profession and discipline of disability studies, wider socio-economic, political and cultural concerns are raised. Viney's Chapter 4 reminds us that the continuation of inadequate legislation and funding of HEIs will undoubtedly fail to support the development of inclusive centres of learning in which students with disabilities can flourish in the same ways that the non-disabled peers are supported to do so. The Community Psychology approach advocated by Kagan *et al.* posits an ecological understanding of marginalisation, where macro-structures and micro-experiences collide. Psychologists need to agitate and argue for institutional changes in order to oppose disabling society.

Promote a psychology of inclusion

Barton (2004) advocates that as critical (educational) researchers we need to (re)explore our key concepts; (re)examine where we are theoretically; (re)consider our models of citizenship and ask what our educational (or, in this case, psychological) institutions are for. Olkin and Pledger (2003) and Levinson and Parritt, Chapter 8 of this book, suggest that if psychologists are going to be culturally competent in working with disabled people then their training should reflect the state of knowledge about disability promoted by the discipline of disability studies in which such knowledge is synthesised and explicated.

Psychological practice must engage with inclusion. Psychologists working in institutional, professional and community spaces should ask:

- What is my understanding of impairment and disability?
- Can my theoretical and professional knowledge help to challenge conditions of disablement?
- How do I understand inclusion and exclusion?
- What role do I play in the exclusion and inclusion of disabled people?
- How do I see disabled people – as active or tragic beings?
- Am I a hindrance or help to the furthering of inclusion?
- What is the aim of my work and how can it contribute to the aims of disability studies, the disability community and disabled people's movement?

This book has only started to answer these questions. Murray, Chapter 3, maintains that education for disabled children is largely one of absence. The 'bottom line' for inclusion lies in (disabled) children being accepted for whom they are by those who support and educate them. Here psychology has much to offer – in terms of promoting empathic forms of practice, of augmenting self and identity through pedagogy and social/health care by undoing the normalising principles of education for the majority rather than for all. The challenge, as we see it, is for psychology to address educational disablement – the exclusion of disabled children and adults – as an immediate and ongoing concern. Rather than seeing inclusion as impacting negatively upon other non-disabled children, inclusion should be seen as positively enriching knowledge and understanding. Ideas around distributed competence (Bird, 1999) present a classroom of selves with distributed ability rather than 'clever' and 'thick' individuals. Education at tertiary level is undoubtedly a struggle (Tregaskis, Stannett and Viney). While access has been granted inclusion is yet to be attained. Reeve's stories, Chapter 7, of non-disabled students avoiding other students with disabilities in case they might be needed to offer help suggests that models of independence at every level of education require critique.

For Todd, Chapter 10, inclusion can only be tackled when one considers the theoretical basis of professional practice. Reflexivity and theoretical resources need interrogating if professionals are to move beyond 'professional thought disorder' – an obsessive classification disorder. Levinson and Parritt, Chapter 8, advocate that disability equality training is formalised across psychology and educational provision and that mentoring systems enable access and progression for disabled people through education and employment. Furthermore, we need to put disability in context (Olkin and Pledger, 2003). Disabled people do not constitute a homogeneous group and their lives intersect the relations of 'race', class, sexuality and gender (see, for example, Morris, 1991, 1993, 1996; Stuart, 1993; Davidson-Payne and Corbett, 1995; Shakespeare and Gillespie-Sells, 1996; Tremain, 1996; Vernon, 1996; Sheldon, 1999; Stone, 1999; Thomas, 1999). Inclusion is not simply a buzz word for the disability industry. A psychology of inclusion should create a psychology that is amenable to diversity. Indeed, the Community Psychology agenda proposed by Kagan *et al.* (Chapter 14) stresses a wider social justice agenda where inequality is systematically tackled.

Critique therapeutic assumptions

It is not our intention here to provide a comprehensive critique of counselling and therapy (see instead Masson, 1990; Parker, 1997). Clearly, though, in assessing psychology from a disability studies perspective, there is an urgent need for therapy to undo a widely held assumption that pathologises people simply on the basis of impairment. Stannett, Chapter 5, identifies inherent problems with therapeutic or counselling services. His account unfolds a version of professionalism in which deviation from the norm is viewed with suspicion and in terms of lacking professional credibility. This is worrying and mirrors some of the critical writings of Omanksy Gordon (2002) in reflecting upon the training of disabled scholars and counsellors which argues that disabled 'students should not have to lose their own stories in favour of anyone else's worldview' (ibid., p. 37). While not necessarily advancing an argument for ontological priviledge – being disabled will inevitably make you better at understanding disability issues than a non-disabled counsellor – we should be reminded that disabled counsellors bring with them a wealth of knowledge that can open up the diversity of psychological practice and value the significance of alternative (life) stories and identities. Marks (2002) reflects upon her own experiences as a psychoanalytic researcher and therapist. Many disabled people that she spoke with about therapy reported that therapists and counsellors tended to frame all their experiences purely in terms of their impairments. Yet, many students with disabilities on her Masters Programme in Disability studies in the Centre for Psycho-therapeutic Studies at the University of Sheffield in the 1990s did not reject the psychological principle of reflecting on experience, but rather objected to the disabling theories and practices. In contrast, Clegg (Chapter 9) promotes a form of therapeutic intervention that builds an enabling meta-perspective, a position from which clients and carers can put the issue into proportion, allowing them to create different ways to respond to one another. This relational concept has many similarities with the interdependent literature in disability studies (Reindal, 1999). Rather than viewing distress or need as necessarily tragic or pathological, Clegg, Chapter 9, recognises distress as something potentially experienced by anyone and a phenomenon to be tackled through a consideration of how the selves are distributed across different environments. For people who occupy a number of service-based contexts, then therapeutic conditions need to be sensitised to the institutionalised restrictions imposed upon people's lives. In Chapter 11, Swain *et al.* tentatively conclude that counselling may well be one route towards confidence building and esteem raising. However, wider questions need to be asked about the epistemological bases of therapeutic interventions into the lives of disabled people.

Seek radical psychological theories

Does disability studies need psychology? Clearly, when psychology disables then it is at odds with the emancipatory aims of disability studies. But the issue is not simply a practical one. All of the contributions to this text raise the question – which psychological theories allow us to understand and challenge the conditions of disablement? Reeve, Chapter 7, illuminates psycho-emotional aspects of disability. But what psychological theories could be used to understand these social and affective components of disablement? In the therapeutic context, as highlighted by Swain and French in Chapter 11, many psychological theories have been embraced throughout the history of counselling and therapy. The question to ask ourselves, then, is which theoretical/disciplinary positions promote enabling understandings and practices for the betterment of disabled people? Olkin and Pledger's (2003) thinking is helpful here, in terms of unpicking the epistemological grounds of theory (Table 13.1):

Paradigm 1 underpins much rehabilitative and mainstream psychological thinking about disability, while paradigm 2 is indicative of a disability studies perspective. Clegg asks whether a psychology of disability can graduate beyond the medical model – or paradigm 1 – in a united, theoretically strong manner? The diversity of positions represented in this book suggest that unity is not the same as homogeneity of theory. Rather, we need to ask:

- Do our theories allow us to understand impairment as a part of personhood rather than being the essence of disabled people?
- Do our psychological theories allow us to unpack the social construction of disability?
- Do our theories support the principle of systematic study and elimination of disablement?
- Do our theories support conceptions of disability and impairment that are socially, politically, historically, culturally and relationally sensitive?
- Do our theories promote hopes for an inclusive society rather than an acceptance of the current status quo?
- Do our theories connect with other radical social theories of critical theory, feminism, critical race, queer theory and post-structuralism in order to theorise and change conditions of alienation and marginalisation?
- Will our theories be resources for the activism of disabled people and the radical practices of practitioners?

Table 13.1 Two paradigms of disability thinking

Paradigm 1	Paradigm 2
Is based on a medical model of disability	Is based on a social model or the new paradigm of disability
Is pathology oriented	Shifts to a systemic and societal perspective
Views differences due to disability (impairment) as deficits or developmental aberrations	Takes a lifespan approach
Is usually cross-sectional	Uses concept of 'response' to disability as a fluid process
Sees people with disabilities (impairments) and their families as at high risk for difficulties	Promotes health and resilience
Focuses predominantly on intrapsychic, personal characteristics or intrapersonal variables	Values disability history and culture
Research on disabled people – which is more likely to be inpatient or treatment settings	Research with disabled people – Incorporates those being researched into the research process
Uses concept of 'adjustment' or 'adaptation' to disability	Sees the major problems of disability as social, political, economic, legal
Uses norms based on non-disabled/able-bodied individuals for comparison	Is grounded in the belief that those with impairments have been denied their civil rights
Is about, but rarely, disabled people	Is usually not just about, but by, disabled people
Perpetuates a we–they model	Seeks remedies in public policy, legislation and systemic programmatic changes

Source: Adapted from Olkin and Pledger, 2003, p. 301.

As Todd notes, we need to move beyond professional thought disorder and its connected ideology of disablement. The contributors to this book offer alternative theoretical resources to those associated with paradigm 1 including systemic, narrative, community, critical, educational, sociological and social psychology. This suggests, to us, that numerous psychological theories share the aims of paradigm 2. For example, a number of chapters in this book touch upon the issue of learning in schools, higher education and professional practice. Psychological theories of learning that readily embrace Vygotskian ideas (see Vygotsky, 1978; Faulkner *et al.*, 1998) promote an environmental view of learning; located understanding in line with the tenets of paradigm 2. Using Vygotsky's zones of proximal development we are drawn to the ways in which collaboration enhances potential. Too often educational systems are organised around individualised activities (such as tests, outcomes, assessment, statementing, etc.) where independence is stressed over interdependence. Vygotsky's theories allow us to consider how impairment is exploited by some educational professionals to justify not working collaborative and inclusively with disabled children. This pitches understanding of the disabled learner in his/her social cultural environment. In this sense, then, it is possible to draw upon psychological theories that are in tune with a disability studies perspective. In Chapter 1 we considered a number of sources of critical theories including discursive psychology, social constructionism, critical psychology and radical psychoanalysis. Each of these positions attends to the ways in which psychological concepts construct and create as they are used in psychological intervention. It is crucial, therefore, for both psychology and disability studies to attend to those wider questions of how theories constitute particularly epistemological and ontological versions of the individual and society. While what we know may be limited, it is not negligible. The different theoretical psychological positions represented in this book bring with them, to varying extents, a vision of disability as (1) social, cultural, political, material, discursive and relational exclusion and (2) a recognition of the resistance of disabled people. These starting points therefore raise questions about the role of research.

Develop emancipatory research practices

The field of disability studies has a long history of promoting research practices that work alongside and with disabled people (Special issue, *Disability, Handicap and Society*, 7(2), 1992; Zarb, 1992; Stone and Priestley, 1996; Barnes, 1997; Oliver and Barnes, 1997; Clough and

Barton, 1998; Goodley and Lawthom, 2005). The underpinning assumptions of the social model of disability have led to a number of core research issues, including:

- *Inclusion* – more and more disabled researchers involved in academia.
- *Accountability* – the disabled people's movement demands researchers and academics to be accountable to the experiences and aims of disabled people, reflected in the slogan 'Nothing about us, without us'.
- *Praxis* – theories of disability emerge from an engagement with the changing nature of disabled people's lives.
- *Dialectical* – research *draws* and *builds* upon the social model of disability.
- *Ontological knowledge* – disabled people understand the conditions of disablement and impairment.
- *Disablement rather than impairment* – disability research should engage with the material, social, cultural, relational and political conditions of disablement.
- *Partisan* – research(ers) are on the side of disabled people.

These issues are, of course, contestable and have provoked major debate in the disability studies literature. What we would hope to see is psychology adopting these considerations in its research practices. Psychology has a history of doing research on disabled people. This cannot be accepted without engagement with research issues that have been raised by disabled people. Ethically sound research is not simply about following professional guidelines on anonymity, confidentiality, withdrawal and the avoidance of distress in research. Ethical research is also about promoting an ethically sustainable vision of disability. Ethics brings with it considerations of values and politics in which the disabling world is changed to give way to more equitable social relationships. Any research endeavour that attempts to link psychology and disability must address these key issues. Furthermore, for psychology and disability studies to learn from one another it is essential that psychology builds relationships with disabled people, disabled professionals and representative organisations of disabled people, as well as the academic context of disability studies.

Conclusion

This book has attempted to bring together an emancipatory disability studies and some theories and practices from the discipline of psychology. We now live in a world of blurred disciplinary genres, competing forms of expertise and rapidly growing forms of human services. It is time for disability studies to engage critically with psychology.

References

AAMR (2002) *Mental Retardation: Definition, Classification, and Systems of Supports*, 10th edn. Washington: American Association on Mental Retardation.

Abberley, P. (1987) 'The concept of oppression and the development of a social theory of disability', *Disability, Handicap and Society*, 2(1), 5–21, reproduced in L. Barton and M. Oliver (1997) *Disability Studies: Past Present and Future*, Chapter 10. Leeds: The Disability Press.

Access to Health Records Act (1990). London: HMSO.

Alanen, L. (1994) 'Gender and generation: Feminism and the "child question"', in J. Qvortrup, M. Bardy, G. Sgritta and H. Wintersberger (eds), *Childhood Matters: Social Theory, Practice and Politics*. Aldershot: Avebury (pp. 27–42).

Albee, G. W. (1982) 'Preventing psychopathology and promoting human potential', *American Psychologist*, 37(9), 1043–1050.

Albrecht, G., Seelman, K. D. and Bury, M. (2001) *Handbook of Disability Studies*. New York: Sage.

Alexander, P. (2003) 'Inclusion: A reality at last', *Counselling and Psychotherapy Journal*, 14(10), 5–9.

Allen, J. (1999) *Actively Seeking Inclusion: Pupils with Special Needs in Mainstream Schools*. London: Falmer Press.

Allport, G. W. (1947) *The Use of Personal Documents in Psychological Science*. New York: Social Science Research Council.

American Psychological Association (2003) *Disability Mentoring Program APA*. Available (on-line) at http://www.apa.org/pi/cdip/mentoring/about.html; accessed 12 March.

Apple, M. (1995) *Education and Power*, 2nd edn. New York: Routledge.

Armstrong, D. (1995) *Power and Partnership in Education*. London: Routledge.

Armstrong, D., Galloway, D. and Tomlinson, S. (1993) 'The assessment of special educational needs and the proletarianisation of professionals', *British Journal of Sociology*, 14(4), pp. 399–408.

Asch, S. E. (1951) 'Effects of group pressure on the modification and distortion of judgements', in H. Gueszkow (ed.), *Groups, Leadership and Men*. Pittsburgh: Carnegie Press.

Ashforth, B. E. and Tomiuk, M. A. (2000) 'Emotional labour and authenticity: Views from service agents', in S. Fineman (ed.), *Emotion In Organizations*, 2nd edn. London: Sage Publications, pp. 184–203.

Aspis, S. (1997) 'Self-advocacy for people with learning difficulties: Does it have a future?' *Disability & Society*, 12(4), 647–654.

Association of Graduate Careers Advisory Services First Destination Survey of recent graduates (AGCAS FDS, 2004) Disabilities Task Group 'What Happens Next? A Report on the First Destinations of 2002 Graduates with Disabilities.' Available from http://www.agcas.org.uk.

Barnes, C. (1991) *Disabled People in Britain and Discrimination: A Case for Anti-Discrimination Legislation*. London: Hurst & Company, University of Calgary Press in Association with the British Council of Organisations of Disabled People.

Barnes, C. (1994) *Disabled people in Britain: A case for anti-discrimination legislation*, Chapter 10, 2nd edn. London: Hurst & Co.

Barnes, C. (1997) 'Disability and the myth of the independent researcher', in Shakespeare, T. (1997) *Rules of Engagement: Changing Disability Research*, both in L. Barton and M. Oliver (eds), *Disability Studies: Past Present and Future*. Leeds: Disability Press (available in the counter collection of the Edward Boyle Library).

Barnes, C. and Mercer, G. (1997) *Doing Disability Research*. Leeds: Disability Press.

Barnes, C. and Mercer, G. (2003) *Disability*. London: Blackwell.

Barnes, C., Mercer, G. and Shakespeare, T. (1999) *Exploring Disability: A Sociological Introduction*. Bristol: Polity Press.

Barnes, C., Oliver, M. and Barton, L. (eds) (2002) *Disability Studies Today*. Bristol: Polity Press.

Barton, L. (ed.) (2001) *Disability Politics and the Struggle for Change*. London: David Fulton.

Barton, L. (2004) 'Social inclusion and education: Issues and questions', Paper presented at the ESRC seminar *Towards Inclusion: Social Inclusion and Education*, 19 July, Institute of Education, London.

Beresford, P. and Campbell, J. (1994) 'Disabled people, service users, user involvement and representation', *Disability & Society*, 9(3), 315–325.

Berger, R. (1988) 'Learning to survive and cope with human loss', *Social Work Today*, 28 April, pp. 14–17.

Beveridge, M., Conti-Ramsden, G. and Leudar, I. (1997) *Language and Communication in People with Learning Disabilities*, 2nd edn. London: Routledge.

Biggs, S. (1997) 'Choosing not to be old? Masks, bodies and identity management in later life', *Ageing and Society*, 17, 553–570.

Billig, M. (1996) *Arguing & Thinking: A Rhetorical Approach to Social Psychology*. Cambridge: Cambridge University Press.

Billington. T. (2000) *Separating, Losing and Excluding Children: Narratives of Difference*. London: RoutledgeFalmer.

Bird, L. (1999) 'Towards a more critical educational psychology', *Annual Review of Critical Psychology*, 1(1), 21–33.

Bishop, B., Sonn, C., Fisher, A. and Drew, N. (2001) 'Community-based community psychology: Perspectives from Australia', in M. Seedat (ed.),

Community Psychology: Theory, Method and Practice. South African and Other Perspectives. Cape Town: Oxford University Press.

Blaikie, A. (1999) *Ageing and Popular Culture.* Cambridge: Cambridge University Press.

Booth, T. and Booth, W. (1994) *Parenting Under Pressure: Mothers and Fathers with Learning Difficulties.* Buckingham: Open University Press.

Brandon, D., Brandon, A. and Brandon, T. (1995) *Advocacy, Power to People with Disabilities.* Birmingham: Venture Press.

Breitenbach, N. (2001) 'Ageing with intellectual disabilities; discovering disability with old age: same or different?', in M. Priestley (ed.), *Disability and the Life Course: Global Perspectives.* Cambridge: Cambridge University Press, pp. 231–239.

Brindle, D. (2004) 'Private care for learning disabled people is a return to Victorian values', *The Guardian*, 4 August.

British Psychological Society (1998) *Code of Conduct, Ethical Principles and Guidelines.* Leicester: British Psychological Society.

British Psychological Society (2001) *Learning Disabilities: Definitions and Contexts.* Leicester: BPS.

Bronfenbrenner, U. (1979) *The Ecology of Human Development: Experiments by Nature and Design.* Cambridge, MA: Harvard University Press.

Brown, R., Bayer, M. and Brown, P. (1992) *Empowerment and Developmental Handicaps.* London: Chapman & Hall.

Bruyere, S. and O'Keefe, J. (eds) (1994) *Implications of the Americans with Disabilities Act for Psychology.* New York/Washington DC: Springer Publishing Company/American Psychological Association.

Burman, E. (1994) *Deconstructing Developmental Psychology.* London: Routledge.

Burman, E. and Parker, I. (eds) (1993) *Discourse Analytic Research: Repertoires and Readings of Texts in Action.* London: Routledge.

Burr, V. (1995) *An Introduction to Social Construction.* London: Routledge.

Burr, V. (2003) *Social Constructionism.* London: Psychology Press.

Burton, M. (1983) 'Understanding mental health services: Theory and practice', *Critical Social Policy*, 7, 54–74.

Burton, M. (2004) 'Decoding "Valuing People"', Paper presented at the UK Community Psychology Conference, Exeter. www.compsy.org.uk.

Burton, M. and Kagan, C. (1995) *Social Skills for People with Learning Disabilities.* London: Chapman & Hall.

Burton, M. and Kagan, C. (2003) 'Community psychology: Why this gap in Britain?', *History and Philosophy of Psychology*, 4(2), 10–23.

Bury, M. (1982) 'Chronic illness as biographical disruption', *Sociology of Health and Illness*, 4(2), 167–182.

Campbell, J. and Oliver, M. (1996) *Disability Politics: Understanding Our Past, Changing Our Future.* London: Routledge.

Carey, M. and Russell, S. (2002) 'Externalising – commonly asked questions', *The International Journal of Narrative Therapy and Community Work*, 2, 76–84.

Carnaby, S. (1997) 'A comparative approach to evaluating individual planning for people with learning disabilities: Challenging the assumptions', *Disability & Society*, 12(3), 381–394.

Carricaburu, D. and Pierret, J. (1995) 'From biographical disruption to biographical reinforcement – the case of HIV-positive men', *Sociology of Health and Illness*, 17(1), 65–88.

Cavet, J. (1998) *'People Don't Understand'*: *Children, Young People and Their Families Living with a Hidden Disability.* London: National Children's Bureau.

Chapireau, F. (2004) 'Environment in the classification of functioning, disability and health', *Journal of Intellectual Disability Research*, 48, 284.

Clay, R. (1999) *Four Psychologists Help Others to See.* Vol. 30, No. 3 http://www.apa.org/monitor/mar99/see.html.

Clegg, J. A. and Lansdall-Welfare, R. (2003) 'Death, disability and dogma', *Philosophy, Psychiatry, Psychology*, 10, 67–79.

Clough, P. and Barton, L. (eds) (1998) *Articulating with Difficulty: Research Voices in Special Education.* London: Paul Chapman Ltd.

Corker, M. and Davis, J. (2002) 'Portrait of Callum: The disabling of a childhood?', in R. Edwards (ed.), *Children, Home and School: Regulation, Autonomy or Regulation?* London: RoutledgeFalmer.

Corker, M. and French, S. (1999) *Disability Discourse.* Buckingham: Open University Press.

Corker, M. and Shakespeare, T. (eds) (2002) *Disability/Postmodernity: Embodying Disability Theory.* London: Continuum.

Corker, M., Davis, J. and Priestley, M. (2001) *Life as a Disabled Child: A Qualitative Study of Young People's Experiences and Perspectives* (www.mailbase.ac.uk/lists/disability-research/files/children.rtf.).

Craig, A. (2003) *Disability and Psychology Studies: Growing into Maturity?* available at http://www.transforming.cultures.uts.edu.au/.

Craig, P. and Greenslade, M. (1998) *First Findings from the Disability Follow-Up to the Family Resources Survey: Research Summary No. 5.* London: Analytical Services Division, Department of Social Security.

Cumming, E. and Henry, W. (1961) *Growing Old: The Process of Disengagement.* New York: Basic Books.

Cutler, D. and Taylor, A. (2003) *Expanding and Sustaining Involvement. A Snapshot of Participation Infrastructure for Young People Living in England* (Spring 2003) Commissioned by the Children and Young People's Unit, DfESCarnegie Young People Initiative.

Dalton, J. H., Elias, M. J. and Wandersman, A. (2001) *Community Psychology: Linking Individuals and Communities.* Belmont, CA: Wadsworth/Thomson Learning.

Davidson-Payne, C. and Corbett, J. (1995) 'A double coming out: Gay men with learning disabilities', *British Journal of Learning Disabilities*, 23, 147–151.

Dent, A. and Atherton, R. (2004) 'A sign of our times: clinical psychologists awareness, concerns and interests in supervising a deaf trainee', *Clinical Psychology*, 33.

Department of Health (2001a) *Children and Young People on Child Protection Registers: Year Ending 31 March 2001: England*. London: Department of Health.

Department of Health (2001b) *Valuing People: A New Strategy for Learning Disability in the 21st Century*. London: HMSO.

Disability Discrimination Act (1995) London: HMSO.

Disability Rights Commission (2000) *DRC Disability Briefing*. Retrieved June 2002, from the World Wide Web: http://www.drc-gb.org/drc/InformationAndLegislation/Page353.asp disabled person, one is observed to be one. *Disability & Society*, 18(2), 2003, 209–229.

Disability Rights Commission (2001) *Disability Discrimination Act 1995 Part 4: Code of Practice for Providers of Post 16 Education and Related Services* http://www.drc-gb.org/education/knowyourduties/highereducation.asp.

Disability Rights Commission (2002) Briefing, October 2002. Cited by *The Employers' Forum on Disability* webpage (http://www.employers-forum.co.uk/www/csr/sttn/sfacts/sfacts1.htm; download date 11.04.04).

Disability Rights Commission (2003) *Code of Practice for the elimination of discrimination in the field of employment against disabled persons or persons who have had a disability*.

Disability Rights Commission (various dates) Various guides relating to the DDA and education including "Learning and teaching". http://www.drc-gb.org.

Dowling, J. and Leibowitz, D. (1994) 'Evaluation of educational psychology services: Past and present', *Educational Psychology in Practice*, 9(4), 241–250.

Doyle, B. J. (2003) *Disability Discrimination: Law and Practice*, 4th edn. Bristol: Jordans Publishing Limited, p. 52.

Duckett, P. S. (2001) ' "Say what[?]": Lessons from the field of learning difficulty', in C. Murphy, J. Killick and K. Allan (eds), *Hearing the Users' Voice: Encouraging People with Dementia to Reflect on Their Experiences of Services*. Stirling: University of Stirling, Dementia Services Development Centre.

Duckett, P. S. (2002) 'Community psychology, millennium volunteers and UK higher education: A disruptive triptych?', *Journal of Community and Applied Social Psychology*, 12(2), 94–107.

Duffy, K. G. and Wong, F. Y. (1997) *Community Psychology*. Boston, MA: Allyn Bacon.

Duncan, N. (2003) 'Awkward customers? Parents and provision for special educational needs', *Disability & Society*, 18(3), 341–356.

Edgerton, R. B. (ed.) (1984) *Lives in Process*. Washington: American Association on Mental Deficiency (now AAMR).

Education Act (1981) *Special Educational Needs*. UK: Her Majesty's Stationery Office (now The Stationery Office).

Egan, G. (1985) *The Skilled Helper*. USA: Brooks/Cole Publishing Co.

Etherington, K. (ed.) (2002a) *Rehabilitation Counselling in Physical and Mental Health*. London: Jessica Kingsley.

Etherington, K. (ed.) (2002b) 'Narrative ideas and stories of disability', *Rehabilitation Counselling in Physical and Mental Health*. London: Jessica Kingsley.

Eurolink Age (1995) *The European Union and Older Disabled People*. Eurolink Age.

Farrar, V. (2003) 'What Happens Next? The Destinations of Disabled Graduates', Higher Education Funding Council for England funded project report, University of Newcastle.

Faulkner, D., Littleton, K. and Woodhead, M. (1998) *Learning Relationships in the Classroom*. London: Routledge.

Featherstone, M. and Hepworth, M. (1991) 'The mask of ageing and the postmodern lifecourse', in M. Featherstone, M. Hepworth and B. Turner (eds), *The Body, Social Process and Cultural Theory*. London: Sage.

Finkelstein, V. (1980) *Attitudes and Disabled People: Issues for Discussion*. New York: World Rehabilitation Fund.

Finkelstein, V. (1990) *Experience and Consciousness* [Internet]. Available from <http://www.leeds.ac.uk/disability-studies/archiveuk/finkelstein/expconsc.pdf> [Accessed 3 October 2003].

Finkelstein, V. (1991) 'Disability: An administrative challenge? (the health and welfare heritage)', in M. Oliver (ed.), *Social Work: Disabled People and Disabling Environments*. London: Jessica Kingsley, pp.19–39.

Finkelstein, V. and French, S. (1993) 'Towards a psychology of disability', in J. Swain, V. Finkelstein, S. French and M. Oliver (eds), *Disabling Barriers – Enabling Environments*. London: Sage and Open University Press, pp. 26–33.

Ford, D. and Lerner, R. (1992) *Developmental Systems Theory: An Integrative Approach*. London: Sage.

Ford, A. B., Haug, M. R., Stange, K. C., Gaines, A. D., Noelker, L. S. and Jones, P. K. (2000) 'Sustained personal autonomy: A measure of successful aging', *Journal of Aging and Health*, 12(4), 470–489.

Fox, D. and Prilleltensky, I. (eds) (1997) *Critical Psychology: An Introduction*. London: Sage.

Frank, A. W. (1992) 'The pedagogy of suffering', *Theory & Psychology*, 2, 467–486.

Frank, Robert G. and Elliott, Timothy R. (eds) (2000) *Handbook of Rehabilitation Psychology*. Washington, DC, US: American Psychological Association.

French, S. (1994) 'Disabled people and professional practice', in S. French (ed.), *On Equal Terms: Working with Disabled People*. Oxford: Butterman-Heinemann, pp. 103–118.

Frosch, S. (1999) *Politics of Psychoanalysis*. London: Palgrave.

Fulcher, G. (1989) *Disabling Policies? A Comparative Approach to Educational Policy and Disability.* London: Falmer Press.

Galloway, D., Armstrong, D. and Tomlinson, S. (1994) *The Assessment of Special Educational Needs: Whose Problem?* Harlow: Longman.

Gatchel, Robert J. and Weisberg, James N. (eds) (2000) *Personality Characteristics of Patients with Pain.* Washington, DC, US: American Psychological Association, pp. xii, 25–35. 311pp.

Gething, L. (1992) 'Judgements by health professionals of personal characteristics of people with a visible physical disability', *Social Science and Medicine*, 34, 809–815.

Gibson, D. (1996) 'Broken down by age and gender – "The problem of old women" redefined', *Gender and Society*, 10(4), 433–448.

Gilleard, C. and Higgs, P. (1998) 'Ageing and the limiting conditions of the body', *Sociological Research Online*, 3(4), U56–U70.

Gillingham, P. (1999) [Information Letter] *The Psychologist*, 12, 228.

Gleeson, B. (1999) *Geographies of Disability.* London: Routledge.

Gleeson, B. (2003) 'After deinstitutionalisation, do we still care?', Keynote address to *Imagination & Innovation*, 38th National Conference of ASSID, Brisbane.

Goffman, E. (1963) *Stigma: Notes on the Management of Spoiled Identity.* Englewood Cliffs, NJ: Prentice-Hall.

Goldner, V. (1998) 'The treatment of violence and victimization in intimate relationships', *Family Process*, 37, 263–286.

Goodley, D. (2000) *Self-Advocacy in the Lives of People with Learning Difficulties.* Buckingham: Open University Press (http://www.shef.ac.uk/inclusive-education/disabledbabies/).

Goodley, D. (2001) '"Learning difficulties", the social model of disability and impairment: Challenging Epistemologies', *Disability & Society*, 16(2), 207–231.

Goodley, D. (2004) '"Learning difficulties" in educational contexts: The life story of Gerry O'Toole' in C. Barnes and G. Mercer (eds), *Disability Policy and Practice: Applying the Social Model.* Leeds: Disability Press.

Goodley, D. and Lawthom, R. (2005) 'Epistemological journeys in participatory action research: Alliances between community psychology and disability studies', *Disability & Society*, 20(2), 135–152.

Greco, V. and Sloper, P. (2004) 'Care co-ordination and key worker schemes for disabled children: Results of a UK-wide survey', *Child: Care, Health and Development*, 30, 13–20.

Gregory, R. J. (2001) 'The spirit and substance of community psychology: Reflections', *Journal of Community Psychology*, 29(4), 473–485.

Hales, G. (1996) *Beyond Disability: Towards an Enabling Society.* London: Sage Publication Limited.

Halliday, J. and Asthana, S. (2004) 'The emergent role of the link worker: A study in collaboration', *Journal of Interprofessional Care*, 18(1), 17–28.

Hanlon, G. (1998) 'Professionalism as enterprise: Service class politics and the redefinition of professionalism', *Sociology*, 32, 43–64.

Hart, J. T. (1971) 'The inverse care law', *The Lancet*, 27 February.

Hasler, F. (1993) 'Developments in the disabled people's movement' in J. Swain, V. Finkelstein, S. French and M. Oliver (eds), *Disabling Barriers – Enabling Environments*. London: Sage.

Hatton, C. (1999) 'Staff Stress', in N. Bouras (ed.), *Psychiatric and Behavioural Disorders in Developmental Disabilities and Mental Retardation*. Cambridge: Cambridge University Press, pp. 427–438.

Heller, K., Price, R., Reinharz, S., Riger, S. and Wandersman, A. (1984) *Psychology and Community Change*, 2nd edn. Homewood, IL: Dorsey Press.

Higher Education Funding Council for England [HEFCE, 1999/2004] 'Guidance on base-level provision for disabled students in higher education institutions'. Available on-line at http://www.hefce.ac.uk/Pubs/hefce/1999/99_04.htm.

HMSO (1995) Disability Discrimination Act 1995. Available on-line at http://www.hmso.gov.uk/acts/acts1995/1995050.htm.

HMSO (2001) *Special Educational Needs and Disability Act 2001*. London: HMSO. Available on-line at http://www.hmso.gov.uk/acts/acts2001/20010010.htm.

Hobbs, C., Taylor, J. and Todd, L. (2000) 'Consulting with children and young people: Enabling educational psychologists to work collaboratively with children and young people', *Educational and Child Psychology*, 17(4), 107–115.

Holland, A. J. (2000) 'Ageing and learning disability', *British Journal of Psychiatry*, 176, 26–31.

Hollway, W. and Jefferson, T. (2000) *Doing Qualitative Research Differently: Free Association, Narrative and the Interview Method*. London: Sage Publications.

Hubert, J. (1991) *Homebound: Crisis in the Care of Young People with Severe Learning Difficulties*. London: King's Fund.

Hughes, B. (1999) 'The constitution of impairment: Modernity and the aesthetic of oppression', *Disability & Society*, 14(2), 155–172.

Hughes, B. and Paterson, K. (1997) 'The social model of disability and the disappearing body: Toward a sociology of impairment', *Disability & Society*, 12(2), 325–340.

Irwin, S. (1999) 'Later life, inequality and sociological theory', *Ageing and Society*, 19(6), 691–715.

Irwin, S. (2001) 'Repositioning disability and the life course: A social claiming perspective', in M. Priestley (ed.), *Disability and the Life Course: Global Perspectives*. Cambridge: Cambridge University Press, pp. 15–25.

Janicki, M. P., Dalton, A. J., Henderson, C. M. and Davidson, P. W. (1999) 'Mortality and morbidity among older adults with intellectual disability:

Health services considerations', *Disability and Rehabilitation*, 21(5–6), 284–294.

Kagan, C. (1997) *Regional Development for Inclusion: Community Development and Learning Disabled People in the North West of England*. Manchester: IOD Research Group.

Kagan, C. (2002) *Making the Road by Walking It*. Inaugural professonial lecture, Manchester Metropolitan University, 30 January 2002.

Kagan, C. and Burton, M. (2001) 'Critical Community Psychology Praxis for the 21st Century', Paper presented at the British Psychological Society Centennial Conference, Glasgow (see www.compsy.org.uk).

Kagan, C. and Burton, M. (2004) 'Marginalization', in G. Nelson and I. Prilleltensky (eds), *Community Psychology: In Pursuit of Liberation and Well-Being*. New York: Palgrave Macmillan.

Kagan, C. and Burton, M. (2005) 'Community psychological perspectives and work with people with learning difficulties', *Clinical Psychology*.

Kagan, C., Knowles, K. and Burton, M. (1995) 'Challenging the system: Advocacy for a person with complex needs who cannot speak for himself', Paper presented at the 1st International Conference of A.R.A.P.D.I.S.: *Psychosocial Rehabilitation in and with Communities*, Barcelona.

Kagan, C., Lewis, S. and Heaton, P. (1998) *Caring to Work: Accounts of Working Parents of Disabled Children*. London: Family Policy Studies Centre.

Keith, L. (1996) 'Encounters with strangers: The public's responses to disabled women and how this affects our sense of self', in J. Morris (ed.), *Encounters with Strangers: Feminism and Disability*. London: Women's Press, pp. 69–88.

Kennedy, J. and Minkler, M. (1998) 'Disability theory and public policy: Implications for critical gerontology', *International Journal of Health Services*, 28(4), 757–776.

Kennedy, M. (1996) 'Sexual abuse and disabled children', in J. Morris (ed.), *Encounters with Strangers: Feminism and Disability*. London: Women's Press, pp. 116–134.

Kilbane, J. and Sanderson, H. (2004) 'Understanding professional involvement in person centred planning styles and approaches: What and how?', *Learning Disability Practice*, 7(4), 16–20.

Kinsella, K. (2000) 'Demographic dimensions of global aging', *Journal of Family Issues*, 21(5), 541–558.

Kitchin, R. (1998) ' "Out of place", "knowing one's place": Space, power and the exclusion of disabled people', *Disability & Society*, 13(3), 343–356.

Kovel, J. (1988) *The Radical Spirit: Essays on Psychoanalysis and Society*. London: Free Association Books.

Kuhn, T. (1965) *The Structure of Scientific Revolutions*, reprinted 1996. London: Routledge.

Kurzban, R. and Leary, M. R. (2001) 'Evolutionary origins of stigmatization: The functions of social exclusion', *Psychological Bulletin*, 127, 187–208.

Labour Force Survey (Spring 2002) Cited by *The Employers' Forum on Disability* webpage (http://www.employers-forum.co.uk/www/csr/sttn/sfacts/sfacts1.htm; download date 11.04.04). The original source is the May 2002 Labour Force Survey Quarterly Supplement, Table 8; http://www.statistics.gov.uk/downloads/theme_labour/LFSQS_0502.pdf.

Laslett, P. (1989) *A Fresh Map of Life: The Emergence of the Third Age*. London: Weidenfeld and Nicolson.

Lawthom, R. (2004) *Managing Diversity: Narratives, Paradigms and Communities of Practice*. Unpublished PhD thesis, Manchester Metropolitan University.

Leveille, S. G., Resnick, H. E. and Balfour, J. (2000) 'Gender differences in disability: Evidence and underlying reasons', *Aging-Clinical and Experimental Research*, 12(2), 106–112.

Levine, M. and Perkins, D. V. (1997) *Principles of Community Psychology: Perspectives and Applications*. Oxford: Oxford University Press.

Lightfoot, J. and Sloper, P. (2003) 'Having a say in health: Involving disabled and chronically ill children and young people in health service development', *Children and Society*, 17, 277–290.

Linton, S. (1998) *Claiming Disability: Knowledge and Identity*. New York: New York University Press.

Longman, P. and Umansky, L. (eds) (2001) *The New Disability History: American Perspectives (History of Disability)*. New York: New York University Press.

Lucas, D. J. (1989) 'Implications for Educational Psychology Services of the Education Reform Act 1988', *Educational Psychology in Practice*, January, pp. 171–178.

Lupton, D. (1998) *The Emotional Self: A Sociocultural Exploration*, London: Sage Publications.

Lyotard, J. (1979) *The Postmodern Condition*. Paris: Minuit.

Maddox, G. L. (1994) 'Lives through the years revisited', *Gerontologist*, 34(6), 764–767.

Madge, N. and Fassam, M. (1982) *Ask the Children. Experiences of Physical Disability in the School Years. 'So what, I'm handicapped... who cares? Not me'*. London: Batsford Academic.

Mansell, J. and Beadle-Brown, J. (2004) 'Person-centred planning or person-centred action? Policy and practice in intellectual disability services', *Journal of Applied Research in Intellectual Disabilities*, 17, 1–9.

Marks, D. (1999) *Disability: Controversial Debates and Psychosocial Perspectives*. London: Routledge Ltd, p. 51.

Marks, D. (2002) 'Some concluding notes – healing the split between psyche and social: Constructions and experiences of disability', *Disability Studies Quarterly*, 22(3), 46–52.

Marsh, P., Rosser, E. and Harré, R. (1978) *The Rules of Disorder*. London: Routledge.

Martin, J., Meltzer, H. and Elliot, D. (1988) *The Prevalence of Disability Amongst Adults*. London: HMSO.

Martin-Baró, I., Aron, A. and Corne, S. (1994) *Writings for a Liberation Psychology*. Belknap: Harvard University Press.

Masson, J. (1988) *Against Therapy: Emotional Tyranny and the Myth of Psychological Healing*. New York: Athenaeum.

Masson, J. (1990) *Against Therapy*. London: Fontana.

McCarthy, M. (1999) *Sexuality and Women with Learning Disabilities*. London: Jessica Kingsley.

McLellan, D. (1997) *Framework for the Qualitative and Quantitative Analysis of Data on the Ageing of People with Disabilities*. Strasbourg: Council of Europe.

McLeod, J. (1998) *An Introduction to Counselling*. Buckingham: Open University Press.

McLeod, J. (1999) 'Counselling as a social process', *Counselling*, August, pp. 217–222.

McLeod, J. (2001) *Qualitative Research in Counselling and Psychotherapy*. London: Sage.

Mehan, H. (1996) 'Beneath the skin and between the ears: A case study in the politics of representation', in S. Chaiklin and J. Lave (eds), *Understanding Practice: Perspectives on Activity and Context*. Cambridge: Cambridge University Press.

Meininger, H. (2004) 'The order of disturbance', *Journal of Intellectual Disability Research*, 48, 448.

Mercer, G. and Barnes, C. (2000) 'Disability: From medical needs to social rights', in P. Tovey (ed.), *Contemporary Primary Care: The Challenges for Change*. Buckingham: Open University Press.

Meyerson, L. (1988) 'The social psychology of Physical disability: 1948 and 1988', *Journal of Social Issues*, 44(1), 173–188.

Miller, A. (2003) *Teachers, Parents and Classroom Behaviour: A Psychosocial Approach*. Maidenhead: Open University Press.

Miller, E. and Gwynne, G. (1972) *A Life Apart: A Pilot Study of Residential Institutions for the Physically Handicapped and the Young Chronic Sick*. London: Tavistock Publications.

Minkler, M. and Estes, C. (eds) (1991) *Critical Perspectives on Aging: The Political and Moral Economy of Growing Old*. Amityville, NY: Baywood Press.

Montero, M. (1998) 'Psychosocial community work as an alternative mode of political action (The construction and critical transformation of society)'. *Community, Work and Family*, 1(1), 65–78.

Montero, M. (2004) *Introducción a la Psicología Comunitaria: Desarollo, Conceptos y Procesos*. Buenos Aires: Paidós.

Moore, M., Sixsmith, J. and Knowles, K. (eds) (1996) 'Conclusions', *Children's Reflections on Family Life*. London: Falmer Press, pp. 135–145.

Morgan, A. (2000) *What is Narrative Therapy? An Easy-to-Read Introduction*. Adelaide: Dulwich Centre Publications.

Morris, J. (1991) *Pride against Prejudice: Transforming Attitudes to Disability*. London: Women's Press.

Morris, J. (1993) 'Gender and disability', in J. Swain, V. Finkelstein, S. French and M. Oliver (eds), *Disabling Barriers – Enabling Environments*. London: Sage.

Morris, J. (ed.) (1996) *Encounters with Strangers: Feminism and Disability*. London: Women's Press.

Morris, J. (2004) *People with Physical Impairments and Mental Health Support Needs: A Critical Review of the Literature*, York: Joseph Rowntree Foundation.

Murray, P. (2002) *Hello! Are You Listening? Disabled Teenagers' Experience of Access to Inclusive Leisure*. York: Joseph Rowntree Foundation.

Murray, P. (2004) *Living with the Spark: Supporting Ordinariness in the Lives of Disabled Children and Their Families*, PhD thesis, University of Sheffield.

Murray, P., and Penman, J. (eds) (1996) *Let Our Children Be: A Collectin of Stories*, Sheffield: Parents with Attitude.

Murray, P. and Penman, J. (eds) (2000) *Telling Our Own Stories: Reflections on Family Life in a Disabling World*. Sheffield: Parents with Attitude.

Nelson, G. and Prilleltensky, I. (2004) *Community Psychology: In Pursuit of Liberation and Well-Being*. New York: Palgrave Macmillan.

Nightingale, D. J. and Cromby, J. (eds) (1999) *Social Constructionist Psychology: A Critical Analysis of Theory and Practice*. Buckingham: Open University Press.

Nikander, P. (1995) 'The turn to the text: The critical potential of discursive social psychology', *Nordiske Upkast*, 2, 3–15.

NWGCPD (ed.) (2003) *'It Doesn't Happen to Disabled Children': Child Protection and Disabled Children*. London: NSPCC.

Öberg, P. (1996) 'The absent body – A social gerontological paradox', *Ageing and Society*, 16, 701–719.

Öberg, P. and Tornstam, L. (2001) 'Youthfulness and fitness – Identity ideals for all ages?', *Journal of Aging and Identity*, 6(1), 15–29.

Oermann, M. and Lindgren, C. (1995) 'An educational program's effects on students' attitudes towards people with disabilities: A 1-year follow-up', *Rehabilitation Nursing*, Jan–Feb, 20(1), 6–10.

Oliver, J. (1995) 'Counselling disabled people: A counsellor's perspective', *Disability & Society*, 10(3), 261–274.

Oliver, M. (1990) *The Politics of Disablement*. Basingstoke, Houndmills: Macmillan.

Oliver, M. (1993) 'Societal responses to long term disability', in G. Whiteneck, S. Charlifue, K. Gerhart, D. Lammertse, S. Manley, R. Manter and K. Seedroff (eds), *Ageing with Spinal Cord Injury*. New York: Demos Publications, pp. 251–262.

Oliver, M. (1996a) 'A sociology of disability or a disablist sociology', in L. Barton (ed.), *Disability and Society: Emerging Issues and Insights*, Harlow: Longman, pp. 18–42.

Oliver, M. (1996b) *Understanding Disability: From Theory to Practice*. Basingstoke: Macmillan.

Oliver, M. and Barnes, C. (1997) 'All we are saying is give disabled researchers a chance', *Disability & Society*, 12(5), 811–814

Oliver, M. and Barnes, C. (1998) *Disabled People and Social Policy*. London: Longman.

Oliver, M. and Sapey, B. (1999) *Social Work with Disabled People*, 2nd edn. Houndmills: Macmillan.

Olkin, R. (1999) *What Psychotherapists Should Know About Disability*. New York: Guilford Press.

Olkin, R. and Pledger, C. (2003) Can disability studies and psychology join hands? *American Psychologist*, 58(4), 296–304.

Omansky Gordon, B. (2002) 'Are birds free from the chains of the skyway: Balancing freedom, responsibility and reflexivity – disability service provision', *Disability Studies Quarterly*, 22(3), 32–38.

Orford, J. (1992) *Community Psychology: Theory and Practice*. Chichester: John Wiley & Sons.

Palmer, C. and Hart, M. (1996) *A PACE in the Right Direction*. University of Sheffield, UK: Mental Health Foundation.

Palmer, S. and McMahon, G. (eds) (1997) *Handbook of Counselling*, 2nd edn. London: Routledge.

Parker, I. (1997) *Psychoanalytic Culture: Psychoanalytic Discourse in Western Society*. London: Sage.

Parker, I. (1989) 'The Crisis in Modern Social Psychology, and how to end it.' London: Routledge.

Parker, I. (1999) 'Deconstructing psychotherapy', in I. Parker (ed.), *Deconstructing Psychotherapy*. London: Sage.

Parker, I. (2002) *Critical Discursive Psychology*. London: Palgrave.

Parker, I., Georgaca, E., Harper, D., McLaughlin, T. and Stowell Smith, M. (1995) *Deconstructing Psychopathology*. London: Sage.

Parritt, S. (2000) 'Disability', in C. Feltham and I. Horton (eds), *Handbook of Counselling and Psychotherapy*. London: Sage.

Phillipson, C. (1982) *Capitalism and the Construction of Old Age*. London: Macmillan.

Phillipson, C., Bernard, M. and Strang, P. (1986) *Dependency and Interdependency in Old Age: Theoretical Perspectives and Policy Alternatives*. London: Croom Helm in association with the British Society of Gerontology.

Pilgrim, D. (1997) *Psychotherapy and Society*. London: Sage.

Pinfold, V., Toulmin, H., Thornicroft, G. and Huxley, P. (2003) 'Reducing psychiatric stigma and discrimination: Evaluation of educational interventions in UK secondary schools', *British Journal of Psychiatry*, 182(4), 342–346.

Popper, K. (1977) *The Logic of Scientific Discovery*. London: Routledge.

Potter, J. and Wetherell, M. (1987) *Discourse and Social Psychology: Beyond Attitudes and Behaviour*. London: Sage.

Pound, P., Gompertz, P. and Ebrahim, S. (1998) 'Illness in the context of older age: The case of stroke', *Sociology of Health and Illness*, 20(4), 489–506.

Prakash, I. J. (1997) 'Women and ageing', *Indian Journal of Medical Research*, 106, 396–408.

Pretorius-Heuchert, J. W. and Ahmed, R. (2001) 'Community Psychology: Past, Present, and Future', in M. Seedat, N. Duncan and S. Lazarus (eds), *Community Psychology: Theory, Method and Practice. South African and Other Perspectives*. Oxford: Oxford University Press.

Priestley, M. (1999) *Disability Politics and Community Care*. London: Jessica Kingsley.

Priestley, M. (2000) 'Adults only: Disability, social policy and the life course', *Journal of Social Policy*, 29, 421–439.

Priestley, M. (ed.) (2001) *Disability and the Life Course: Global Perspectives*. Cambridge: Cambridge University Press.

Priestley, M. (2003a) *Disability: A Life Course Approach*. Oxford: Blackwell.

Priestley, M. (2003b) ' "It's like your hair going grey", or is it? Impairment, disability and the habitus of old age', in S. Riddell and N. Watson (eds), *Disability, Culture and Identity*. London: Pearson Education.

Prilleltensky, I. (2001) 'Value-based praxis in community psychology: Moving towards social justice and social action', *American Journal of Community Psychology*, 29(5), 747–778.

Prilleltensky, I. and Nelson, G. (2002) *Doing Psychology Critically: Making a Difference in Diverse Settings*. London: Palgrave.

Quality Assurance Agency '*Quality Assurance Agency: Code of Practice: Students with disabilities*', Retrieved 2004, available on-line at http://www.qaa.ac.uk/public/COP/COPswd/contents.htm.

Rabinow, P. (ed.) (1984) *The Foucault Reader*. Middlesex: Penguin.

Race, D. G. (2002) *Learning Disability: A Social Approach*. London: Routledge.

Ramcharan, P., Roberts, G., Grant, G. and Borland, J. (eds) (1997) *Empowerment in Everyday Life: Learning Disability*. London: Jessica Kingsley.

Rapley, M. (2003) *The Social Construction of Intellectual Disability*. Cambridge: Cambridge University Press.

Rapley, M. and Antaki, C. (1996) 'A conversation analysis of the "acquiescence" of people with learning disabilities', *Journal of Community & Applied Social Psychology*, 6(3), 207–227.

Rappaport, J. (1977) *Community Psychology: Values, Research, and Action.* London: Holt, Rinehart and Winston.

Reason, P. and Heron, J. (1995) 'Co-operative inquiry', in R. Harré, J. Smith and L. Van Langenhove (eds), *Rethinking Methods in Psychology.* London: Sage.

Reeve, D. (2000) 'Oppression within the counselling room', *Disability & Society*, 15(4), 669–682.

Reeve, D. (2002) 'Negotiating psycho-emotional dimensions of disability and their influence on identity constructions', *Disability & Society*, 17(5), 493–508.

Reeve, D. (2004a) 'Counselling and disabled people: Help or hindrance?', in J. Swain, V. Finkelstein, S. French and M. Oliver (eds), *Disabling Barriers – Enabling Environments*, 2nd edn. London: Sage Publications, pp. 233–238.

Reeve, D. (2004b) 'Psycho-emotional dimensions of disability and the social model', in C. Barnes and G. Mercer (eds), *Implementing the Social Model of Disability: Theory and Research.* Leeds: Disability Press, pp. 83–100.

Reeve, D. (2005) *Negotiating Disability in Everyday Life: The Experience of Psycho-Emotional Disablism*, PhD, Lancaster: Lancaster University.

Reindal, S. M. (1999) 'Independence, dependence, interdependence: Some reflections on the subject and personal autonomy', *Disability & Society*, 14(3), 353–367.

Reinders, H. S. (2000) *The Future of the Disabled in Liberal Society: An Ethical Analysis.* Notre Dame, IN: Notre Dame Press.

Reinders, H. S. (2003) 'The ambiguities of "meaning": A commentary', *Philosophy, Psychiatry, Psychology*, 10, 91–98.

Rieser, R. (2004) 'Disability education in higher education: How do we moved from integration to inclusion? Some thoughts arising from training to meet the challenges of the Disability Discrimination Act', Paper presented at the ESRC seminar *Towards Inclusion: Social Inclusion and Education.* 19th July 2004, Institute of Education, London.

Robertson, S. (2004) 'Men and disability', in J. Swain, V. Finkelstein, S. French and M. Oliver (eds), *Disabling Barriers – Enabling Environments*, 2nd edn, London: Sage Publications, pp. 75–80.

Roller, J. (1998) 'Facilitating pupil involvement in assessment, planning and review process', *Educational Psychology in Practice*, 13(4), pp. 266–273.

Rose, N. (1989) *Governing the Soul.* London: Routledge.

Rothwell, P. M., McDowell, Z., Wong, C. K. and Dorman, P. J. (1997) 'Doctors and patients don't agree: cross sectional study of patients' and doctors' Perceptions and assessments of disability in multiple sclerosis'. *British Medical Journal*, 314, 1580–1583.

Rubin, H. J. and Rubin, I. S. (1995) *Qualitative Interviewing: The Art of Hearing the Data*. Thousand Oaks, CA: Sage.

Saetersdal, B. (1997) 'Forbidden suffering: The Pollyanna syndrome of the disabled and their families', *Family Process*, 36, 431–435.

Salvatori, P., Tremblay, M., Sandys, J. and Marcaccio, D. (1998) 'Aging with an intellectual disability: A review of Canadian literature', *Canadian Journal on Aging-Revue Canadienne Du Vieillissement*, 17(3), 249–271.

Salzberger-Wittenberg, I. (1970) *Psycho-Analytic Insights and Relationships: A Kleinian Approach*. London: Routledge & Kegan Paul.

Sánchez Vidal, A., Zambrano Constanzo, A. and Palacín Lois, M. (eds) (2004) *Psicolgía communitaria Europea: Comunidad, Poder Ética y valores. European Community Psychology: Community, Power, Ethics and Values.* Barcelona, Universitat de Barcelona.

Sanderson, H. (2001) 'Critical Issues in the Implementation of Essential Lifestyle Planning within a Complex Organisation: An Action Research Investigation within a Learning Disability Service', Unpublished PhD Thesis. Manchester: Manchester Metropolitan University.

Sanderson, H. (2002) 'A plan is not enough: Exploring the development of person-centered teams', in S. Holburn and P. M. Vietze (eds), *Person-Centered Planning Research, Practice, and Future Directions*. Baltimore: Brookes.

Sarason, S. B. (1977) *The Psychological Sense of Community: Prospects for a Community Psychology*, 3rd edn. London: Jossey-Bass Publishers.

Scandinavian Journal of Disability Research, 6(1), 2004.

Segal, J. (1997) 'Counselling people with disabilities/chronic illness', in S. Palmer and G. McMahon (eds), *Handbook of Counselling*, 2nd edn. London: Routledge.

Shakespeare, T. (ed.) (1998) *The Disability Reader: Social Science Perspectives*. London: Cassell.

Shakespeare, T. and Gillespie-Sells, K. (1996) *The Sexual Politics of Disability: Untold Desires*. London: Cassell.

Sheldon, A. (1999) 'Personal and perplexing: Feminist disability politics evaluated', *Disability & Society*, 14(5), 645–659.

Short, A. (2004) *Families Leading Planning* (with Colleagues). Manchester: Helen Sanderson Associates (www.helensandersonassociates.co.uk).

Sinason, V. (1992) *Mental Handicap and the Human Condition*. London: Free Association Books.

Skelly, A. (2002) 'Valuing people: A critical psychoanalytic perspective in reply to Baum and Webb', *Clinical Psychology*, 18, 42–45.

Skill: The National Bureau for Students with Disabilities, http://www.skill.org.uk.

Sloper, P. (1999) 'Models of service support for parents of disabled children. What do we know? What do we need to know?', *Child: Care, Health and Development*, 25(2), 85–99.

Sloper, P. and Lightfoot, J. (2002) 'Involving disabled and chronically ill children and young people in health service development', *Child: Care, Health and Development*, 29(1), 15–20.

Smail, D. (1993) *The Origins of Unhappiness: A New Understanding of Personal Distress*. London: Constable.

Smail, D. (1996) *Getting By Without Psychotherapy*. London: Sage.

Smail, D. (2001) 'De-psychologizing community psychology'. *Journal of Community & Applied Social Psychology*, 11(2), 159–165.

Smith, A. and Twomey, B. (2002) Labour Market Division, Office of National Statistics 'Labour market experiences of people with disabilities'. Labour Market Trends, August 2002 http://www.statistics.gov.uk/CCI/article.asp?ID=238&Pos=5&ColRank=2&Rank=320.

Smith, C. and Nylund, D. (eds) (1997) *Narrative Therapies with Children and Adolescents*. London: The Guilford Press.

Smith, L. and Daughtrey, H. (2000) 'Weaving the seamless web of care: An analysis of parents' perceptions of their needs following discharge of their child from hospital', *Journal of Advanced Nursing*, 31(4), 812–820.

Special Educational Needs and Disability Act (2001). London: The Stationery Office.

Special issue on disability research, *Disability, Handicap and Society*, 7(2) 1992.

Stanley Milgram (1983) *Obedience to Authority: An Experimental View*. New York: Harper/Collins.

Stead, J., Lloyd, G. and Kendrick, A. (2004) 'Participation or practice innovation: Tensions in inter-agency working to address disciplinary exclusion from school', *Children and Society*, 18, 42–52.

Steinberg, A., Lezzoni, L., Conhill, A. and Stineman, M. (2002) 'Accomo-dating Medical School Faculty with Disabilities. LDI Issue Brief, Vol. 8, No. 4, Leonard Davis Institute of Health Economics.

Stevens, G. R. (2002) 'Employers' perceptions and practice in the employability of disabled people: A survey of companies in south east UK', *Disability & Society*, 17(7), 779–796.

Stone, E. (ed.) (1999) *Disability and Development: Learning from Action and Research on Disability in the Majority World*. Leeds: The Disability Press.

Stone, E. and Priestley, M. (1996) 'Parasites, Pawns and Partners: Disability research and the role of non-disabled researchers', *British Journal of Sociology*, 47(4), 699–716.

Stuart, O. (1993) 'Double oppression: An appropriate starting point?', in J. Swain, V. Finkelstein, S. French and M. Oliver (eds), *Disabling Barriers – Enabling Environments*. London: Sage.

Sutherland, S. (1999) 'With respect to old age: long-term care – rights and responsibilities'. Research Volume 1, Cm 42191-11/1, HMSO.

Swain, J. and Walker, C. (2003) 'Parent-professional power relations: Parent and professional perspectives', *Disability & Society*, 18(5), 547–560.

Swain, J., Finklestein, V., French, S. and Oliver, M. (eds) (1993) Disabling Barriers – Enabling Environments. London: Sage Publications.

Swain, J., Gillman, M. and French, S. (1998) *Confronting Disabling Barriers: Towards Making Organisations Accessible*. Birmingham: Venture Press.

Swain, J., French, S. and Cameron, C. (2003a) *Controversial Issues in a Disabling Society*. Buckingham: Open University Press.

Swain, J., Griffiths, C. and Heyman, B. (2003b) 'Towards a social model approach to counselling disabled clients', *British Journal of Guidance and Counselling*, 31(1), 137–153.

Swain, J., Clark, J., Parry, K., French, S. and Reynolds, F. (2004) *Enabling Relationships in Health and Social Care: A Guide for Therapists*. Oxford: Butterworth-Heinemann.

Thomas, B. (2001) ' "I've taught you once already": Forgetting the disability in learning disability', *Clinical Psychology Forum*, 148, 26–28.

Thomas, C. (1999) *Female Forms: Experiencing and Understanding Disability*. Buckingham: Open University Press.

Thomas, C. (2004) 'How is disability understood? An examination of sociological approaches', *Disability & Society*, 19(6), 569–583.

Thomas, D. and Veno, A. (eds) (1996) *Community Psychology and Social Change: Australian and New Zealand Perspectives*, 2nd edn. Palmerston North: Dunmore Press Ltd.

Thomson, M. (1998) *The Problem of Mental Deficiency: Eugenics, Democracy and Social Policy in Britain c1870–1959*. Oxford: Clarendon Press.

Todd, E. S. (2000) 'The Problematic of Partnership in the Assessment of Special Educational Needs', PhD Thesis, Newcastle University.

Todd, L. (2000) 'Letting the voice of the child challenge the narrative of professional practice', *Dulwich Centre Journal*, 1 and 2, 73–79.

Todd, L. (2003a) 'Consulting the children', *Special Children*, 155, 15–19.

Todd, L. (2003b) 'Disability and the restructuring of welfare: The problem of partnership with parents', *International Journal of Inclusive Education*, 7(3), 281–296.

Todd, L. (2003c) The views of the child: Enabling pupil participation', *Special Children*, 154, 22–25.

Tomlinson, S. (1982) *A Sociology of Special Education*. London: Routledge & Kegan Paul.

Tomm, K. (1987) 'Interventive interviewing part II. Reflexive questioning as a means to enable self-healing', *Family Process*, 26, 405–413.

Towell, D. and Sanderson, H. (2004) 'Person-centred planning in its strategic context: Reframing the Mansell/Beadle-Brown Critique', *Journal of Applied Research in Intellectual Disabilities*, 17(1), 17–21.

Traustadottir, R. (2004) 'Disability studies: A Nordic perspective', Keynote lecture, British Disability Studies Association conference, Lancaster, June.

Tregaskis, C. (2004) *Constructions of Disability: Researching the Interface between Disabled and Non-disabled People.* London: Routledge.

Tremain, S. (ed.) (1996) *Pushing the Limits: Disabled Dykes Produce Culture.* Canada: Women's Press.

Trickett, E. J., Watts, R. J. and Birman, D. (1993) 'Human diversity and community psychology: Still hazy after all these years', *Journal of Community Psychology*, 21, 264–279.

Trickett, E. J., Watts, R. J. and Birman, D. (eds) (1994) *Human Diversity: Perspectives on People in Context.* San Francisco: Jossey-Bass.

Turner, B. (1989) 'Ageing, politics and sociological theory', *British Journal of Sociology*, 40(4), 588–606.

United Nations Secretariat (1998) *World Population Prospects, The 1998 Revision, Volume II: Sex and Age.* New York: The Population Division, Department of Economic and Social Affairs, United Nations Secretariat.

UPIAS (1976) *Fundamental Principles of Disability.* London: Union of the Physically Impaired Against Segregation.

Ussher, J. (1991) *Women's Madness: Misogyny on Mental Illness?* New York: Harvester Press.

Vernon, A. chapter in Morris, J. (ed.) (1996) *Encounters with Strangers: Feminism and Disability.* London: Women's Press.

Vincent, J. (1999) *Politics, Power and Old Age.* Buckingham: Open University Press.

Vygotsky, L. S. (1978) *Mind in Society.* Cambridge: Harvard.

Wagner, P. (1995) 'A consultative approach to the educational psychologist's work with schools', *Educational and Child Psychology*, 12(3), 22–28.

Waitman, P. and Conboy-Hill, S. (eds) (1992) *Psychotherapy and Mental Handicap.* London: Sage, pp. 150–170.

Walker, A. and Maltby, T. (1997) *Ageing Europe.* Buckingham: Open University Press.

Walker, A. and Naegele, G. (eds) (1999) *The Politics of Old Age in Europe.* Buckingham: Open University Press.

Walkerdine, V. (2001) *Growing Up Girl: Psycho-Social Explorations of Class & Gender.* New York: New York University Press.

Warnock Report (1978) Great Britain. Department of Education and Science. 'Committee of enquiry into the education of handicapped children and young people (1978)'. Special Educational Needs (Cmnd. 7212). London: HMSO.

Watson, N., Shakespeare, T., Cunningham-Burley, S., Barnes, C., Corker, M., Davis, J. and Priestly, M. (1999) *Life as a Disabled Child: A Qualitative Study of Young People's Experiences and Perspectives.* ESRC Research Programme. Children 5–16: Growing into the Twenty-First Century. Grant number L129251047.

Wechsler Adult Intelligence Scale-III (UK) (1998). London: The Psychological Corporation.

Wetherell, M. (ed.) (1996) *Identities, Groups and Social Issues*. London: Sage in Association with the Open University Press.

White, M. and Epston, D. (1990) *Narrative Means to Therapeutic Ends*. London: W.W. Norton.

Williams, S. (2000) 'Chronic illness as biographical disruption or biographical disruption as chronic illness? Reflections on a core concept', *Sociology of Health and Illness*, 22(1), 40–67.

Wilson, A. and Beresford, P. (2002) 'Madness, distress and postmodernity: Putting the record straight', in M. Corker and T. Shakespeare (eds), *Disability/ Postmodernity: Embodying Disability Theory*. London: Continuum.

Winslade, J. and Monk, G. (1999) *Narrative Counselling in Schools*. Thousand Oaks: Corwin Press.

Winter, D. (2004) Co-director, University of Hertfordshire post-graduate training course in clinical Psychology.

Wolfensberger, W. (1992) *A Brief Introduction to Social Role Valorization as a High-Order Concept for Structuring Human Services*, 2nd edn. Syracuse, NY: Training Institute for Human Service Planning, Leadership and Change Agentry, Syracuse University.

World Health Organization (2001) International classification of functioning, disability, and health (ICF). Geneva: Author.

www.compsy.org.uk UK Community Psychology website.

Xenitidis, K., Henry, J., Russell, A., Ward, A. and Murphy, D. (1999) 'An inpatient treatment model for adults with mild intellectual disability and challenging behaviour', *Journal of Intellectual Disability Research*, 43, 128–134.

Zarb, G. (1992) 'On the road to Damascus: First steps towards changing the relations of disability research', *Disability, Handicap & Society*, 7, 125–138.

Zarb, G. and Oliver, M. (1993) *Ageing with a Disability: What Do They Expect after All These Years?* London: University of Greenwich.

Zola, I. (1989) 'Towards a necessary universalizing of disability policy', *Millbank Memorial Quarterly*, 67(2), 401–428.

Index

acceptance of difference, 30
Access to Health Records Act
    (1990), 80
access to services, 28–9
acquiescence, 177
action, 174–6
active view of disability, 192–3
ageing identities, 86–7
aggression, coping with, 136–9
American Association on Mental
    Retardation, 127
anticipating barriers, 118
application for jobs, 77–82
appointments
    inflexibility of, 28
    use of time, 28

blind/partially sighted, 44, 46, 48
bodily ageing, 84–6
British Psychological Society,
    74, 111

cerebral palsy, 19–33, 71–83
change
    in enabling practice, 144–6
    in institutions, 196–7
Clarkson House, 64
clinical psychology service, 124–5
cognitive limitation, 131–2
colleagues' reactions, 113–15
    denial, 115
    inappropriate concern, 114
    projected anxiety, 115
    rejection, 114
    stereotyping, 113–14
communication skills, 77

community psychology, 8–9, 170–86
    definition of, 170–3
    ecological approach, 173–4
    and learning difficulties, 176–83
    paradigm and principles, 173–6
    roles of, 184–5
community social psychology, 15
compliance, 177
copers, 55
counselling, 155–69
    individualistic nature of, 164
    social model, 168–9
critical psychology, 7
critical theories, 6–8
cultural otherness, 87–9

deaf/hearing impairment, 44,
    46, 48
denial, 115
    of psychological reality, 38–40
developmental disability, 126
developmental systems theory, 32
Disability Bill (2005), 57
Disability Capital Allocation
    Funding, 63
Disability Discrimination Act
    (1995), 3, 42–70, 71, 80,
    111, 193
    institutional responses to, 58–9
Disability Equality Training, 74–5,
    79, 106, 118, 169
Disability Living Allowance, 28, 60
Disability Rights Commission,
    57, 177
disability studies, 190–1
disability thinking, 201

disabled babies, 19–33
  birth, infancy and childhood, 20–6
  later life, 27–33
disabled families, 20–6
Disabled Students' Allowance, 11,
  53, 59–61
disablement, 3
disabling society, 94–107
discrimination, 24–5
  in education, 34–41
  expediency, 76–7
  in job seeking, 71–83
discursive psychology, 7
diversity, 174–6
dysarthric speech, 74, 77
dyslexia, 43, 44, 46, 48

education, 24–5
  exclusion from school, 34–41
Education Act (1970), 24
emancipation, 1–2, 9, 202–3
empathy, 40
empowerment, 131–2
enabling practice, 141–54
  definition of, 143–4
  inclusion, 40, 152–3
  need for change, 144–6
  need for theory, 146–52
equipment, 30–1
exclusion, 40
  from school, 34–41
expediency, 76–7
externalisation, 151

funding for Higher Education, 59–67
  evaluation of, 63–7
  gaps in, 61–2
  institutional funding, 62–3

Higher Education, 42–70
  copers, 55
  and employability, 53
  funding, 59–67
  impairment labels, 55–6

implications of legislation for
  academics, 67–9
increasing numbers in, 53–5
national and international
  legislation, 56–9
psychology, 71–83
returners, 55
setting targets, 52–3
strugglers, 54
Higher Education Funding Council
  for England, Equality Challenge
  Unit, 58
Human Rights Act, 56

impairment, 3
  rethinking, 188–90
  social model, 3
impairment labels, 55–6
impersonality, 31
inappropriate concern, 114
inclusion, 40, 152–3, 197–8
institutions, transformation of,
  196–7
intellectual disability, 7, 14, 24, 45,
  47, 49
intellectually disabled clients,
  123–40
  aggression, 136–9
  clinical psychology service,
    124–5
  empowerment and cognitive
    limitation, 131–3
  meeting tragedy, 134–6
  recognition of people needing
    help, 125–8
  relating to, 128–9
  responding to self-harm, 130–1
interactions with patients and
  clients, 115–16
internalised oppression, 101–3
International Classification of
  Functioning, Disability and
  Health, 126–7
inverse care law, 128

job seeking, discrimination in, 71–83
  application process, 77–82
  expediency, 76–7

landscapes of exclusion, 97
learning difficulties, 126
  role of community psychology,
    176–83
  see also intellectual disability
legislation, 56–9
  implications for academics, 67–9
  use of to support requests, 119

mental retardation, 128
models, 116–17
multiple disability, 45, 47, 49

narrative practice, 150–2
National Disability Team, 58
normalisation, 4–5

older age, 12–13, 83–92
  ageing identities, 86–7
  bodily ageing, 84–6
  cultural otherness, 87–9
  politics, 90–1
  social structure, 89–90

patients/clients
  intellectually disabled, 123–40
  interactions with, 115–16
person centred planning, 178
personal care support, 44,
    46, 48
politics, 90–1
pop-labels, 4
post-structuralism, 147–50
power, 174–6
projected anxiety, 115
psycho-emotional dimensions of
    disability, 95–103
  internalised oppression, 101–3
  social interactions, 98–101
  structural disability, 97–8

psychology, 4–9, 71–83
  advantages of opening up to
    disabled people, 120–2
  community psychology, 8–9
  critical, 7
  critical theories, 6–8
  discursive, 7
  pop-labels, 4
  radical psychoanalysis, 8
  social psychology, 5–6

radical psychoanalysis, 8
rejection, 114
relationships, 38–9
returners, 55

school, exclusion from,
    34–41
self-harm, 130–1
self-reporting of disability, 51
  type of impairment, 52
sense of humour, 119
service integration, 28–9
social constructionism, 6
social death, 87–9
social interactions, 98–101
social model of disability, 2, 3,
    155–69
social model of impairment, 3
social psychology, 5–6
social structure, 89–90
social understanding of disability,
    191–2
Southampton University,
    64–7
Special Educational Needs and
    Disability Act, 56
special needs, 126
stereotyping, 111–22
  colleagues' reactions,
    113–14
  work settings, 12–13
structural disability, 97–8
strugglers, 54

students, disabled, 42–70
successful functioning,
    117–19
    anticipating barriers, 118
    establishing openings, 118
    extra financial costs, 119
    professional skills versus necessary
        adjustments, 119
    sense of humour, 119
    use of legislation to support
        requests, 119

tragedy, coping with,
    134–6

under-estimation of abilities, 72–3
unseen disability, 45, 47, 49

wheelchair user/mobility
    impairment, 44, 46, 48
Widening Participation funding, 63
work setting
    colleagues' reactions, 113–15
    interactions with patients and
        clients, 115–16
    models, 116–17
    stereotyping in, 112–13
    successful functioning, 117–19
worksearch, 73–5